reading for wine lovers everywhere and anyone dreaming a vineyard dream.'

Mike Veseth, author of *Wine Wars* and *Extreme Wine* and editor of *The Wine Economist*

Praise for *Grape Expectations*:

'*Captivating reading for anyone with dreams of living in rural France.*'

Destination France

'*I was moved and delighted by this book, which has vast and useful amounts to say about wine and the passion of wine-making, about France and the great adventure of family life, and above all about the trials and challenges that build a marriage... splendid book.*'

Martin Walker, bestselling author of the *Bruno, Chief of Police* series

'*Really liked Caro's book; it's not the usual fall in love with France story, it's warts and all – including horrific accidents! Definitely the best – and most realistic – tome coming from the 'A Year in Provence' genre.*'

Joe Duffy, Irish radio personality

'*bright, passionate, inspiring, informative and absolutely delicious*'

Breadcrumb Reads blog

'*Filled with vivid descriptions of delicious wines, great food... a story of passion, dedication, and love*'

Bookalicious Travel Addict blog

ALSO BY CARO FEELY

Grape Expectations

Saving Our Skins

*Wine: The Essential Guide to Tasting,
History, Culture and More*

GLASS HALF FULL

The Ups and Downs of
Vineyard Life in France

CARO FEELY

summersdale

GLASS HALF FULL

Summersdale Publishers Ltd
46 West Street
Chichester
West Sussex
PO19 1RP
UK

www.summersdale.com

Printed and bound by CPI Group (UK) Ltd, Croydon, CR0 4YY

ISBN: 978-1-84953-991-3

Substantial discounts on bulk quantities of Summersdale books are available to corporations, professional associations and other organisations. For details contact general enquiries: telephone: +44 (0) 1243 771107, fax: +44 (0) 1243 786300 or email: enquiries@summersdale.com.

ABOUT THE AUTHOR

Caro Feely can usually be found juggling vineyard, wine school, accommodation and writing deep in south-west France. She and husband Seán produce wine and much of their own food, with the help of their daughters Sophia and Ellie, on their certified organic farm. No matter what she is juggling, at the end of the day, one hand usually has a glass (half full) of wine in it.

NOTE FROM THE AUTHOR

This is a true story. However, some names and the order of events have been changed for privacy and for the flow of the story. Speech is based on memory and seeks to capture the essence of the moment.

In memory of Peta-Lynne 'Blossom', our beloved Mum Feely

*This is a story about the ebb and flow of life and love,
of living and dying, a shout for the earth, for nature,
for us and our future*

It doesn't matter if the glass is half full or half empty –
there is always room for more wine.
Anonymous

CONTENTS

PART I

FIRE
AND FRUIT

Nature... has more votes, a longer memory,
and a sterner sense of justice than we do.
Wendell Berry

CHAPTER I

HAIL THE DESTROYER

Lemon-coloured reflections skittered across the table as I lifted the glass to my nose to check the aroma. Satisfied, I poured two more tasting samples and handed the glasses to Christophe and Seán. They sniffed, swirled and sniffed again.

'How do you make this wine?' Christophe asked after tasting and aiming an expert jet into the spittoon, the motion coming as naturally to him as it did to us.

'Oh, easy,' said Seán. He laughed and his solid six-foot-two body reverberated. I knew how that laugh felt when I had an arm resting on his shoulders: it rolled through him. I hadn't felt that in a long time. We didn't have time to sit together – or, if we did, it was on opposite sides of our large kitchen table to talk business. Now his laughter spread as we shared the conspiratorial humour of knowing how much work went into making wine.

Seán lifted his head, his face framed by a mane of wavy hair, streaked blond from working in the sun, and by his stubble, worn to mark the start of harvest, displaying a dash of salt and pepper I hadn't noticed before.

'We follow a simple process: harvest, press, cold stabilise, rack, ferment, rack the finished wine into a new vat with the fine lees, mature for six months then into the bottle.'

He ran through the steps; simple, swift words masking how complex and physically demanding the process was. Each step included a myriad of decisions. As the winegrower and winemaker at each point, our senses were taking in information and processing it to make the right decisions. For example, in the first step of the harvest, in making the call about when to harvest, we analysed the grapes for sugar level and acidity but, more importantly, we walked through the vineyard tasting grapes. Our senses took in taste, texture, colour, tannins. We considered each part of the grape individually – skin, pulp and seeds – but also the grape as a whole.

'Simple, like we do with our dry Riesling,' said Christophe.

I smiled knowing their 'simple' was not the average person's 'simple'.

'What do you call this wine?' he asked.

'*Sincérité*,' said Seán, holding up the bottle, showing the name and logo, an embossed mosaic three-way spiral called a triskell.

'I like the names you have given to the wines,' said Christophe. 'More interesting than putting a varietal on it like we do in Germany.'

'But for wine lovers it's easier if the varietal is clear and on the front,' I said. 'Most people buy wine based on the varietal.'

'It's crazy that there are more than a thousand grape varietals and the majority of wine drinkers only know and buy the top few,' said Seán. 'Bang goes our biodiversity.'

The room was quiet for a moment. Outside, vine-covered hills ran into the distance, filling the expansive windows. Inside, walls of limestone and a ceiling of poplar and oak enclosed the scene, bringing a sense of solidity and calm. But it was harvest time, impossible to feel calm.

After spitting I looked up out of the window again and saw a small thunderhead in the distance. It spread like a charcoal-coloured duvet being shaken over the blue sky then hung still for a few moments before growing and moving closer, its dark grey curves plumping out as if being spread by an unseen giant. I felt a tinge of fear.

'The taste is our *terroir*,' said Seán, seemingly oblivious to the storm cloud. 'We take what it gives us. I shepherd what nature provides rather than "making" wine. With our natural farming, the wine reflects the limestone that underpins our vineyard; you taste the ancient seabed in the glass. If you lick the roof of your mouth you'll find a hint of salinity, like a sea breeze.'

'Hmm, yes, I see what you mean,' said Christophe.

Seán's description transported me back to a visit years before when a Loire Valley winegrower had sparked our dream to go wine-farming in France. We had planned and saved for almost a decade. After years of searching, we found our vineyard, the one we were looking on to now. It had been in liquidation, a 'fire sale'. We told ourselves it had potential but we had to look beyond the rotten shutters, un-trellised vineyards, rusted fences and mouse infestation. Seán returned from his fact-finding visit and said, 'It looks like the vineyards of the *premier grand cru classés* we visited in St-Émilion.'

We were idiots without a clue but, after tasting the wines and seeing the views, we were smitten, our rational selves swept away by an unaccountable force, a passion, a deep need to grow and make our own wine. We sold up, left our jobs and put everything into the failing farm. Since that shaky beginning, we had farmed organically and it showed. The Sauvignon Blanc was clean and carried notes of grapefruit, gooseberry and lemon on the cool undertow of limestone.

'We harvested the Sauvignon Blanc this morning,' said Seán.

'What was it like?' said Christophe.

'Smooth,' replied Seán.

They were men of few words.

'It's rare for it to be smooth,' I added. 'Simple; yes. Smooth; no.'

They laughed.

'Every year we're guaranteed some breakdown and the expensive repairs that go with it,' I said. 'We need to re-equip but that will cost a fortune.'

'I know the feeling,' said Christophe, whose family owned a vineyard. 'It's a juggling act.'

I pushed the thought of machinery breakdown out of my mind and opened the *La Source* red, a classic St-Émilion-style blend of Merlot, Cabernet Franc and Cabernet Sauvignon. As I poured, the room darkened, as if following the change in colour in the wine. We gathered close to the windows, fascinated. The cloud mass grew larger with each second, the initial dark bank expanding like a tidal wave rolling in slow motion across the sky and throwing the room into darkness as if night was falling. The top of the almond tree in front of the tasting room began to thrash, then the lower level cherries and hazelnuts followed. I felt a shiver of dread and saw a similar thought on Seán's face.

The poplars on the driveway began to swirl like mops shaken by angry cleaners. A few large dark circles splatted on the terrace outside. I felt anxiety rising and tried to calm myself. *It will be OK – it's only rain.* As if hearing my internal voice, the wind upped the ante, thrashing the trees more ferociously and making the vines on the hillside dance like dervishes. With each passing second the drama notched up like a Wagner symphony.

The first hailstones clattered on the terrace and I felt a cold bolt of adrenalin.

My attention was drawn to a car pulling in alongside the tasting room. Michael and Lisa, architect and artist from London, were regular guests to the Wine Lodge. I waved from the window, not chancing going out into the violent weather. They waited a few minutes, hoping the storm would ease. It got worse. They threw caution to the wind and raced inside. We kissed hello and I introduced them to Christophe.

'I'd better get you over to the Lodge before it really comes down,' I said, taking the Lodge keys from the counter, delighted to have something to take my mind off the brewing disaster.

'What does this mean for the harvest?' shouted Michael as we stepped into the maelstrom. I could barely hear him above the noise of the storm.

'I don't know. We have to wait and see,' I yelled. 'Be careful you don't slip.'

In the few seconds crossing the uncovered section of timber deck from the tasting room to the Lodge we were soaked. I opened the door and hung on to it with all my strength to stop the wind giving it a life of its own.

'*Bonne installation!* Happy settling in. I'll be back with a gift bottle of wine when the storm eases. Cross your fingers that it isn't too destructive!' I shouted, laughed hysterically, then forced the door closed behind me, the wind like a magnet, keeping it from closing then throwing it forward, so it took all my power to stop it from slamming.

A pile of hail had gathered at the door of the tasting room. I felt a jolt of panic for our future – something I had felt many times since we had given up relatively secure city jobs for farming in south-west France. I steeled myself, pulled the tasting-room door open and rushed in before I got any wetter.

It felt safer inside the protective capsule of glass, stone and wood, but I felt dizzy with worry. We had only harvested the Sauvignon Blanc, about a tenth of our harvest. The rest was still on the vines and not quite ready. My brain flipped through potential outcomes. The only acceptable one was for the hail to stop.

Hail was more frequent than it had been a decade before. Global warming was creating unstable weather, including more storms, and farmers like us were experiencing it up close. I felt my stomach twist with worry.

Seán was going through the motions of the tasting, trying to ignore the unfolding disaster. The darkest part of the storm was still the other side of Saussignac but it was only a matter of minutes before it hit us full on. There was nothing we could do. Seán commented on this aroma and that tannin, what he had done in the vineyard and in the winery. It was like making small talk while watching a car crash.

Then the dark mass boiled out, as if an invisible force holding it back had let go. It rolled like angry water released from a dam wall and raced over Saussignac Castle. The hail drumbeat on the roof increased. We stopped talking. The noise outside reached fever pitch; rain and hail pounding, and wind thrashing the trees and vines relentlessly.

I felt like our lives were suspended over a void. In a few minutes our harvest could be shredded. Some long seconds passed as we stood mesmerised, then the mass split into two and the destructive darkness raced away; one part towards Gageac-et-Rouillac in the east, the other to Razac-de-Saussignac in the west. The battering of the hail calmed, then stopped.

'Holy smokes,' I said.

'That was close,' said Seán.

Christophe was wide-eyed.

'I wonder what the damage is?' I said.

'Not as bad as it could have been,' said Seán as he rinsed the glasses.

'We should go and check now,' I said.

'Relax,' said Seán. 'If we see it now or in ten minutes it's not going to make any difference.'

I swallowed my panic and tried to concentrate on the wine.

The sun came out. Like the returning light, the last wine was golden: our Saussignac botrytis dessert wine.

If it were not for the hailstones thick against the tasting-room door, it would have been hard for a newcomer to believe a storm had passed.

'This is very good,' said Christophe after taking a sniff and a sip. 'It's like a *trockenbeerenauslese*.'

He took another sip, savoured it and spat into the spittoon, then set his glass down.

'Your wines are great. Real *terroir*. I would love to stay and talk more but I should leave you as I know you're anxious to check the grapes.'

He had a reserved Northern European way about him. We were in the midst of a crisis and he acknowledged that but was calm. I wondered what they would do in southern Italy, Sicily or Corsica in a similar situation – probably scream and race out into the vineyard as I felt like doing.

'It is what it is,' said Seán. 'I think we missed the worst of it.'

We exchanged bottles with Christophe. The tradition of swapping wine with other winegrowers was one we cherished. Since becoming winemakers we rarely drank wine made by someone we didn't know. It added a special dimension to our enjoyment of our favourite drink.

As we waved his small white car farewell, our minds were already in the vineyard. Before the car had turned up the hill to Saussignac I was pulling on my boots. Night was falling. We needed to get out there fast.

With a worker lamp in hand, we followed the track below our house, a long stone building covered in grey concrete. Beneath the seventies concrete that the locals called *crépi* we knew there were original cut stones that had been quarried on the farm. Removing it was one of many tasks that would keep us busy far into the future. If the hail damage was bad, that and other projects would be pushed out. Sometimes I felt like we took one step forward to take two steps back.

The Dordogne Valley spread below us like a quilt of perfect country scenes. Vineyards, plum orchards, forests and pasture were sewn together, patterns of green and gold with the river in the middle. The scene looked so peaceful and safe. Yet the village of Mardenne's only water source was one of 500 community wells that had special project status because it was so polluted by local farmers' activities. A programme of phone calls and meetings had been initiated to cajole farmers to stop using the legal poisons that were showing up in the water. So far it wasn't working. Recent analysis of the town's water showed the herbicide level to be so high that there wasn't a scale for it. A farmer had weed-killed a field hours before a storm and it had washed the herbicide directly into the community's water. The herbicide was glyphosate, classified by the World Health Organization (WHO) as 'probably' carcinogenic. It was still legal in the EU and should have been banned long before. Mardenne's well showed glyphosate but also traces of chemicals that had been banned for more than ten years, including atrazine and arsenic. Atrazine was a popular herbicide in the twentieth century but has been shown to be a persistent endocrine disrupter and carcinogen. Arsenic is a famous poison – it was a favourite method for murder in the Middle Ages and the Renaissance – but was considered a great idea as an agricultural pesticide in the 1900s. It is a poison that can kill and in smaller doses it leads to nervous-system disruption that can be the cause of diseases like Alzheimer's. When I thought about it I felt desperate, frustrated and very grateful that our tap water didn't come from there.

Our local Saussignac district was slowly transforming to organic farming. A large percentage of winegrowers had already converted: around 20 per cent of the vineyard surface area, compared to an average in France of around 4 per cent at the time. Local farmers had started on the road to organic for different personal reasons. One neighbouring couple were driven to find an alternative to chemical farming when their five-year-old daughter got leukaemia. Their research concluded that systemic chemicals were behind their daughter's terrible disease and they went organic. With treatment their daughter recovered. Another close friend went organic after realising chemical farming was bad for the quality of his wine and for his long-term yield despite what the agricultural advisers said. Not surprisingly, many of the 'advisers' were connected to the sale of agricultural chemicals.

I set aside my thoughts about Mardenne's water calamity and focused on our immediate one – the hail. The vines alongside us were covered in green plumage and, without getting closer, I knew the storm had not been as devastating as the one in St-Émilion a couple of years before. Then the vines had been hit so hard that it looked like winter, the leaves and just-set fruit shredded off the trellis, leaving only the solid wood and cane structures like emaciated skeletons.

But, given the fragile state of our almost ripe fruit, even a small amount of hail could wreck our crop and the old Sémillon vines that ran down the east-facing slope looked ruffled. There was no mistaking that the storm had passed through.

I stepped into a row and lifted leaves so I could scrutinise the grapes.

'No broken skin here,' I said, feeling a flood of relief.

'Nor here,' said Seán, doing the same on the next row. 'A bit windblown, that's all.'

'Thank God.' I popped a grape into my mouth. After chewing and tasting the skin and pulp, I spat the pips into my hand to look at the colour. There was still a line of bright green along the centre. They were almost ready. In a few days the green would diminish and the pips would brown and start to taste a little nutty instead of bitter astringent.

'I think we should pick on Thursday as planned,' said Seán after doing the same.

Each year we started harvest with a vague idea of which days would be ideal for each grape and then adjusted our plan based on the weather and development of the grapes. We were on target.

We kept walking, hurrying but stopping every few rows to check the bunches. The vines changed from Sémillon to Sauvignon Blanc.

'The further we go the more roughed up the vines look,' I said. 'Thank God this Sauvignon is safe in the winery.'

Seán nodded.

'There are a few perforated leaves here,' he said, lifting one to show me.

I felt anxiety rising and wondered what we would find around the corner in the Hillside Merlot, our last parcel on this stretch of land, a steep east-south-east slope already dark with the shadows of the evening.

In the first row of it I found grapes with broken skin.

'We've been hit,' I said, my heartbeat pounding in my ears and my mind racing to the implications.

Seán looked up from the next row.

'Here too. It looks bad but I don't think it's as serious as you might think, Mrs C,' he said, using a nickname he had given me years before. 'We hand-pick this parcel so we can remove any damaged grapes when we harvest.'

'But won't damage bring bugs? And rot?' I said.

'It could. But is there enough to hit the emergency button? This is one of our best red vineyards. We need it for red. If we pick now it will only be good for rosé. Let's count how many damaged grapes we find on the last two rows.'

We each took a row.

'Around one broken grape every three bunches,' I said as I reached the end of mine.

'You see. Less than one per cent,' said Seán. 'It was the same for me. Definitely not enough to warrant picking when it isn't ripe.'

'But even a little damage could bring rot,' I repeated.

'That's a risk,' said Seán. 'Let's go and check the other Merlot.'

Feeling a little light-headed with a combination of anxiety and relief, we crossed a semicircle of grass cupped by a curved wall of limestone that we called the amphitheatre, home to a giant fig tree. It presided over the area like a dark-green wise woman. Its gorgeous lush leaves offered deep shade; its fresh fruit fed us for weeks in season and its jam the rest of the year. Through the summer its tantalising scent reached way over to the vineyard, an aroma so uplifting that French perfume producers sold a home fragrance called *Sous le Figuier* (Under the Fig Tree). Passing it, I couldn't resist picking a fig despite our haste. I was a figaholic. When Seán visited the farm for the first time and told me it had copious fig trees, I declared, 'It was made for us!' If it had figs I was ready to buy.

A few metres past the fig, a staircase of wood and stone wound up the cliff from the amphitheatre to the tasting room. Clambering up the uneven steps – the fastest route – I thought of Ad and his son Adrian, friends from Holland, who had made the steps. Back then there was no tasting room, wine school or Wine Lodge accommodation. Now the view above us was filled by two structures built on to the original stone walls of abandoned workshop, pigsty and stables from the nineteenth century. Each time I saw the buildings I felt a wave of gratitude. Their oak frames were works of art, like the ever-changing views they offered on to the vineyards. We reached the top and stopped.

'What a view,' said Seán. 'Even after the storm.'

We took in the scene for a few moments, then he sighed deeply and said, 'We had better get on or the light will be gone.'

That sigh was the first sign of how worried he was. It said so much about the care, attention and sweat that had gone into the vineyard and the disillusion that the grapes could be destroyed in a few minutes. Even if the damage was slight, the hail was a reminder of how fragile we were in the face of nature.

To keep up with Seán's long stride, my fast walk broke into a trot. We passed our herb *potager* (kitchen garden) and turned towards Saussignac along a grassy track that ran alongside baby Cabernet Sauvignon vines we had planted three years before. Setting up the tiny vineyard had taken tenacity – first to get the vineyard-planting rights (an archaic quota system), then to establish the vines. Like the buildings, it was a vote for the future.

We reached the end of the baby vines and the start of the last Merlot vineyards.

'The same procedure as the last vineyard?' I asked, using a phrase from a favourite film, *Dinner for One*.

'The same procedure,' said Seán, giving me a weak smile – another sign that he was worried.

'What do you think?' I said as we reached the end.

'I think the arguments are the same though it's clearly worse. We'll lose more by jumping the gun and turning it into rosé than by waiting and removing the damaged grapes when we hand-pick. I'll do some research on what we can do to limit the risk of rot. A clay spray can help the healing but this close to harvest I'm not sure there's much we can do.'

A little further on, we reached our last small triangle of Merlot. It was worse again.

'What will we do?' I said.

'This vineyard isn't big enough to call the machine out and picking by hand with just the two of us isn't viable. Anyway it would make such a small volume it would cost more to harvest than it would generate. We may have to forget this section,' said Seán. 'We'll see closer to harvest.'

I nodded. It was a tiny area but we were a small producer and every grape mattered. I felt a wave of worry wash over me.

Beyond the triangle were another five rows of Sauvignon Blanc picked that morning. It was the most southerly point of our farm and it looked battered. I held my hands together in a gesture of gratitude to the sky, thankful we had harvested it before the storm struck.

As we walked back we went through our options again. Seán was adamant that we shouldn't do anything and that there wasn't enough damage to jump the gun. I reticently agreed.

That night after dinner and saying goodnight to our two daughters, I turned back my old sleeping bag that served as our duvet and heard the sound of harvest machines clattering and beeping high-pitched warning signals in the surrounding vineyards. Seán opened our bedroom window to close the shutters. The smell of the night, filled with harvest aromas of fresh grapes and crushed leaves, rushed into the room. I loved those aromas but they brought a flutter of nerves. Since becoming winegrowers, the month of September always held a hint of promise, nervous anticipation and fear.

Our neighbour's courtyard lit up. His tractor and trailer rattled back from the vineyard. I felt a chill run down my spine. He was emergency-harvesting everything on a Saturday night because of the hail.

'Maybe we have underestimated the damage,' I said. 'Perhaps we should be harvesting.'

'I don't think so,' said Seán. 'We checked the grapes. We know the state of them. Anyway, like I said, we'll hand-pick those sections and remove the damaged grapes at harvest. Our neighbours machine-harvest so they don't have that option.'

He was probably right but the noise of the harvest machines still made me doubt. Maybe they knew something we didn't.

'You saw how that cloud split,' added Seán. 'We were incredibly lucky. The vineyards the other side of Saussignac were hit worse than us.'

We stood in the dark, observing, our arms just touching. The bright lights of a harvester lit up the vines nearest the village and the clattering started again. Seán took a deep breath, sighed, reached for the shutters and closed them decisively as if to say, 'Don't say another word.'

That night I thrashed back and forth, unable to sleep with the noise of the machines. I flushed hot and cold and wondered if I was getting sick. As soon as it was light enough I went out to check again. The damage was there but no worse than the night before. Our equilibrium was so finely balanced, one knock and we could fall. I wondered if as a wine business we could weather the coming challenges of global warming – or if I even wanted to. I was passionate about wine and organic farming but the work overload, stress and uncertainty of life as farmers had already taken its toll on our relationship. I didn't know how much more I or it could take. But stopping the train we were on, especially in the middle of harvest, was not possible. There was no emergency brake.

CHAPTER 2

HARVEST THRILLS

The cold pre-dawn air stung my nostrils and the gravel crunched under my boots as I crossed the courtyard. Above me the heavens were brilliant with stars. I could see Seán's outline through the insulation curtain of the winery. Sensing my arrival, he looked through a slit and inclined his head to listen.

'He's on his way,' he said, ears fine-tuned to the harvest machine's whine across the valley.

I heard it and felt a flutter of adrenalin.

Seán dropped the curtain and I stepped forward and put my head through to see him blast a final jet of rinsing water over the vat destined for the day's Sémillon. Then he attached the harvest pipe that would serve to move fresh harvest from trailer to vat using elastic guy ropes.

A whine sounded in the courtyard and I turned to see the three-metre-tall harvester light up the darkness like a cruise ship. Benoît, the driver, waved and climbed down the ladder to ground level. We exchanged the obligatory kisses and a few words about the harvest. After explaining the section we were harvesting, I ran ahead to indicate the rows to harvest, marked with baby-pink Lycra bows, a tradition at Château

Feely. He gave me a big smile that dissolved into giggles before straightening up and earnestly calibrating the machine.

He was setting simple things like the height and width of the rows but also more sophisticated information like the grape variety to be harvested. Given the varietal, the machine would know the range of weight the grapes should have. For example, a Cabernet Sauvignon grape is smaller and weighs less than a Merlot grape. The sorting system inside would vacuum away the bits that weighed less than the lower point of the set range, while the sticks, whole bunches and other parts that were larger and weighed more would be caught by the sorting grille and vibrated to the back to be sorted into whole clusters to be de-stemmed and waste to be ejected. It was a sophisticated piece of equipment worth the equivalent of a modest house in France.

I jogged back up to the winery and found Seán climbing down from the scaffolding we had set up beside the vat.

'Everything's ready,' he said. 'Let's watch the progress so we know when to get into position.'

From the terrace we watched the machine lumbering down the vineyard like a high-tech dinosaur. It straddled the row and shook the vines with metal bow-shaped arms that ran parallel across the inside, making the grapes fall into a conveyor belt of silicon baskets and leaving the stems behind. A stream of rejected matter exited the sorting system at the back, creating a green, brown, yellow and gold cascade that shimmered in the rear lights.

We knew that the stream contained critter collateral (lizards, mice, snakes and insects) and some were making it into the harvest bins despite the sorting – another reason we wanted to move to hand-harvesting everything. We didn't enjoy machine-harvesting but economically and organisationally it was the only option for our whites, rosé and everyday red. We were committed to a ten-year cycle with the harvest machine cooperative so we were stuck. Already by hand-picking the top reds and the dessert wine we weren't using what we paid for each year. No 'get out' or flexibility was a downside to joining a machine cooperative, something we only realised once we were in.

I took a deep breath. At harvest time we were stretched even more than usual. We expected to finish in time for me to take our daughters, Sophia and Ellie, to school and to allow time to change into more suitable attire for welcoming guests due for a day of wine school. Seán was focused on the culmination of his year's work in the vineyard while I tried to keep up with the cadence of visits and shoehorn harvest activity in alongside the constant stream of administration and emails generated by our growing business.

We stood quietly for a moment. At the top of the next row the harvester turned back on to the main track.

'Let's go,' said Seán. 'We don't want to keep him waiting.'

The harvester pulled into position and Seán backed the tractor up behind him. I felt nervous. From the pavement of our house I was perfectly positioned to see how well aligned the tractor and harvester were but also well away so I wouldn't be crushed. Safety was always in our minds. Every year farmers died in the process, either by a false step with a machine, falling from the top of a vat or ladder, electrocution or asphyxiation from the carbon dioxide given off in fermentation.

Seán and Benoît lined up and prepared to empty the bins. It was almost right but I could see that grapes would hit the lip of the trailer and be lost. I yelled and held my hand up. Benoît inclined the left bin then saw me and stopped the tip just in time. Seán pulled away and reversed back in. It was perfect. I gave the thumbs up and the harvest flowed smoothly across. The harvester took off again, while I turned back to the winery and watched Seán back the trailer into the entrance of the winery. The next step was connecting the trailer to the harvest pipe that would transfer the grapes to the vat. It was always a tough connection.

'Feck!' said Seán. 'Doesn't this make you dream of hand-harvesting?'

'Too right,' I said, panting with the effort of holding a pipe that was the thickness of a rugby player's thigh, with heavy metal ends, while Seán tried to close the join.

'Are you sure we have the right connector for this trailer?'

Seán gave me a withering look and cussed again.

The pipe got the message and clamped on.

He reached into the tractor cabin and switched on the power take-off (PTO) shaft that turned the auger, the screw conveyor, of the trailer. It hummed to life and fresh harvest began pumping into the pipe. The first splat hit the vat next to me and was followed by a rhythmical flow. Satisfied that the load was transferring smoothly, I climbed down the scaffolding. As I stepped on to the ground, the sound of pouring stopped. The auger was still going but harvest was not flowing through. I waved to Seán and climbed back up the scaffolding.

'Nothing's coming through,' I shouted and held my fingers in a cross.

A couple of years before, the auger was jammed by a metal hook and we had had to empty a trailer-load by hand. We learned the lesson well and hadn't used those metal hooks to repair the trellising since.

Seán turned off the trailer.

'It can't be a hook – it's still turning,' he said as if reading my mind. 'Stay up there. I'll turn it back on and up the power – maybe it needs a little more encouragement.'

Power made no difference. The auger just macerated our precious harvest more furiously for no result.

I shook my head, feeling a tiny stream of panic. Benoît would soon be back with the second load.

Seán stopped the tractor and came around to join me.

'It must be the angle of the pipe. The slope's too steep,' he said. 'We have to lift it.'

Seán crossed the winery floor to fetch an A-frame ladder then set it up at the middle point, raising the centre of the pipe half a metre above the original position on a stack of wooden pallets.

'Maybe that'll do it.'

'Could it really be as simple as that?' I said.

'Basic physics,' said Seán. 'You climb up there and make sure it stays in position.'

'Easy for you to say,' I said, clambering back up the scaffolding to hang on to the pipe. With hundreds of kilograms of harvest pumping through, it could be as dangerous as a python.

Seán looked back to check I was in place and started the auger. Harvest throbbed through the pipe, the ladder stayed firmly in position and, seconds later, grapes splattered into the vat. I gave a thumbs up and a relieved smile. In minutes the load was finished. I felt like we had climbed a mountain. Seán turned off the PTO.

I relished that there was no noise for a moment then realised the vineyard below the winery, where the harvester should have been working, was silent. I flung open the winery shutters. The dawn had painted a strip of pale orange and yellow across the top of Gageac hill. Above it a range of blues progressed up through the sky still filled with stars. But below that beauty the machine had stopped about ten metres into a vineyard row.

'Feck,' said Seán, looking over my shoulder. 'We'd better go and see what's happening.'

Breaking harvest part way was bad for us work-wise but it also meant oxidation for the juice that was already in the harvest-machine bins. Out in the vineyard, the harvested grapes were not protected by inert gas as they were once they were in the winery.

'Maybe we should take some sulphur dioxide,' I said.

'I'll come back if it's necessary,' said Seán. 'The earlier we start dosing the more it needs.'

Sulphur dioxide (marked as 'sulphites' on wine bottles) is a preservative for wine but it is also like a drug – if we started now our juice would be addicted, and we preferred to use as few sulphites as possible.

Seán closed the insulation curtain and the metal sliding door of the winery, and we jogged round to where the harvester was.

Benoît was pulling at a trellis pole that poked out of the machine at a nasty angle. The section of vines above him and all its trellising had been ripped out.

'A part of the trellis got caught,' said Benoît. 'I stopped as soon as I realised but it was already too late for them.'

He pointed to the uprooted vines, ancients that had lived happily on this hillside for nearly seventy years. I felt like crying.

Seán moved to help Benoît pull the pole. They yanked it with all their shared force and nothing moved.

'It's too far in. We can't pull it out,' said Seán.

Something about the situation made me want to laugh. The craziness of it, the sadness of the dying vines, the phrase Seán had just used. Seán glared at me and I put a face on that matched the seriousness of the scene.

'Do you have a chainsaw?' asked Benoît.

'*Bien sûr*,' Seán said and turned to fetch it.

'I am very sorry,' said Benoît.

'Don't worry, Benoît, it's only a few vines,' I said, trying to downplay the situation since I could see he felt bad. 'I hope the machine isn't damaged.'

He pulled a face that said it all. It was the start of the harvest season. The CUMA, our agricultural cooperative, needed both machines working. From us he was due to go to another farm and then another. It wouldn't only be our morning that was affected. The machines worked around 16 hours a day – two driver shifts and sometimes more.

In minutes Seán was back, large chainsaw in hand. He and Benoît discussed the best approach then the telltale buzz split the dawn and the pole succumbed piece by piece. They worked like surgeons, careful not to damage themselves or the harvester. The chainsaw went silent.

'At first glance the harvester looks OK,' said Benoît.

Seán rolled away the wires and the uprooted vines, and Benoît leaped up the ladder into the cabin. He drove ten metres then stopped, leaned out and gave us the thumbs up.

'Crisis over,' said Seán. 'Back to work.'

'We've been out here half an hour at least. Won't our fruit be oxidised from sitting exposed to the air for this extra time?' I said.

'There was very little in the bins. He had only done a couple of rows when it happened. It'll be all right,' said Seán.

In the winery I kept looking out of the window to check on Benoît's progress. With the delay we would finish close to when my group was due to arrive.

The sun was up when he came back. The transfer went smoothly and while Seán backed the trailer up to the winery and set about preparing for the next part, I signed Benoît's harvest papers.

'You can apply to the CUMA for insurance for the damage,' said Benoît. 'It must have been a loose trellis pole.'

'Well, thank goodness the machine is working fine,' I said, ignoring the delicate pass of the blame.

We checked the vineyard for loose vines and poles before the harvest machine passed but it was possible that one had seemed OK to human touch but not to a thwack of a three-ton harvest machine.

'Would you like an espresso before you go?' I said.

With the pressure I felt about the day ahead, I already regretted making the offer. As if sensing my stress, Benoît unusually declined.

'I need to get on and I know you do too,' he said, nodding his head in the direction of Seán waiting for me. Our harvest couldn't be delayed another second.

'Thank you so much, Benoît,' I said and kissed him on each cheek.

He waved farewell from the top of the ladder then swung into the cabin and closed the door. The harvester whined and beeped, its tyres turning up the gravel of the courtyard, then took off up the road, its bulk dwarfing the adult cherry trees at the entrance to the farm.

'Come on, come on,' shouted Seán.

Back in the winery, I climbed the scaffolding to hold the pipe that was now finely balanced over the A-frame ladder and Seán started the auger. In minutes, most of the harvest had made it into the vat and Seán was scraping the fruit from the edges of the harvest trailer. He chased them with a bucket of water, the extra pressure from behind necessary to get some of the last fruit through. Then he switched off the auger and tractor. Jointly we unhitched the pipe and hiked it, still heavy with fruit, into a food grade bin to collect the last few litres.

I rolled the nitrogen gas bottle – almost the same size as me – to the tank as Seán climbed up, then passed him the gas wand.

Nitrogen is an inert gas and created a good blanket to protect our harvest from oxidation. He filled the tank with gas then handed it back to me and I rolled the bottle back into position.

Seven years of harvest and our motions were like a choreographed ballet. We moved automatically through the activities; no need to speak. Each year we improved our set-up and became more familiar with what we needed to do. We were old hands.

But the word 'hand' reminded me how important it was to not let familiarity allow our guard to drop. Seán had lost a third of his finger to the auger of the trailer we were using that day. It was the last day of our first harvest. Seán's finger still ached at times; the part that was missing itched like it was still there. It had recently started to grow a sharp bit of bone out of the side of the stub. He rubbed it subconsciously.

'We should have a cup of tea,' I said. 'I need to check on the girls anyway.'

Since the accident we had learned to take appropriate breaks during intense days. Being overtired created lapses in concentration that could be fatal on a farm and in a winery.

In the kitchen, Sophia and Ellie were putting on their shoes, preparing to go to school. They had dressed and eaten breakfast. Since they were too small to remember they had had to get on with their lives like tiny adults when we were in the midst of moments like harvest. I gave them each a hug and turned on the kettle.

'Are your bags ready?' I said.

They nodded sagely.

The kettle boiled as Sonia, our neighbour, arrived to pick them up. I quickly poured water into the two cups – black tea for me and rooibos for Seán – then went out to kiss Sophia and Ellie goodbye and help them up into Sonia's car. She had saved us on many occasions like she was that day, doing the school run for me at short notice.

'*Bonne journée!*' I shouted as they drove off.

In the kitchen plumes of steam rose over the cups and the fragrance of the two teas mingled in the air. I poured a drop of milk into mine and took the cups outside.

Seán and I sat down on a pallet and sipped our tea.

'I'll be OK doing the clean-up on my own,' he said. 'You get ready for your group. I can't help with the prep today.'

'I'll be busier than a one-legged man in a butt-kicking competition,' I said and laughed as I pictured the saying, a favourite of one of my sister's exes. With large groups, teaching all day plus preparing, serving and cleaning up was manic.

In the garden, the last of the baby tomatoes hung on the vines. I picked a few red orbs for my basket then tasted one, marvelling at the flavour. The view of the Dordogne Valley from the *potager* was like a scene from a fantasy film; mist swirled across the surface, parallel eddies snaking away from the river in constant movement. Immediately below us in the flat of the valley, two blue firs and the *château* of our neighbour's property peeked up through the mist as if they were floating on an enchanted cloud. I took in the view like a quenching drink of peace, then popped another tomato into my mouth, picked a few more for my basket and went inside to change into a dress and pearls. I slicked on lipstick and checked my face for sunscreen marks.

In the tasting-room kitchen, I set eight plates on the preparation table then cut the cheeses for the lunch and made the salad dressing. As I placed the cheeses back in the fridge, a minibus pulled up outside. My group had arrived, right on time.

For the next few hours, I was engrossed in sharing my passion for wine, *terroir*, vineyard, organic and biodynamic agriculture. After serving lunch, I jogged across the courtyard and wolfed down a slice of bread and tomato. Seán was stretched out on the sofa in the lounge for a half-hour siesta. Doing physical work all day, he needed a moment to recharge. There was no chance of that for me. I raced back to continue the lunch service and afternoon session.

The group left with warm farewells, promising to return and to share our address with friends. They were happy. The feedback forms on the table filled me with a warm sensation. Many said they left with a new appreciation for wine and particularly for organic wine. Of everything we were doing, this gave me the most satisfaction. It didn't feel like work. I loved it.

The cleaning up was another matter. I stacked as many glasses and plates as would fit into the dishwasher and set it to go so I could unload it and reload before closing up for the night.

It was already time to fetch Sophia and Ellie. I grabbed our dog Dora's lead and she barked with excitement.

We trotted up the last row of the hail-damaged Merlot to the village so I could see what it was like five days after the event. I didn't see any flies hovering or pick up smells of vinegar or rot as we passed, but there was no time to look closely – we were late. Dora sensed the urgency and raced ahead, pulling me up the hill like a sledge dog.

Sophia and Ellie were waiting at the school gate, the last to be collected. They gave me a look of reproach.

'*Mes excuses pour le retard*,' I said to Krystel, who ran the after-school service. ('Sorry I'm late.')

'*Pas de problème*,' she replied, her tone implying a little extra flexibility was allowed for winegrowers in the thick of harvest.

I kissed the girls on their foreheads.

'Sorry I'm late,' I said. 'Today has been hectic.'

'Don't worry, Mum,' said Sophia.

Ellie gave me a glare that said, 'Don't do it again.'

'So, how's life?' I asked as we set off back down the hill.

'OK,' said Sophia.

'*Bof*,' said Ellie.

Despite their downbeat replies I felt happy, filled with gratitude for where we were; for the soft autumn air; for the joy of walking; the grand panorama of the valley spread below us.

'Let's sing!' I said and waited a moment then started a song. 'There is fun everywhere, Olé olé olé, Swing your arms in the air, Olé olé olé.'

Ellie joined me and we sang the refrain again, then she added a section, '*et fait caca par terre*' ('and do a poo on the ground'). In French it worked perfectly with the rhyme of the song. I felt a little disgusted but found myself laughing.

'One of my friends made it up,' said Ellie gleefully, her class at an age where potty humour was still a hit.

'Oh no,' I said, laughing all the more. 'I'll never be able to sing it normally again.'

We turned down the second Merlot row and I stopped to check bunches and taste grapes every few metres. A few had fuzzy rot and I felt a pinch of anxiety. We were still a couple of weeks off the ideal moment for harvesting the reds. It would take some nerve to hold out.

As we entered the courtyard that formed the U-shaped centre of the house and outbuildings, Seán came out of the winery, arms wide, and the girls ran to give him hugs and kisses.

'Make yourselves a *goûter*,' I said. 'A drink, some fruit, some bread and jam, then do your homework. OK?'

'Yes, Mum,' said Sophia.

'Help Ellie if she needs it,' I added.

We expected Sophia to take the lead ever since she was tiny. Now, at nine years old, she was super responsible. I knew I could rely on her to do her homework without being asked, to get up on time, to have her breakfast and be ready. With Ellie, who was two years younger, it wasn't so certain. She found it hard to get up and needed follow-up supervision unless it was something she loved. She was timid with people she didn't know and rebellious at the same time, but she had an iron will and had been capable of staring down an adult at a couple of months old.

Leaving them to fend for themselves, I returned to my clean-up. After emptying and refilling the dishwasher and vacuuming the floor, it was 6.30 p.m. I had been on my feet almost non-stop for 14 hours. My dad was probably right with his 'if you keep going at this rate you'll be dead before you retire' comment, no matter how much I loved it.

We needed to find a solution to being overstretched but the cost of hiring someone, even at the minimum wage, made it difficult despite the growing demand for our visits and our wines. I set the dishwasher to run again, all the while thinking about what to do. To make the business financially sustainable we needed to sell out and sell everything in the bottle at higher prices than we were at that moment. But I wasn't sure how to get there, especially given the impasse of not having help. Selling more wine would take time I didn't have. We needed another pair of hands; to get that we needed more income. It was a chicken-and-egg situation I knew I wouldn't solve immediately, particularly since Seán and I took turns to cook and it was my night. I locked up the tasting room.

Realising the time, I turned to run to the house, tripped on the outside mat and flew across the gravel. I came down hard, knocking the breath out of myself. Head pounding, I picked my body up. I was dazed, and my knees and hands were bleeding, but there didn't appear to be any serious damage. Inside the house I cleaned myself off and found my lip was bleeding too. I disinfected the scrapes.

Oblivious to the flying mum act that had taken place, the girls had finished their homework and were preparing to play a game of Wii on our ancient, fat TV. I left them to it and went to prepare dinner. I didn't know what to cook but almost everything started with onions chopped and sweated in butter so I did that. Then I saw a bag of Seán's home-made tomato sauce in the fridge. I threw that in with crushed garlic, a pinch of sugar and salt, a twist of black pepper and a few sprigs of oregano from the garden and left the pan to simmer.

A pasta sauce like this needed a glass of Italian wine – for the sauce and for the chef. Taking a medieval-looking key from the cupboard, I walked down to the wine cellar under the house. Stepping into the ancient cellar filled me with awe at the weight of history, its sense of solidity and the bottles of wine – including our own from back vintages that were sold out. It was a crossroads of architectural history and wine. The back wall of perfectly cut square stones blackened with age dated, according to a local expert, to around 700 AD, the time when a monastery was constructed in Saussignac. The other walls were 'young', dating to the fourteenth and eighteenth centuries respectively. I still found it hard to believe it was ours and we were slowly building our own vineyard history in the wondrous liquid wine. I felt a little bipolar at times, as if my relationship with wine and our vineyard was love–hate. It was such a hard taskmaster, such a roller coaster, and yet I loved it.

Ours was nothing like the bottled history of some of the *châteaux* I visited in St-Émilion. At Château Guadet they had vintages going back to 1914. Ours was modest, a mere seven vintages. We knew them all, down to the details of 'Maeve and Conor were here for that harvest' or 'that was the year of the frost'. Each bottle and its year were a tapestry of memories, of hiccups and of successes. For all the angst of winegrowing, there was something profound about this *métier* (profession), where we worked with nature and made a living product that could last a lifetime.

The swap stock I had exchanged at the last organic wine fair we attended was piled up against the back wall. Like other fairs, it had been a good opportunity to meet other growers, but it had delivered little in terms of sales. Many buyers would walk past the appellation of Bergerac, not even bothering to stop and taste. If they did, we were too small and our volumes didn't come near their minimum requirements or our prices were too high for what they expected from the appellation. In the dim light I rifled through bottles stacked in cardboard boxes.

'Perfect!' I said out loud, spotting a Chianti, the ideal match for my pasta supper. I lifted the bottle that recalled a frantic swap with a handsome Italian at the end of the show but not much else. I wouldn't tell Seán that. 'Horse piss,' he would say, 'and he probably wore pointy shoes.' Seán had a thing about pointy shoes. For him they were a sign of a salesman, a slippery, shifty character and an instant write-off for the unsuspecting wearer.

The wine was a young Chianti DOCG (*Denominazione di Origine Controllata e Garantita*), made with organic grapes; mostly Sangiovese with a little Merlot. Since 1996, under pressure from the success of renegade wines known as 'Super Tuscans', Chianti had allowed up to 20 per cent of the blend to be international varieties like Cabernet Sauvignon, Merlot and Syrah (Shiraz).

'What's going on?' said Seán, passing the open cellar door as he walked up from the vineyard.

'Wine for tonight,' I said, holding it up without a word about the maker. I took my treasure and locked the cellar door.

'What happened to you?' Seán asked, noticing my lip then seeing my hands and knees.

I explained.

'You've got to slow down, Mrs C,' he said.

'Easy to say, not easy to do,' I said.

'I know,' he replied.

We walked back up to the kitchen together.

The sauce bubbling on the gas flame filled the kitchen with the delicious aromas of tomato and garlic. I took two glasses from the cupboard, pulled the cork and poured, savouring the sound of the wine passing from bottle to glass.

My nose picked up a waft of cherry then I gave the glass a good swirl and sniffed again, this time more deeply, allowing the aromas to expand through my nasal passage and into my brain. Images of cherry, cinnamon, scrub herbs and tea formed. I took a sip and slooshed it all around my mouth. On the palate it was light and fruity with good acidity.

'It's good,' said Seán.

'Not bad for a man with pointy shoes,' I said.

Seán's face dropped and I burst out laughing.

'He-he. Only joking.'

I crossed the courtyard for fresh parsley, snipped it into my sauce and served it on to just-cooked tagliatelle.

'Cheers, everybody!' I said, lifting my glass as I sat down. 'To a successful harvest!'

'Cheers, Mummy,' said Ellie, clinking her glass of elderflower juice and making eye contact then moving to do the same with Sophia and Seán.

We made our way around, careful not to cross each other in the process. It was a family ritual.

Eating together was a sacred moment but it was a weeknight so we didn't linger. Seán had started a routine where Sophia and

Ellie cleaned up so at the end of the meal we got up and left them to it. It was precious extra time. I went to catch up on the emails that had come in through the day. In amongst the work mail was one from a biodynamic truffle farm in Quercy, near Cahors, offering a truffling weekend in February. We farmed in the biodynamic way, like 'organic plus', so my ears pricked up.

To go biodynamic a farm must already be certified organic. In plant and tree farming – including vines – being organic means no chemical fertilisers, herbicides, systemic pesticides or systemic fungicides. Put simply, biodynamics includes three additional elements. The first is to think of the farm as a whole farm system, a living ecosystem that can be self-sufficient. The second is working with the farmer's almanac, a calendar of the earth's movements in relation to the moon, planets and constellations. Each cosmic entity is associated with one of the four elements of our world: fire, air, water and earth. By plotting them and their position in relation to our planet, the calendar identifies which element is strongest at a given moment. Each element is linked to a part of the plant: fire to fruit, air to flower, water to leaf and earth to root. The ideal moment to do different activities is when its associated element is strongest. For example, we plant carrots on a root day, lettuce on a leaf day, roses on a flower day, tomatoes on a fruit day. We prefer to harvest our grapes on a fruit day. It sounds crazy but think of the effect of the moon on the tides of the sea – if it can move that volume of water it's a seriously powerful force. Third, in biodynamics we use plant- and animal-based preparations and sprays, ideally from our farm, to aid the plants to grow and protect themselves.

I was a sceptic until I saw what a difference biodynamics made to our vineyard and to our wines. Since going biodynamic, we had decreased our dose of copper for combating downy mildew, one of the most dangerous fungal diseases in our region, from

6 kilograms per hectare (the maximum that was allowed in organic) to under 1.5 kilograms per hectare (less than a quarter of the maximum dose allowed for organic). With biodynamics, our vines were becoming more resistant to disease and our wines tasted better. Our experience made me want to visit more biodynamic farms.

St Amour's truffle weekend fell on our fifteenth wedding anniversary. In Dublin Seán and I would go out every year to celebrate but since moving to France all funds were siphoned into the farm and we hadn't been out to celebrate at all. This looked like an ideal opportunity to find out what the truffle hype was about, to learn from another biodynamic farm and to catch up on years of missed celebrations. I knew our relationship needed attention. It was like anything – ignored for long enough, it would wither and die. We needed to act before it was too late. Before I had time to think about whether we could afford it, I sent an email to book it.

Over the next month harvest progressed peacefully. We hand-picked the hailed Merlot on our annual vine shareholder weekend. Our diligent pickers carefully removed all rot. We lost a quarter in the sorting but the result tasted good. With the worry about hail damage assuaged and visits calming with the cold season, I should have felt more relaxed but instead I felt more on edge. I struggled to sleep and when I did I had nightmares about dying. I flushed hot and cold and felt out of sorts. My temper flared at nothing. Seán remained calm. He swept the chimney of our wood-burning stove. Winter closed in. Soups and stews took over from salads and barbecues. Sophia and Ellie began working on their Christmas lists.

CHAPTER 3

HUNTING BLACK GOLD

Real Christmas came and went. It was one I chose to forget as Seán gifted me a household steam-cleaning machine. He must have missed the How to Avoid Divorce 101 course.

I considered cancelling the truffle weekend but decided that I deserved it even if he didn't. He was halfway through the pruning when I gave him the card for our truffle experience at St Amour on our anniversary.

'I hope you booked the truffle menu,' he said. 'No point in going truffle-hunting if we aren't going to eat the truffles.'

I laughed nervously. He knew me too well and he didn't know how much the truffle menu cost. I had pre-booked the cheapest menu for both of us. I wanted to experience the place but the cost made me hyperventilate.

On the appointed day, we delivered Sophia and Ellie, bubbling with excitement about a night of fun with their friends Florence and Martha of *Famille* Moore. Dave and Amanda had transformed their run-down farmhouse, bought a couple of years before, into a *manoir*. There was no trace of the fire that had ravaged their living room when they looked after our daughters during our trip to California a couple of years before.

The stink that persisted for months was gone and the chimney that caused the fire had been erased. The progress they had made on the house and on the wine their vineyard produced was extraordinary.

After goodbye kisses, our daughters scampered off to play with their friends without giving us a second glance. As we drove away I felt sad to leave them. It was strange going away for a lovers' weekend.

St Amour was expecting us mid-afternoon so we had time for sightseeing. En route via small district roads the farming I observed passing by slowly changed from vines to grains and pasture. Through the window I drank in the sight of ancient Monflanquin, a *bastide* (a fortified town), bound by vestiges of a security belt of stone ramparts that were studded with five city gates in the Middle Ages.

The further inland we travelled the colder it became. The houses were more enclosed; windows were smaller; roofs steeper and colours more sombre. At Fumel, we parked the car and walked up through the village, around the famous castle with its terraced gardens and panoramic views, on to the Lot river. We looked for a guided visit but it was deserted and silent, a classic winter scene on a Saturday in modern rural France. A few boards told the history of the nobility of the castle but it was bone dry and I struggled to concentrate.

Feeling hungry we wandered back down, looking for a place to eat. I wanted something light and Seán wanted something solid after pruning for two hours that morning. We found a dark tavern that offered both and was the only place open.

Fumel was on the border of the region we were heading for: the Quercy, famous for Cahors wine, a strong and tannic red made from at least 70 per cent Malbec with blending partners of Merlot and Tannat. The region's food did a good impersonation of the Dordogne and was famous for all things duck. We knew it was best to stick with regional specialities that were certain to be local products. Seán selected *confit de canard* (duck confit) and a glass of local wine, and I chose *salade de Quercy*. When it arrived it looked exactly like a Périgourdine salad: a pile of fresh lettuce and tomato loaded with duck gizzards, smoked duck breast, walnuts and a vinaigrette dressing made with walnut oil. Both delivered more than we expected from the outer appearance. We were fortified and ready to truffle.

In the tiny village of Lariolle a sign pointed up a track to St Amour. It was remote and isolated; a cluster of houses rather than a village. We wound up to a small parking area in front of imposing gates. A dark green Porsche, a black Mercedes sports car and a red Audi cabriolet were already parked up. We squeezed our Mazda into the last space.

'Perhaps we should have brought the Louis Vuitton,' I said, taking out my beat-up kitbag received as a corporate gift years before.

Seán laughed, rubbing his old leather shoes with a cloth. He made to close the car boot.

'Don't forget the bag with the boots. We need them to go truffling,' I said.

'No way am I taking that old shopping bag in here,' said Seán. 'I'll come back for them later.'

Wrapped in coats and scarves, our bags slung over our shoulders, we passed through the gate and followed a stone path up to the main building, a double-storey Quercy farmhouse. A wide set of stairs led to a terrace where the door opened into a dining-room reception area. We heard voices and a slight blonde woman, dressed in jeans and collared shirt, appeared from their direction.

'*Bonjour*. Caro et Seán Feely,' I said, introducing us both.

'*Bonjour et bienvenue. Inés,*' she said and shook our hands. '*Enchanté.*'

'Sorry we're a little late,' I said.

'*Pas de problème.* We're having tea. I'll show you to your room so you can install your bags then you must join us.'

We followed Inés down the steps and up another staircase on to the terrace of a separate part of the farmhouse complex. She opened the door of a cosy-looking room and spread her arms in a gesture of welcome.

'Make yourselves at home. We don't have keys so just close the door behind you to keep the heat in. As soon as you are ready please join us.'

The room was cold but the bed had layers of inviting covers. Within, cream stone walls, a solid oak floor and exposed-beam ceiling provided the backdrop for antique bedside tables and a large bed, a walnut armoire, a flame-coloured sofa, a low table and a writing desk. I dropped my bag on to a chair and threw myself on the bed.

'Do you know truffles are an aphrodisiac?' I said, bouncing up and down to see how it felt.

'But you're on the cheapest menu that doesn't include truffles,' said Seán. 'Bad luck for you.'

We laughed. We had agreed that Seán would go for the middle menu that had some truffles but I was going to stick to the original low-cost booking to keep our spending within reason.

I jumped up and looked into the bathroom.

'A bath! Total luxe!' I said. At home one tiny shower room sufficed for four of us. When the Wine Cottage was empty in winter I sometimes stole across to enjoy the luxury of a bath, but since that part of the house wasn't heated unless there were guests, it was a pleasure tinged with pain.

'I'll get the boots,' said Seán.

I looked out of the window; vegetable gardens terraced down to a dam, with fields and forests beyond. It was beautiful and organised. Seán returned, boots in hand, not a shopping bag in sight.

'Thanks,' I said, taking my old leather hiking boots. I pulled them on and did up the laces. 'We'd better get over there – I don't want to miss the truffling.'

'Hang on, let me finish reading this article about the place,' said Seán, sitting on the sofa with a file of press clippings in front of him.

'No, we need to go! You can read that later,' I said, grabbing Seán's coat and pulling him like an excited kid.

'OK, OK!' Seán said and followed. 'Don't forget to tell them I want the middle menu that includes truffles.'

Despite having lived in France for many years, Seán still felt self-conscious talking French to people we didn't know. With friends he was at ease in the knowledge that they would accept his grammatical and pronunciation errors. In his lonely job in the vineyard he didn't get to practise as much as I did and he had started with less French than I had, having taken French at school.

In reception the sound of voices led us to the next room. It looked like a Louis Vuitton winter advert: blazing log fire, long dining table and six people outfitted in luxurious leather, fur and fine fabric, sipping from delicate cups.

Inés introduced us to the three couples, Parisians retired to a quieter life in La Rochelle. I got two names but even those I wasn't sure about. When we arrived in France I had had to replay a voicemail message eleven times to take down the name and number. Since then I had improved but traditional French names said quickly were still difficult to compute and more difficult to store. It was even more complex when people introduced themselves with surname then first name, as they were obliged to do at school.

Guillaume, Inés's husband, farmer and master chef, came through the kitchen door as she finished the introductions. We shook hands.

'*Enchanté*,' he said. 'Can I interest you in a coffee or something stronger before you go truffling? We have a local prune liqueur that these gentlemen are enjoying.'

'A coffee sounds magic,' I said.

'Liqueur please,' said Seán.

'A good choice,' said a portly fellow dressed like a tsar.

Guillaume reappeared with a small silver tray holding a tiny china cup and a tot glass.

'Is it possible to have a touch of milk?' I said.

'Of course,' Inés said and returned with a minute jug of cream. In France there was seldom a *nuage de lait*, a cloud of milk for coffee or tea. I poured and a rich yellow web spread through the dark brew. The powerful aroma drew me in; the coffee was luscious.

Guillaume moved to check a pot hanging over the fire. He adjusted a metal structure and, seeing me approach, explained.

'I can hang multiple pots and adjust their height according to the heat required. We can also roast a whole carcass or portions of meat.' He pointed to a spit and a small metal cage, like a barbecue grill but round. I felt like I had stepped back a few hundred years.

'Speaking of cooking, have you decided which menu you wish to book for tonight?' he said. 'While you are out I will start my preparations.'

'Thanks for reminding me,' I said. 'I had booked for the short menu for both of us but Seán would like the middle menu.'

'Unfortunately we can't offer different things for everyone as we are a very small team. You both need to book for the same menu,' said Guillaume. 'The short menu doesn't include truffles, and it seems a pity not to have truffle when you are here for the truffle weekend.'

Like any good Libra I deliberated for a moment, weighing the scales this way and that despite it being obvious which choice I had to make – we only had our fifteenth anniversary once in our lives.

'OK, we'll go for the middle menu,' I said and glanced at Seán.

He was following the banter, oblivious to the fact that I would be having an aphrodisiac dinner too. The group – including Seán – was settling in, the effects of prune liqueur and the warmth of the fire manifesting magnificently. It looked like it would be difficult to get them to move.

'*Alors*, are you going truffling or not?' said Guillaume, sensing the same thing.

'*Bien sûr!*' said the portly man's wife. 'Let's go!'

Wrapped in coats, scarves, hats and gloves, we descended the terrace steps. The temperature had dropped another degree or two.

'Wait here a minute while I get the dogs,' said Inés.

She went up to an outbuilding some 20 paces above the main house and opened the gate. A large black short-haired cross and a young blonde Labrador ran out in glee.

'It's cold but it's going to get colder,' said Inés as she rejoined us. 'Snow is forecast,' she added, pulling her jacket in.

I felt a shiver as I recollected our three-day siege in Burgundy due to exceptional snow a couple of years before.

Inés led the way out of the main gate and up a farm track that took us into a forest. A few minutes later, sensitive to the puffing of the corpulent tsar, she stopped.

'We'll take a break here so I can tell you some history of the truffle,' she said. 'The Quercy, the name given to this region, comes from the Latin word "quercus" for oak tree. Before organised agriculture what thrived on the high limestone and poor soil were oak trees. The truffle loves to live on the roots of oak trees so the region became famous for it. At the end of the nineteenth century, the *paysans* in France harvested around three thousand tons of truffles. Today it is a great year if we harvest thirty tons across the country. One hundred times less. Why this massive drop?' She looked around. 'Any ideas?'

'Chemical agriculture?' I said.

'Yes, that is a key reason,' said Inés. 'Any other suggestions?'

She looked around at our expectant faces then continued.

'What Madame said is correct – truffles are fungi and they need a living soil. In "modern" agriculture we use chemical fertiliser, systemic pesticides and weedkiller; these kill the life in the soil and hence the truffles.'

I could see question marks on the faces of the rest of the group. It didn't look like they had thought much about what form of agriculture was being used for their food.

'For the magic of the truffle to occur we need a living soil and that means farming organically at a minimum. Here we farm biodynamically as a way to take the life in our soil to a level beyond organic.'

I knew Inés could go a lot further with that thought but, like me with a group where the majority hadn't considered what organic farming was, delving into biodynamics was a step too far.

'But it's also our mode of living that has changed,' said Inés. 'For truffles to develop, the forest needs to be cleared of undergrowth. The light needs to reach the soil. In the past people collected the small bits of wood for kindling; browsers like deer and goats cleared the undergrowth and fertilised the soil at the same time. This light and the clearing of the undergrowth and animal presence are important for them to thrive. Does it make sense?'

We nodded.

'Any questions?' Inés paused a moment. 'Perhaps that's enough talking. Are you ready to see the truffles? The dogs are.'

They were racing back and forth, eager to get going like Dora, our dog, when I did visits at the vineyard.

'*On y va!*' said Inés, using the French term that means 'let's go' but directly translates as 'one goes there'.

Beyond us the end of the tall forest formed a window over the track that opened on to neatly manicured smaller trees. We stepped through the gap and entered a different world. The plateau rolled like a great undulating blanket of green stubble dotted with truffle trees in perfect rows.

'*Ça y est!* Here we are!' said Inés. 'We keep the trees pruned so that there is light on the ground. You see here?' She pointed to a stone circle at the base of the nearest tree. 'This is *le brûlé*, the burnt; this plant-free zone means there are probably truffles developing here. It is a telltale sign. We had better hurry – we have to follow the dogs to find the truffles.'

Inés sped off tracking the dogs. We followed, walking fast but not feeling the urgency that she did. The air was so cold it chapped my air passages as it passed through to my lungs. It smelt clean and clear. A great cloud of moisture formed with each out-breath. The rolling plateau – studded with precise white circles of limestone under each tree – felt remote, isolated and wild. Apart from the sounds made by our group there was deep silence; no cars, no planes, no machines.

'Show me, Bacchus, where is the truffle?' said Inés, bending over the black dog who was digging about a metre from the base of a tree.

He looked up expectantly.

'Look for it. Come on, look for it!' She pointed into the hole with her small trowel.

He continued a little more frantically then lifted his head again. Inés scraped away some dirt.

'There it is! Good dog! Bravo, Bacchus,' she said, and gave him a treat from her pocket then took the truffle out of the hole. She refilled the hole with earth, rose and passed the truffle to the nearest person.

'Smell that and pass it round,' she said. 'Our black gold.'

I took the nugget from Seán's outstretched hand. It was the size of a large walnut, with a bumpy, dusty, dark-brown surface. I saw why chocolate truffles were called such. It felt weighty and good in my hand. I lifted it to my nose. As I breathed in I closed my eyes. The smell was floral and earthy. It was like being transported to a field rich with late summer aromas and at the same time to the warm comfort of a winter fireside filled with umami notes of the finest *cèpes*, a meaty forest mushroom. It felt like magic, like it was connecting heaven and earth, summer and winter. In that breath I understood the excitement of truffles and why they cost so much. Years before I bought a tiny jar of oil with a truffle the size of a one-cent piece for Seán as a gift. It cost a fortune. He judiciously seasoned scrambled eggs and a roast chicken with it. We liked it but we didn't understand why it created such genuflection in the world of gastronomy. Now I knew. A sense of eureka filled me as I reluctantly handed it back to Inés.

The dogs charged off again and started sniffing at the base of a tree about 20 metres further on. It was the young dog's turn. Cosette dug frantically and soon found treasure, but she hadn't learned to give it to her mistress yet. Inés prised her mouth open, scolding all the while, and took the truffle, then tried to explain to Cosette that finding it was good but eating it was bad, and gave her a treat from her pocket.

Bacchus had found another spot and was digging like a dog in a cartoon, his paws whirring with limestone and clay flying out behind him. Inés ran over to him. Meanwhile, the younger dog had found a different spot and this time, with Inés's attention taken by Bacchus, Cosette ate what she found, gobbling truffles worth more than gold like they were dog biscuits. I called to Inés. She left one of the others to watch Bacchus and ran over to Cosette to salvage a piece of black gold from her jaws.

'We have to be vigilant and it's difficult with two dogs, but while she's learning I have to take them out together,' said Inés. 'It's best to be at least two with two dogs.'

Both dogs had taken off again, the older dog Bacchus streaking back up the slope towards the track that ran along the edge of the plateau. We raced after him and Inés called Cosette.

'It's incredible!' I said to Inés as I trotted next to her. 'From how far away can they smell the truffles?'

'Oh, we are not sure, but I think about thirty metres. Perhaps more,' she said.

As if to prove her point, Bacchus swerved into another row and came to a halt about thirty metres further on. He started digging and Inés caught up just in time to save the next nugget. It was like a strange game of hide-and-seek. She turned the metal bucket to show us how many she already had, a good five-centimetre layer of truffles of all sizes.

'How much are those truffles worth?' I asked.

'I don't know,' said Inés.

'It looks like about half a kilogram,' said the portly man. 'At least five hundred euro.'

'Phew!' I said. 'That's a good day's work for the dogs.'

'Yes, I think we have enough for today. We'll keep going up this way. The next section is young trees – there are no truffles there yet. We're experimenting with different companion plants between the truffles. We've made the rows wide enough to cultivate wheat between them. There are two benefits: the wheat aerates the soil with its root system and we get to harvest wheat that is delicately perfumed with truffle. But it's getting really cold so I think we should head back now,' said Inés as we reached a limestone track that dropped down off the plateau.

We followed her down a descent so steep it was almost vertical. I took teeny steps to keep my balance and hung on to Seán's hand. To our left and right the slopes were packed with trees holding the soil in place and stopping erosion. At the bottom a lower road took us back along the valley floor.

'We used to keep pigs, the traditional black pig of Gascony,' said Inés, pointing to an abandoned pigsty in the trees. 'They lived free and wild in this forest. But it became too much work with everything else that we were doing and made it difficult to travel so we decided to focus on truffles and hospitality. Now we have partners that raise the pigs as we would and we do the maturation of the hams and some other pork products. You will taste them later. We grow grain and sunflowers over there.' She pointed to a flat fertile field. 'We use local products in our cuisine, many of them directly from our farm.'

We continued chatting as we walked back. I was keen to understand as much as I could about how they developed and managed their farm.

'For heating we use solar and wood,' said Inés, pointing to rows of solar panels. 'We selectively thin the woods on the steep slopes. That is good for the forest and also forms the core of our heating in winter. We recycle our used water through a reed-bed system and we bottle pure water from the source on the farm.'

'Impressive,' I said. 'I hope we will be as self-sufficient one day.'

'It didn't happen overnight. It has been an ongoing project for more than twenty-five years. And of course we have new projects every year and trials with new techniques. We keep evolving.'

We reached the house and Inés invited us inside to warm ourselves while she put the dogs back into their run. The fire was blazing. We happily removed a few layers and revelled in the heat.

Guillaume burst through the kitchen door as Inés came in to join us.

'So what treasure did you unearth?' he said.

'A little,' said Inés, lifting the can.

'*Ah oui*, enough for supper tonight, I think,' Guillaume said and laughed. 'Have a seat and relax by the fire.'

We threw ourselves into the chairs around the table and allowed the warmth to infuse.

'Take your time. We'll be preparing the dinner. We look forward to seeing you at seven p.m.,' said Guillaume, making to leave.

'Before you go, Guillaume, I have a little question. Why no keys for the rooms?' said one madame dripping with jewels – little wonder the question.

'Oh, I have a funny story for you. We stopped using keys because people kept taking them – by mistake *bien sûr*. Our doors are old doors and replacing a lost key is not as easy as a quick trip to the key cutter. We didn't want to lose the character and charm of the place by changing the locks. Anyway, we are so isolated here, the farm is secure, we have dogs, there is no one around but us. So we decided to get rid of the keys. Everything is open – our house, the guest rooms. One day about five years ago, we had a couple from Paris for the weekend. They looked like they would have been more at home in St Tropez than St Amour. On Sunday evening the woman came running into reception saying, "My jewels have been stolen!"'

He looked around the room, enjoying the suspense of his story. 'We asked them to look everywhere. They looked again but returned adamant that the jewels, worth about fifty thousand euro, were gone. I called the local police. Half an hour later they arrived. The atmosphere was very strange. We were all potential perpetrators of the crime. With the crisis we weren't able to continue the normal service. Everyone staying at St Amour was gathered together in this room and questioned one by one next door in the parlour by the police, who also searched all the rooms. By midnight we were all exhausted and still there was no sign of the lost jewellery. The couple and the police went back to their room to search one last time. Hidden underneath the Madame's underwear they found her jewels!'

'But it is not possible!' one of the ladies said and clapped her hand over her mouth.

'*Mais oui*. The jewels had been found but we couldn't get the evening back. It was our night of Agatha Christie. We laugh about it now but I wasn't laughing then. The lesson is: don't hide your jewellery in your underwear.'

He went out laughing heartily while we, sharing in the laughter, dispersed to our respective rooms.

Seán and I decided to walk the route we had taken to the plateau to see the enchanting truffle fields again. This time we took the longer road back, one that extended further into the new truffle tree section. The air was icy and it was dark by the time we returned.

To recuperate I lounged in a luxurious bath filled with organic bubbles, one of the bathroom treats provided. I felt like a queen. While I soaked, Seán read the newspaper, appreciating the comfortable sofa. It was a life of luxury we hadn't experienced in a long while.

After drying myself in a soft-as-down bath sheet, I slipped on a gold G-string – as close as I was getting to jewellery in my underwear. Then I added sheer dark stockings, a little black dress, leather boots and lipstick. I was ready to go and Seán hadn't even hit the shower.

We exchanged places. I sat reading and relaxing. It felt quite extraordinary. I breathed deeply, enjoying the moment of peace, and sipped on a glass of our *Grâce* red wine that Seán had poured for me.

I felt in a state of grace, grateful beyond measure for this long overdue interlude. Seán emerged from the bathroom dressed in beige chinos and a blue collared shirt that matched his eyes. His golden mane was brushed, tamed into a halo, and his cheeks were shaved – rare in winter, when they needed hair to protect them from the cold while he was out pruning. I almost didn't recognise him. He looked so much younger without a beard.

'You shine up well,' I said, rising from the sofa. 'Ready?'

'Ready.'

The dining room had the perfect ambience of low lighting and intimate chatter. We greeted our truffling friends with a '*bonsoir*' and a wave. Inés had changed from farming gear, jeans and a cowboy hat to stockings, miniskirt and high heels. She showed us to our table and returned with a wine list.

As Seán perused the list and my hands itched to get hold of it, Inés explained quietly that the others were on the seven-course truffle menu and, so that we could keep pace with them, they would offer us a few extra truffle surprises. It was our lucky night. I had gone from no truffle to full-blown truffle in a couple of hours. If the aphrodisiac promise was for real, the place would be steaming.

Inés was welcoming but we felt a little ill at ease. It was so long since we had dined at an upmarket restaurant that we felt rather out of place.

Inés returned with a tiny square of lard for each of us, home-made bread and the aperitif Seán had ordered.

'The idea is to eat the lard on its own. It is to show that a simple product like this when well raised is delicious. It also gives you appetite. The bread is made from our own wheat, sea salt, water from our source and our own living yeast.'

'Thanks, Inés. That looks delicious,' I said, referring to the bread rather than the lard. You couldn't get more local than that: grown, ground and baked on the farm. The lard on the other hand didn't sound gourmet to me. It was a strange start.

'What do you recommend for the wine?' asked Seán. 'We would prefer local and organic.'

'Unfortunately the ones from Cahors available right now are not certified organic,' said Inés. 'We prefer organic and biodynamic wines but in the local selection we don't always have them.'

Seán made his selection from the Cahors list and Inés left to find our order. I was disappointed that this icon of organic and biodynamic farming was not selecting organic wines for their wine list. It didn't make sense.

Feeling a little reticent, I tasted the lard. It was delicious, full flavoured and nutty; my preconception was proved incorrect.

The arrival of the bottle of wine was accompanied by a small plate of *jambon de porc noir*, ham from black pigs of Gascony home-cured for 24 months. Inés explained that these black pigs could not be raised in intensive conditions. They needed to be free to range, ideally in the forest eating acorns and having fun.

We began to chat about the day: the truffles, the dogs, the freedom we felt in this isolated place, the ideas it sparked.

The menu followed like a symphony. A *velouté du curé*, a velvet-smooth, pastor's soup of *potimarron* (a small, gourd-like, bright orange pumpkin), laced with truffle and a hint of foie gras, started the adventure. There was more truffle in the soup than had been in the jar I bought for a king's ransom many years before. The flavours were divine, fit for a priest as the name suggested; I felt like singing hallelujah. I sipped my Cahors, appreciating the dense dark fruit and tannin, then took my last scoop of soup and sighed. How could things get any better?

But there was more – *bien sûr*. Next was a *risotto à la truffe* – home-grown wheat cooked risotto-style with truffle and leeks. Once again the 'simple' dish had a depth of flavour and a fragrance of truffle that filled the stomach and the soul. The aroma of brioche turned our heads as it came through the door. Each tiny savoury brioche had its own whole truffle inside. We ate slowly, savouring each bite; the infusion of truffle through the soft bread was intense. At that point our neighbours were served a layered potato dish, a *dauphinoise à la truffe*, and we had a much-needed break. It was the only part of the seven-course truffle menu we weren't served and it provided welcome time to talk instead of eat.

'That soup and risotto were *exceptionels*,' I said. 'It's the combination of the quality of ingredients and their heritage, the raising of it and all the steps in the transformation. All three were *juste*. They respect the product through the entire process from the growing to the processing to the final cooking. It's simply perfection and perfect simplicity at once.'

'I wonder if truffles would grow at Garrigue?' said Seán.

Garrigue was the old farm name and also the sector name of our part of the commune of Saussignac. We had changed it to Château Feely, our family name, a few years before because there were so many Garrigues on the market already and it was difficult to say.

'The limestone of their plateau looks like our *terroir*,' I said.

'Hmm, perhaps Dora could become a truffle dog,' said Seán.

'He he. Maybe. But Inés said it took fifteen years for the trees to start giving truffles,' I said. 'I'm not sure our loving Dora will be around for that.'

'But if you're lucky you might get them after five,' said Seán. '*Exceptionnellement*.'

Seán looked longingly at his empty glass.

'Wine and truffles – they just go together.'

'Absolutely. One for us to look into a little more.'

Inés served the main, *filet mignon de porc aux truffes*, pork tenderloin with truffle reduction sauce, and Seán ordered a glass of another local red.

When it arrived he took a deep sniff.

'Dark berries, a hint of truffle,' he said. 'This could be a perfect match.'

He took a bite of the pork and truffle sauce and a sip of wine. 'Delicious.'

'I'm jealous,' I said. 'One little sip?'

'No way, you'll leave lipstick on my glass and the wine won't be the same. Petrochemicals.'

Seán was a Luddite when it came to cosmetics.

'No petrochemicals, only natural products,' I said.

'How do you mean natural products? All lipsticks are petrochemical.'

'Not this one,' I said and whipped it out of my bag.

I had converted to organic and natural products, including my lipstick, but even those Seán didn't like. Perfumes and deodorants weren't allowed in our house, only a natural deodorant – and even that wasn't allowed in our bedroom because it brought on a sneezing fit for Seán.

He passed the wine glass over reluctantly and I took a small sip. It was a little softer than the bottle we had ordered but with a good body, dark colour and fruit typical of Cahors Malbec.

'I think the whole idea of what they are doing is inspirational,' I said. 'The basic products grown on the farm, the transformation of local unique products like the ham made with their ancient method, the restaurant that highlights their own produce. It's a circle like the one we have with the visits, the wines and the accommodation.'

'Hmm. The idea of a restaurant showcasing the farm's products is good but I don't like the hours a restaurant requires. We don't have any spare time anyway.'

'True,' I said.

'We need to work smarter,' said Seán.

We were talking about work again. It was inevitable when our lives took place at our work and we worked together. It was an upside and a downside. We loved what we did and were passionate about it – something that was a luxury in itself – but I wasn't sure how we would ever achieve a normal balance in our lives with this situation. For the previous eight years we had to focus on the business and neglect our personal life for our survival. Now we were inching closer to financial equilibrium as a business and our challenge was to achieve balance in our lives before it took an irreversible toll on our health and our relationship.

Inés removed our empty plates and soon returned with *pomme à la truffe*, apple in a rich egg custard laced with truffle. I ate the fruit and left the custard – a step too far for me. I offered it to Seán and he held his hand up.

'I love the isolation of this place,' said Seán.

I knew what he meant. Saussignac, our village, and the valley below us were constantly expanding with new houses. The main road beneath the farm had little traffic when we arrived but now carried an almost endless stream at peak hours. In addition we were aggravated by the conventional farming around us. We were fortunate that most of our vineyard borders were with other organic farmers, like our neighbour Olivier, or with wild areas. But when a chemical farmer sprayed, even miles away, we could smell it. The products were not innocent and they didn't stay on the targeted area. Looking down at the area around Mardenne we could sometimes see plumes of spray drifting well beyond where the sprayer was operating, on to neighbouring farms and into the Dordogne River. I had read that 92 per cent of France's waterways and rivers were polluted with pesticides from agriculture.

'It looks less intensively farmed here but I bet they have the same problems,' I said.

'But their farm is much bigger. Their buffer areas are way larger than ours.'

'We couldn't cope with more land. We're stretched as it is,' I said. 'And anyway, I'm not moving.'

Seán laughed. He knew that I wanted to be buried on our farm. I had always felt a need for an anchor, a root, and I wanted that for me and my family. I loved the solidity, the settledness, of a farm and a family's shared place like we had. I wanted our daughters to know they had a place to come back to when they flew the nest, that there was this solid base in the world. Sometimes the weight of the responsibility of that solid base made me feel like running away. Sometimes it didn't feel that solid, but it was there.

Inés reappeared with a small rectangle of chocolate *à la truffe* that signalled the end of the night's feast. It was delicious and heavily laced with black gold. The quantity of wine and food we consumed that night should have sent us straight to sleep. But it didn't. I can attest to the aphrodisiac effect of truffle.

In the morning I woke with the energy of a young lover. Seán was still asleep so I pulled on my boots for a walk instead. The dawn was just breaking and I had the world to myself. Even the dogs didn't stir as I tiptoed across the courtyard, let myself quietly out of the gate and took the path up to the truffle forest. As I stepped on to the open plateau, snow began to fall, soft white flakes lit up like a silver shower in the light of the dawn rising to the east. Over the white stones and perfectly manicured truffle trees it was like something out of Narnia; a magic land. It took my breath away.

I kept walking, pleased to have my insulated boots and barely able to believe the beauty was real. With the snow the silence was even greater. My footsteps were soft in it; no hard sounds, just the soft touch of the white blanket forming around me. It was extraordinary. The dark clouds above showered down flakes that shimmered silver and gold in the dawn light. I reached the point where we had turned down with Inés and considered going further, to where Seán and I had been the night before. I kept walking. The trees stretched out ahead of me in the swirling flakes. At the next corner I stopped and looked back, hesitating for a moment about whether to turn back.

Under the trees the *brulés* had less snow, their limestone circles a creamy colour against the pure white, punctured every now and then with grass stubble. Beyond the plateau the land plunged away to the valley floor and layers of hills disappeared into the distance, folds of lemon, gold and amber. The light and depth created between the snow and the cloud above me and the rising sun were like nothing I had experienced before. I stayed there, breathing the cold and calm and taking in the magic, until the cold in the tips of my fingers drove me home. I thought better of the long route. If the snow was building Seán might want to get home sooner rather than later to avoid Burgundy take two.

I teetered down the steep shortcut – even more treacherous with the snow – then stepped it out back to the farmhouse via the lower road.

Seán was up and had packed the car. As expected, he wanted to hit the trail before the snow worsened. Even without snow we had decided that the truffle egg breakfast, while tempting, was beyond our bellies and budget. Besides, another dose of that hefty aphrodisiac could have been dangerous.

We found Inés in the main house.

'I hope you enjoyed it,' she said.

'Oh yes,' I said. 'Especially hearing about the truffles on our walk with you and the dinner. We're organic and biodynamic farmers. In fact, we brought two bottles of our wine for you to try.'

'That is very interesting and kind,' said Inés. 'But it isn't me that decides on the wines. Let me see if Guillaume has a moment to talk to you before we serve the breakfast.'

Minutes later we were ushered into the cocoon of their professional kitchen. Their youngest child descended the stairs wrapped in pyjamas and gown. She looked sleepy, like she needed a quiet Sunday with her parents. It was their home as well as their workplace. We knew the feeling. Now I felt like we were invading their private space but Guillaume drew us in.

'Come, come,' he said. 'Tell me a little about yourselves. Can I get you a coffee?'

'I would love an espresso,' I said, the idea of a shot before our long drive very tempting.

Seán declined. He had been off caffeinated drinks for years and I guessed was also sensitive to our hosts' right to family time on Sunday.

We took turns to share our story and why the triskell, a three-way spiral, in a mosaic form, was the logo on our label. After many failures and a label 'hall of horrors', we had found our emblem.

'The triskell is an ancient Celtic sign. You can see it carved into rocks at Newgrange in Ireland, a site dating to 3500 BC,' said Seán. 'It's a nod to our Irish roots but we grew up in South Africa. My grandparents that came from Ireland farmed a vineyard in the Cape.'

'Springboks!' Guillaume said and lifted his jacket to show us a Springbok logo on his shirt.

A look of complicity passed between him and Seán. They were both rugby men.

Guillaume passed me a tiny cup of espresso. Inés took a jug of cream from the fridge and placed it on the counter. I mouthed *merci* so as not to interrupt Seán.

'We thought we would go wine-farming in South Africa but we moved to Dublin and on a holiday to France we fell in love with French wine and vineyards. It took years to find our farm in Saussignac. We have great *terroir*, a section of limestone plateau similar to yours but much smaller.'

'Interesting,' said Guillaume, lifting the bottle for a closer look at the triskell.

'We're passionate about organic and biodynamic,' I added. 'The triskell symbolises the biodynamics too since the spiral is emblematic of nature and of dynamisation. We're excited and inspired by what you're doing here, your self-sufficiency, the truffles, the food you served last night. It's an experience we'll never forget.'

'Thank you,' he said.

'I have one question,' said Seán. 'How did you make the truffle risotto?'

'Ha ha, you need a lot of truffles,' Guillaume said and opened the fridge to show us a bowl of dry spelt grains with several large nuggets of fresh truffle nestling inside. 'It is a good way to store the truffles and it gives truffle flavour to the grain.'

'Thank *you* for a fantastic stay,' I said. 'And Inés for the truffling – the afternoon was *magnifique*.'

'Thank you for the wine. We will taste them and let you know,' said Guillaume.

We left them to serve breakfast. The retired Parisians had appeared and were limbering up to start their truffle egg feast. We were happy to leave them to it, the extravaganza of the previous night a strong cerebral and corporeal memory.

At home, we were thrown straight back into the cycle of long days and constant work. I followed up about the wines but we never heard back from St Amour. It left a little bitter note in the experience. They probably didn't have time to deal with individual producers plus it would be impossible to deliver to them for a reasonable cost. Or perhaps they hated our wines – I still had a sense of anxiety and momentary lapses of confidence in them. Like Bo Barrett in the film *Bottle Shock*, I hadn't learned to trust our wines and my taste buds.

A friend in St-Émilion, Vince Lignac, often said, 'I make the wine I like. I can't please everyone so I make the wine that reflects my *terroir* – a true wine, not a wine for a market.' That was what we were doing. I had to have confidence in them as much as we had to find balance in our lives. The fact that we had sold out of old vintages, despite the horrific labels that had graced them in our early years, was a sign that the wine was good.

But whatever Inés and Guillaume's reasoning, I had to get on and make wine sales. The *gîte* bookings were slow. I kept getting requests for a swimming pool and a television. We had made a decision to not install TV, wanting the experience for our guests to be about wine, nature and outdoors. With our precarious finances a swimming pool had been out of the question. A quick online review of competing *gîtes* showed that we had to have one if we wanted our accommodation to be successful. That and the rising summer temperatures of recent years made it a necessity.

The getaway had been good for our relationship but a single swallow didn't make a summer. We returned to our bad habits. Seán barely acknowledged my presence when he came through in the morning. I got a grunt rather than a hello or a kiss. We were supposed to be married but we were no closer than business partners. My concern about our relationship compounded my sleepless nights. I woke up at 3 a.m. and started writing my second book. I had to make something positive out of the situation.

CHAPTER 4

ORANGE EGGS

Seán stomped into the kitchen, back after four hours of pruning. I was oblivious to the time, wrapped up in front of my computer working on the final edit of *Grape Expectations*, my first book, due out that summer.

'Where's lunch?' he shouted. 'I'm starving!'

He was frozen and exhausted.

'I didn't notice the time,' I said.

'Yeah, yeah, sitting toasty in the warm house. Couldn't even be bothered to make a hot soup for her husband.'

I unbent myself from the keyboard and pushed back the old wicker chair that had travelled from South Africa with us decades before. Its feet scraped across the wooden floor. I needed a proper desk chair with support and wheels – for my back and for the floor. I hobbled from the 'office', a room in our house, through a dark landing and into our small galley kitchen. After being hunched over the computer for so long I felt stiff as a board.

We dreamed of renovating our house but it would be the last renovation on the list. Since the St Amour truffle getaway, we were crackling with ideas of how to broaden our farming base;

thoughts of truffle trees, farm animals and how to make our tourism offer an even better experience. Years of investment and effort were required for these initiatives, all of which would take priority over our home renovations.

'Sorry,' I said as I entered the kitchen. Seán's disgust that I didn't turn out a fine farmer's lunch every day was an ongoing tussle with a pinch of joking and a tablespoon of serious.

'Guess I'll make it myself,' he said, putting a handful of just-picked wild leeks and kale on the counter. 'What's wrong with you?'

'Nothing. Just a bit stiff,' I said. 'Should have taken some breaks to stretch but I was so engrossed I didn't.'

'Every hour, Mrs C. You have to get up and stretch every hour. Or come and do some vineyard work – that would be even better.'

He stepped back on to the porch to take off his boots, put on his house clogs then washed his hands. He turned from the sink and took two homegrown onions from the vegetable rack, a thick wood board and the Henckel knife my sister had given us years before, then returned to the counter nearest the oven.

He chopped like a pro. His right hand took a bit of leftover butter and threw it into the iron pan, just warm from the gas flame. When the butter sizzled the chopped onions went in, then the wild leeks followed by kale and a handful of organic mushrooms that had been sitting in the back of the fridge. Cooked potatoes from a few nights before were chopped and followed the rest.

'Won't you grab a handful of parsley for me?' he said.

'Sure.'

As I stepped out into the courtyard the cold wind smacked my face. It felt good, fresh and alive. I needed to get out. I missed the outdoors when I was stuck inside doing administration or writing for days on end. The mass of parsley that Seán had planted in an old cut-out *barrique* was in good shape. Second-hand barrels made perfect plant troughs cut in half or laid sideways with a window cut out of the top like this one. The parsley was cold and damp to the touch. I lifted it to my nose and sniffed deeply. It mingled with the aroma of Seán's cooking wafting on the air, getting stronger with each step back to the house. My mouth started to water.

I rinsed the parsley and passed it to Seán. In a flash it was finely chopped like I could never do. Seán was a perfectionist chef. He chopped fine. I chopped rough. He threw the parsley in then piled two stacks of the mix on to our plates and popped them in the oven.

He placed two of Blanchette's eggs into the pan alongside two eggs bought from the supermarket to supplement our now tiny supply. We had kept chickens for years but only one, Blanchette, was left of the original batch of eight. Our homegrown egg supply had been a key part of our self-sufficiency. Blanchette still laid the odd egg but nowhere near what we needed for our family of four. The shop ones were a light yellow and Blanchette's were dark yellow, almost orange. Seán took the plates out of the oven and placed one of each on top of the mix. The aroma was savoury and delicious.

'Thanks, SF,' I said and took the plate. I sat down at my end of the old pine table and Seán settled into his end.

'Salt and pepper please,' he said.

I got up from my chair and leaned across the table to pass them. Even when it was just us we sat at the far ends, nearly two metres apart.

'Thanks,' he said, reaching to take them.

I cut into the home egg and the orange yolk spread across the mushroom, kale and potato mix. I took a forkful. It was bliss; the textures and flavours were in perfect harmony. I closed my eyes for a moment to appreciate the gourmet sensations in my mouth.

'That is so good, SF,' I said. 'I can barely find words to describe it. Earthy, salty, umami. Yummy.'

Next I cut into the shop egg and took a bite. It was egg but it was not bliss. The harmony was gone.

'What a difference!' I said. 'That shop one is a pale rendition of egg.'

'Exactly. That's what I've said all along,' said Seán. 'When we don't have our own we have to get the eggs from the organic lady on the Bergerac market.'

'It's like the truffle I bought in a jar compared to the real thing,' I said. 'It's crazy that such anaemic eggs can be called "organic free range". I guess at least we're sure the chickens aren't battery-style and they aren't eating genetically modified grain and antibiotics.'

'They are *industriels*,' said Seán, almost spitting the word out in disgust. 'They're following the letter of the organic law but not the spirit. That's what happens when it's all about lowest cost.'

Like some of the organic vegetables in the supermarket they had lost their soul, but at least they weren't packed with pesticide residues. I moved the shop-bought egg aside and took another mouthful of the heavenly food on my plate.

'We need to think about getting new chickens,' I said.

'Not until we've had our summer holiday,' said Seán.

Friends had offered us their holiday house in Provence for a week. We had been before and were looking forward to another break at their beautiful *mas*, a traditional Provençal farmhouse. We needed it.

'But we need to have animals. To be truly biodynamic our farm needs to be a closed circuit. We need their presence, their energy and manure.'

'I know. But look at us. We don't have time to scratch our bums,' said Seán.

Whenever he used that expression I couldn't help but laugh.

'Anyway, before I forget, I need a new mower,' said Seán, looking at me drily. 'The old one won't fit down the new Cabernet rows.'

That stopped my laughter. The vineyard and winery were a bottomless pit of expense. My mind cast around.

'But what about sheep instead of a mower? Couldn't we get a band of sheep? Like we saw at Benziger and at the Fetzers' new place, Ceàgo, in California?'

'Someone has to look after the sheep. Animals take money and attention,' said Seán.

'But they'll generate income as well. Meat and wool,' I said.

'You can't give the wool away,' said Seán. 'In Europe it costs more to get a shearer than you can sell the wool for. I looked into that already. For the meat, yes, that will perhaps generate some revenue but there's a lot of red tape if we want to sell the meat. We need to research it more. But regardless of that, in spring when the first vine shoots are out and the grass is growing gangbusters, I'll still need the mower since the sheep would eat the young shoots.'

'*Alors* you'd better find out how much the mower will be and we'll have to build it into the budget,' I said.

'And you had better make sure you find the right eggs,' said Seán.

'Ecologically it makes total sense to get sheep,' I said. 'I met a couple at the Vinexpo Expression Bio Show last year. They've successfully run sheep on their vines for years. I'll contact them to ask if we can visit.'

Our lunch had been a working lunch again. Our work was our life and our life was our work. To be truly good at what we were doing we had to find a balance. We had to be more disciplined about taking time out for ourselves but the rising tide of our growing business needed all the hours we had.

That afternoon I called Andrea and Fearn, winegrowers and shepherds near Castillon, and re-introduced myself.

'You must come soon so your daughters can see the lambs,' said Andrea. 'Why don't you visit us on Wednesday afternoon? We can show you the sheep and then have afternoon tea.'

I felt Andrea's warmth and open spirit over the phone.

'Thanks, Andrea. That would be perfect,' I said.

We chatted a little about the season before I hung up, delighted to have the sheep research visit lined up.

Wednesdays were half days for schools in France. French school had gone from a four-and-a-half-day week with Wednesday off and a half day on Saturday to the half day on Wednesday then to a four-day week to save money on school transport and then back to the half day Wednesdays when the state realised the teachers couldn't fit all the work into a four-day week. We had barely got used to one programme when it changed again. Each time the days were changed or the order was switched, the teachers' unions would call for a day of strike action and no one would go to school. I wondered if it wasn't all just an excuse to have a day off.

'Wait for us, Mum,' said Sophia.

She and Ellie were a few steps behind me on the library stairs. I stopped and waited for them to catch up.

Seán had started a Saturday routine of library and market in Bergerac, a working town with a beautiful historic medieval centre, 20 minutes from Saussignac. In season, I was hectic with *gîte* changeovers and clients on Saturday; now, in winter, I had time while Seán had to be out pruning on all the good-weather days God gave us. Some days, like today, the expedition would stretch to include a cream tea at the Victoria Café, offering a touch of glamour to the outing.

From the library we followed the main street to the market, the place to find our artisan organic egg producer. The eggs had dark yellow yolks and a taste that told us the chickens were outside eating grass and insects, not only grains. It was not merely the taste that was affected: eggs from outdoor 'grazing' chickens had up to twice as much vitamin E, 40 per cent more vitamin A and three times as many omega-3s. Our egg mission addressed both health and taste.

The winter sun's cool rays played across the streets packed with stalls, light and shade changing with the constant movement. People's breath rose like smoke in the air. Sometimes an unknown salesman would take up prime position in front of the church. That day the product was a plastic kitchen utensil and the presenter had a large crowd looking on as he played out his routine. He promised that his gadget would transform your life. It seemed so out of place. I felt like chasing him out of town. We had learned to buy equipment that would last our lifetimes, if not generations; iron pans, solid metal graters with no plastic attachments. We knew the real thing, like a metal pan or a cast-iron pot, was good value if you considered the lifetime value rather than the one-time cost. My most recent purchases, of dustpans, were metal. Already they had lasted longer than any of the plastic ones in my past. The price was 25 per cent more than the plastic version and I had already recouped that in longevity.

We found a passage through the crowd growing around the salesman and I led the way down the side street to the left of the church. Our first stop was our organic baker, a shy man. I had bought from him many times but never struck up a conversation. With the church towering above us, we stocked up on wholegrain bread and perfumed chocolate brioche buns for Ellie and Sophia, ending the transaction with a quiet 'thank you'. With bread and brioche safely stored in our cloth shopping bag, we took off again. I found pleasure and satisfaction shopping on the market and getting to know our suppliers. Here a person's product was an extension of themselves. Like us, their products reflected their personalities.

'Wait for us,' shouted Sophia a few steps behind me. 'You're going too fast, Mum.'

I stopped and hung the bag over my shoulder so I could take their hands, gave them both a squeeze and slowed down the pace. Usually I was in such a hurry I raced around the market circuit like it was a Formula One track. I had to learn to slow down, to take in the environment with all my senses.

I became aware of the smells as I passed, the pungent freshness of the vegetable stands and the rich yeasty aroma of the *boulangers*, the conversation between market goers and stallholders, the cooing of the pigeons on the church above us and the hum of cars on the main street nearby. I looked at the stalls more closely, as if seeing the patchwork of colours and movement for the first time.

There were large stands packed with masses of produce; traders rather than producers. There were farmers' stands, sometimes two generations or even three, working side by side. At one stand, a couple, weathered and well into their seventies, sat behind a small wooden table garnished with plastic containers of walnuts and mushrooms. Behind the containers were a few jars of honey and home-made jam. I wondered how much change they had seen in this town and market in their lifetimes. I was tempted to stop but a quick look at my watch told me that if we wanted to get to the Victoria Café before the lunch rush we had to keep moving.

On the lane that hugged the other side of the church I found Valérie, a natural organic cheese and yoghurt producer that created *tarin*, an unpasteurised cow's-milk cheese that came in small and large rounds and in bricks. It was creamy and delicate and we loved it. We joined the queue. The tall grey-haired man in front of me ordered his cheese.

'I like your cheese so I buy it but I don't see the difference between organic and not organic when it comes to dairy,' he said to Valérie. 'I don't see why I should pay more for organic milk. Aren't they all out eating grass?'

Valérie took a deep breath and a dose of internal patience. She reached for the cheeses he had requested and started to wrap them. Once composed, she looked up and gave him a little smile.

'Well, Monsieur, a few things are different. With conventional you could be drinking milk laced with wormicide, antibiotics and weedkiller, to take a few. Organic dairy means no herbicides, no pesticides, no genetically modified feed and no antibiotics in your milk. They can be part of your daily dose if you consume conventional dairy.'

'I never thought of that,' he said.

'*Beh oui*, Monsieur. There are many differences. To get back to what you said about the grass, conventional dairy cows can be fed grain indoors for part or all of their lives so they may not be eating grass at all, whereas with organic dairy pasture-fed is guaranteed. And of course, the organic rules mean better care and better health for the cows. I could talk for a long time on this but I must serve Madame. Thank you in any case.'

He looked like he could have uttered the French term '*bouche bée*' ('mouth wide open') as he took his order off the counter. I felt like running round and giving Valérie a pat on the back but my daughters found me embarrassing enough so instead I gave her a wide smile, ordered my cheese and yoghurt and quietly moved on to make space for the next person.

Valérie probably had stats at her fingertips like I had for wine, including studies showing that artisan organic milk like hers had up to 50 per cent more vitamin E, 75 per cent more beta-carotene and 70 per cent more omega-3 fatty acids than conventional milk. It also had more than double the amount of certain antioxidants, like those that keep your eyes healthy as you age. It wasn't only that you weren't getting the bad things like wormicide, herbicide and antibiotics; you were getting a product naturally packed with good things.

The number of organic stalls had grown over the years but it was still relatively low. Based on a quick stall count I estimated less than five per cent. For the average person there was little awareness of what organic meant and why it was worth seeking it out. As producers we knew why so deeply that we only ate organic food. We knew that our health was too precious to compromise on what went into our bodies. We didn't have the latest mobile phone and we shared one old car but we only ate organic.

A few stalls on was our egg producer. I still didn't know her name but I could tell she recognised my face. She and her partner also grew organic vegetables and produced home-made pasta, including one that was a delightful shade of green thanks to a dose of stinging nettles. It tasted so good – with salad and a little olive oil and garlic, it was a meal in itself.

Stinging nettle was a plant we used in biodynamics. The Latin name of 'nettle' is *urtica*, from *urere*, to burn or scorch, because of how it burns or stings when you touch it. We had masses of it on the farm. I loved nettle soup but we also dried the leaves to use as a tea for the vines. Sprayed on the leaves it acted as a mild antifungal. Macerated fresh, the leaves could be used as a fertiliser or a compost spray. The leaves are high in nitrogen and contain magnesium, sulphur and iron, thus are a good compost activator too.

Loaded with our shopping, bulked up with stinging-nettle pasta and eggs, we walked down the cobbled streets of old Bergerac to the pedestrianised lane that held the Victoria. An olde English-style metal sign hanging on a gold chain announced the location of the tiny café wedged in above a tea shop. The French couple that ran it were tea fanatics.

Inside, the cramped space was like a *Harry Potter* film set except that instead of magic sweets or sorcery books there was tea and every type of tea accessory you could imagine. The wooden beams were hung with hooks carrying mugs; the walls were lined with shelves crammed to bursting with teacups, pots, caddies and related decor. Display cabinets filled the floor space save for a skinny corridor that passed by the sales counter and went up a steep set of wooden stairs to the cosy teahouse. Deep armchairs and tea tables lined the outer walls, and bistro-style tables and chairs filled the middle. The walls were hung with English-style memorabilia of horses, rugby and gardening. Ellie and Sophia made for the armchairs closest to the window.

'Luxury!' I said, taking the bistro chair that was left.

'*On est bien la, hnn,*' said Ellie, looking smug and sounding so French.

Monsieur Victoria appeared and handed us the menus. 'On special today we have tiramisu and black forest cake.'

'It is a special day *alors,*' I said. 'Sophia and Ellie love tiramisu.'

'Hot chocolate and tiramisu please,' said Sophia.

'The same,' said Ellie.

'Please,' I said.

'Please,' added Ellie.

'Organic Earl Grey tea and scones for me please,' I said.

Monsieur Victoria thanked us and whisked himself away, swishing behind the pink cotton curtain that marked the entrance to the small galley kitchen where they worked their wonders.

I tried to inculcate in my daughters how important it was to say 'please' and 'thank you' and to take time to be grateful each day, but sometimes it felt like a losing battle.

'I'll have to give you punishment like I had at boarding school,' I said. 'Early rising. That was getting up at five thirty to do an hour of hardcore exercise before the school day. We had to run so much that some kids would vomit. We were so stiff the following day we could barely walk up the stairs.'

'Ha ha,' said Ellie.

'You laugh. But if you don't remember to be *gentille* then I'll have to start doing that. There'll be a double benefit because you won't forget your manners and you'll get fit.'

'Oh, Mum, that was of your days. Of our days we don't do things like that,' said Sophia, using her own special English expression 'that was of your days' based on the French '*de nos jours*'.

'But we should,' I said, barrelling ahead. 'And I think we need a six-day week like we had – a full work week with a half day on Saturday. None of this four-day week nonsense.'

A look of horror spread across their faces. I burst out laughing and they did too.

Monsieur Victoria swooshed back to our table with a tray loaded with goodies.

'A hot chocolate and tiramisu for mademoiselle, a hot chocolate and tiramisu for the other mademoiselle and the Earl Grey and scone for Madame.'

'Thank you,' I said.

'Thank you,' chimed Sophia and Ellie, clearly frightened by the threat of early rising.

'*C'est moi. Bon appetit,*' he said.

The term '*c'est moi*' directly translated as 'it's me', a short way of saying 'it's me that thanks you'.

I took a sip of Earl Grey and a bite of my scone with jam and cream. I was not like many of my daughters' friends' mums, who were into clothes, make-up, city living and things like shopping. I was into walking, farming, wine and the outdoors. I had to find things for us to enjoy together without doing what I didn't like or what they didn't like. Before we knew it they would be grown up and gone.

'Yum,' I said and took another bite of scone loaded with jam and cream.

'You have cream just there,' said Sophia, pointing to a glob of cream on my top lip.

'Thanks,' I said, wiping it away. 'Thinking of school days, wouldn't it be great to go to South Africa?'

'Oh yes!' said Sophia.

'So good,' said Ellie.

'So long as there's no "early rising" there,' said Sophia. She frowned then laughed.

'When can we go?' said Ellie.

'I don't know. It depends on how quickly we can save enough money,' I said. 'We'll have to work towards it. It means saving our money instead of going shopping and having fancy cream teas.'

They looked crestfallen.

'It will be worth it,' I promised.

It was 12 years since I had been back to South Africa, the land of the first 27 years of my life. Sophia and Ellie had never visited it. We had been so focused on our farm and so financially stretched that a trip had not entered my head. Now, as I thought about it, I felt a wave of homesickness, of missing South Africa, a feeling I had kept at bay by necessity. I added the cost of flights to my long list of budget priorities. For the balance of our lives, for our daughters to know their roots, to see Seán's parents, for so many reasons, we had to go.

We had become a Demeter certified biodynamic farm and with that certification came the obligation to have animals. Demeter is the largest biodynamic certification body in the world. They ensure that products that carry their logo and the 'certified biodynamic' label meet the rigorous standards of biodynamic farming and production. We knew we would continue to keep chickens but not as free as they had been. A reckless chicken had trashed the tasting-room table the previous year, smashing glasses and creating mayhem. They were so friendly they left their manure gifts near the front door and on the terraces of the *gîtes* and the tasting room. A wine-tasting experience that included the stink of chicken poo was not one that we wanted. We had to rethink our chickens.

If we couldn't control a few chickens, considering more animals didn't seem like a great idea but it didn't stop us visiting Château Brandeau, the vineyard in Castillon. They had been mowing their vines with sheep for decades. I loved the idea of a closed circuit where the sheep ate the grass and returned the manure to the fields as they browsed – and gave us meat in the process. But we were frightened by the extra responsibility and bureaucracy animals would bring. Already it was difficult to get away. If we had farm animals it would be even more so.

Château Brandeau was in a small valley bowl nestled against the plateau of Castillon. The final stretch up to the farm was a swathe of rolling hills filled with vines and patches of forest. In the gravelled entrance a black *deux chevaux Citroën* added a touch of French cachet to the natural beauty. Alongside the parking area a lean-to shed packed with farming equipment rested on a limestone cliff, and on the opposite side an old farmhouse with climbing roses and a brand-new winery smacked contrasting facades uncomfortably together.

A tall solid man with shoulder-length white hair stepped out of the front door and crossed the gravel.

'Fearn,' he said, stretching out his hand.

'Andrea,' said a wiry, strawberry blonde, a few steps behind him.

'Caro, *enchanté*,' I said, shaking hands. 'Thank you so much for inviting us. Your farm is beautiful.'

'It's home,' said Andrea after greeting us. 'Perhaps we should start outside and then visit the new winery before we have tea.' She looked at our footwear somewhat dubiously. 'I have some spare boots.'

She and Fearn were well shod for the season, sporting serious wellingtons. Seán was the only one on our team with the right equipment; I felt like a right 'townie', the name country kids gave to city kids when I was growing up. Andrea headed inside for extra wellies.

'A fire took out the winery two years ago,' said Fearn, noticing that we were looking at the modern winery building. 'We were lucky we didn't lose the house and the insurance paid for this new, better insulated version.'

'How frightening,' I said.

'It was.' A look crossed his face that said he wouldn't enjoy stirring up the memory.

Andrea returned with boots and we pulled them on. She went back inside and came out again with two wine bottles fitted with teats.

'To feed the lambs,' she said, seeing our questioning looks.

'All ready?' said Fearn.

We nodded.

'*Alors*, let's go!'

We followed him down the muddy track with Ellie staggering after us in boots five sizes too big.

'You were asking about the administrative part of the livestock,' said Fearn. 'We went the simple route. We keep the sheep to mow the grass but we don't sell the meat. We have to declare them but the administration is relatively light. If we wanted to sell them as organic meat there would be a lot more hoops to jump through.'

'That's what we were worried about,' said Seán.

I left the two men talking and pulled back to help Ellie, who was trailing a way behind. Andrea drew back too.

'Don't worry, Ellie, it isn't far,' she said. 'You'll see. And it'll be worth it. There are new lambs.'

We passed through a wide farm gate into a vineyard enclosed by brush and forest. I spied the sheep at the top end and pointed them out to Ellie. Some had already seen us and were running down the hill, their long tails flapping. In the group were two black lambs with white faces and a touch of white on their tails.

'I'll show you how to feed them then you can do it yourselves. OK?' said Andrea to Sophia and Ellie.

They were a little scared at first. They had never been this close to sheep before. I felt as if I were in a time warp – growing up, my favourite pet was an orphan lamb called Mini, shortened to Min. She was born premature and at night my grandmother woke up to feed her with an eyedropper every couple of hours.

Min made it against the odds. She would hear my voice when I returned home from school and race across the paddocks and cry, '*Maaa maaaaa*' at the gate until I came and let her out to be with me. She was closer to me than my dog.

'They are so cute,' said Sophia as the lamb sucked on the bottle she was holding.

'I want one, Mummy,' said Ellie.

'They are very cute, my kiddies. But if we get sheep they have to pay for themselves. They would mow the grass and we would eat them.'

'Never!' said Sophia.

'No way!' said Ellie.

'Well, you do need to find a use for the excess rams and eating them is a good solution,' said Andrea. 'Officially we don't eat ours – they die of natural causes. They're only here to mow the grass and they do it very well.'

Andrea was a wise woman. She didn't talk a lot, and when she did you listened.

'It's getting cold. Would you girls like to see the horses before we go in for tea?' she said.

'Yes please!' said Sophia and Ellie in unison.

I was pleased to see my lesson in *politesse* at the Victoria Café was paying off.

'Fearn, you show Seán and Caro the new winery and I'll take Sophia and Ellie via the horses,' said Andrea, leading the way back out of the gate. Sophia and Ellie happily followed. Usually they would have been shy of someone they had just met but Andrea was already their friend.

Leaving them with the horses, I caught up with Seán and Fearn in the new winery. It was a dramatic contrast to the rest of the farm. The clinical, square space housed large, stainless steel tanks and an upper level of two drywall offices and a washroom.

'It's easier to keep things clean in this new space,' said Fearn. 'The last vintage was great. Perhaps the best we ever made.'

He moved along and led the way out. We passed from the modern block into the house through a narrow stone passage that seemed as old as time. We popped out into a warm, aroma-filled living room with large oak beams overhead.

Andrea was making tea. Sophia and Ellie sat on a brown sofa next to a wood-fired stove, stroking a cat. I felt like a time traveller. Fearn invited us to sit and I sank into a deep threadbare chair near the fire. It felt snug as a hug. The large open-plan kitchen, dining area and lounge oozed comfort. It was ancient and loved. Andrea cut into a loaf of freshly baked banana bread and the aroma spread through the room, adding another layer of comfort.

Fearn and Seán talked about farming while the girls continued to stroke the cat and I joined Andrea at the well-worn counter.

'When we started nearly thirty years ago we quickly realised we had to find another income. The farm couldn't support both of us. I ended up having to teach to make ends meet.'

'I know the feeling,' I said. 'That's what led us into the tourism activities we offer but for me it was a lifesaver. After being an IT consultant and project manager, being a lonely farmer's wife in rural Dordogne was a culture shock. The wine school saved my sanity.'

'I can see that,' said Andrea as she passed me a cup of steaming tea and a plate of fragrant bread.

'We did it for necessity but I love being with people and running workshops so it was the perfect fit,' I said.

'Not like me. I didn't really want to teach. I wanted to be in the vineyard. I spend all my spare time with the vines. I love it. I can't wait for next year when I retire so I can be back in the vines full-time.'

'Gosh, Andrea, it seems unfair that you couldn't do that and pursue your passion. It's a tough wine market.'

'Hmm, and it hasn't got any easier. Our costs have gone up every year but the price we are paid has often gone down. I'm thankful I did the teaching so I'm guaranteed a better retirement than a farmer. But I still can't wait to stop and get back to the vines.'

We handed out tea and bread then settled around the fire.

'So you're going to get some sheep then?' said Fearn.

'Perhaps in a year or two,' said Seán. 'I'm not sure we're ready.'

'Just dive in and do it the way we do,' said Andrea.

'You're probably right, Andrea, but we're saving for a dream holiday to South Africa. To make it worthwhile we need to be away at least three weeks. Until we've done that trip we don't want to have more animals to worry about... And the trip isn't going to happen tomorrow.'

'I see. Well, it is possible to get an automatic water trough filler and if they're out on pasture in a secure enclosure you could leave them for a couple of days, but not three weeks. But for so long you'll need to get a house-sitter to keep an eye on the place, won't you?'

'Hmm, I hadn't thought of that,' I said, realising that it wasn't just money that needed to be saved for our trip to come to fruition.

When we said our farewells I felt like we knew Fearn and Andrea well even though we had only shared a couple of hours with them. We felt deeply satisfied: a corporeal satisfaction thanks to our bellies full of banana bread; a 'thinking being' satisfaction thanks to another key piece of research for biodiversity on the farm; and, above all, a satisfaction of the spirit for the richness of the interaction with this peaceful couple.

'You won't believe it!' shouted Seán that weekend. He was in the lounge and I was in the kitchen. 'There's an article about Brandeau here!'

He was clearing out a trunk of old journals and found an article he had kept from a Canadian smallholder magazine we bought on a trip ten years before. The writer had visited Fearn's parents in the early eighties then visited Fearn and Andrea 20 years later. He wrote about how, when he first visited, the farms in the locality were small mixed farms and you could buy all your food from local artisans within walking distance of the farm: milk, cheese, bread, honey, vegetables, meat, fruit and wine *bien sûr*. By his second trip, many farms had consolidated; they were bigger and had specialised in winegrowing. There was no other local food. Now the only food supply was a huge shopping centre a car journey away. It was a sign of the times we were living in. It was necessary to get big and specialise in one crop, with all the mechanisation that went with it, or get out. But ironically that was not good for us as humanity, for our food security, for the quality and freshness of it, for local employment. The stranglehold of global markets with their focus on price had turned farmers' work – that was about life and creativity – into factories. But the uncertainty of farming, with its dependence on nature and weather, was as far from a factory as you could get. Farmers had given up the joys and benefits of being farmers and kept the bad parts. It was little wonder the suicide rate among farmers was five times the national average in many countries. Farmers were being crushed between suppliers who set the price for seed and agrochemicals and buyers who set the price for the purchase of the farmers' products. They felt like they had no power and no choice. By doing what we were doing – going back to natural methods and thus avoiding the supplier stranglehold and selling direct to avoid the buyer stranglehold – we took back that power. The growth in farmers' markets, organic producers and consumer interest in food provenance and quality were trends that were helping to change the situation.

Even on our own farm the mixed part was dwindling. Our last hardy chicken, Blanchette, had made it through the hard winter with snow so thick we were sledging, snowboarding and skiing down Saussignac hill. My video of her tramping through snow that came to her chest showed an old lady full of energy and life. Seán had moved her private chicken house next to the front door beside the boiler room so she had some warmth now her friends were gone.

The head chicken Poc Poc was killed under the wheel of a hit-and-run passer-by. The rest of the chickens had quietly died of old age: one settled in the woodshed; another snuggled up against the kitchen door. We felt sad but they were ready, unlike the sudden death of Poc Poc.

Soon after our visit to Brandeau, Blanchette began to sleep more and stayed close to the kitchen door. Then her breathing was laboured and there was a little stain of blood on her rear end. She took a walk outside and made it back into the henhouse that evening. Seán took her water and food and said goodnight. The following morning she was on the floor of the henhouse motionless, gone to the long sleep from which we do not return. Seán dug a hole to bury her up near the top orchard. He asked Sophia and Ellie if they wanted to see Blanchette for one last time. Sophia didn't want to but Ellie did. Seán carefully lined the hole with straw and wrapped Blanchette in one of our old baby blankets.

'She looks like she's asleep,' said Ellie.

We said a prayer for her. It was a beautiful moment of giving thanks for a chicken that had given us many eggs over her lifetime, a real character. We said goodbye and Seán filled the hole.

We missed having chickens. They were part of our farm life. We could see how animals helped keep a balance. They were individuals and they brought a level of respect for life that was not the same as on a farm without animals. They were also part of our biodiversity and of the energy of our farm, like our vegetable garden, forest and hedgerows.

'We need animals. I want us to get chickens and sheep,' I said to Seán as we ate lunch.

'But we want our week of holiday in Provence. Dora can go to the kennels but chickens and sheep are another story. And what about South Africa?' said Seán.

'But we need chickens,' I said, beginning to get irrationally angry.

'I know, Mrs C, but you know that we don't have a neighbour we can rely on, especially now that Sonia and Fred are moving. We can think about chickens after Provence and then we can think about sheep after South Africa.'

'And another thing,' I said, feeling aggressive and taking off on a different tack. 'We don't talk about anything but business – you don't even say good morning to me. We're no better than people sharing a house. We have to sort it out or stop.'

Seán looked at me wide-eyed and I stormed out like an angry toddler. With my broken nights I was tired and irritable. I felt like I couldn't keep up with the demands being made on me. I wanted to run away, to be free from the incessant work of our growing business. On the outside people looking in thought we were successful, that things were going so well. On the business front it was true that things had turned around. Each month was no longer a precipice like it had been in the early days.

But despite the relative financial stability I was so stretched I couldn't appreciate it. I wanted to write more but I didn't have the time. We had made it through another harvest and our fruit was safely in the winery. We had a fire to keep us warm in winter, and a garden and food store filled by Seán's green fingers. I reminded myself how much I had to be thankful for but I couldn't overcome the darkness that kept creeping over me, a film of depression and insomnia that had appeared out of nowhere, sapping my energy and my optimism.

PART 2

AIR AND FLOWERS

Wine brings to light the hidden secrets of the soul,
gives being to our hopes, bids the coward flight,
drives dull care away, and teaches new means for
the accomplishment of our wishes.
Horace

CHAPTER 5

CHANCE MEETINGS IN THE TIME OF FLOWERING

The weather turned dark like my mood. It was late spring, time for the vines to set their flowers, and it should have been sunny. We needed the bees buzzing and the kids blowing dandelion fuzz. We should have been running through the light-filled vineyards singing gleefully, 'The vines are alive with the sound of buzzing.' Instead temperatures plummeted and it poured with rain. It had been hot so the vines flowered since they knew they had to follow their unstoppable seasonal progression but cold and damp wrecked the transformation from flower to fruit.

Like harvest, the flowering can be a scary time for a winegrower. Each tiny cream flower has the potential to turn into a grape given the right conditions. The conditions were not right and a toll had been taken but we didn't know the extent of the toll. To know the damage we had to wait for the bunches to form but industry pundits predicted significant losses.

I consoled myself that my mum and dad's golden wedding anniversary was around the corner. In a few weeks, friends and family from South Africa, Zimbabwe, the UK, USA and Canada would converge on our farm, a place to meet in the middle. My brother, who I hadn't seen in more than a decade, and his family were coming from British Columbia and my sister from California. I felt a little shaft of happiness shine through my dark funk.

Then my brother called to say that they couldn't make it after all. His IT support business had been hit with some nasty surprises that quarter and he needed to be at work. He didn't have anyone to fill in for him on crucial projects. Our children had never met. It had been too long already and now it was going to be even longer. The news added to my grim mood.

Vinexpo, one of the largest wine fairs in the world, took place every two years in Bordeaux, usually just after the flowering. A few years before I had participated in the Expressions Bio, an exclusively organic show that took place at the same time. Back then the show had delivered nothing but a severe dose of no-confidence. We rarely participated in wine shows; they were an expense that was hard to justify with the volumes we produced. Now our local organic winegrower association announced that Expressions Bio was being held within the Vinexpo halls and I was tempted to try it again.

Wine shows were a great way to meet other winegrowers, as much an inter-winegrower networking event as they were a selling event. I loved meeting other people that were as passionate about organic wine as I was. It was also a chance to swap wine with those growers to keep our cellar stocked so we didn't get 'cellar palate', a well-known trap that winegrowers could fall into: drinking only their own wine so in the end it was the only one they liked.

I didn't hold out great hope for the show but I was excited since I was sharing a stand with my friends Clément and Francine Klur from Alsace. Spending two days with them would be like taking a tonic – and I needed one. On the way into the show I shared a ride with a friend, Thierry, who farmed about five kilometres away from us. The drive into Bordeaux offered a chance to catch up; to talk about everything from the state of the wine market to our business with Naomi Whittel of Reserveage for our dried grape skins. Naomi was a part of the small miracle that had turned our failing farm around a few years before. Instead of the grape skins left after pressing going to compost or to the government distillery we dried them and sold them to Naomi. She created a resveratrol antioxidant food supplement from our skins and other ingredients, essentially an anti-ageing vitamin supplement. Thierry's relationship skills had developed her initial contact through our website into something enduring. Chatting non-stop, the 90-minute drive felt like 15.

We unpacked Thierry's red *forgon* (utility van) and set up our wines on our respective stands. I had received the first few copies of a Polish translation of my book, *Grape Expectations*, and I laid a copy of the original in English and the Polish one alongside our wines. Having my book translated felt grand, like I had hit the big league. Perhaps a Polish wine buyer would be tempted to stop.

A few minutes before the show opening, Clément and Francine came flying down the alley, arguing with each other. Their partner rivalry reminded me of Seán and myself. It took a very strong relationship to work together like they did. They pulled in next to me behind our shared table.

'*Caaarrrrooooo, comment va?*' said Clément, letting go of his wine trolley and hugging me close. Clément was a happy Bacchus with curly brown hair, beard, apple cheeks and a smile that took your cares away. He was always upbeat and ready for a laugh.

Francine drew in behind him, a second wine trolley in hand. She was delicate with long hair and fine features, but beneath the calm-looking exterior was a cauldron of energy and an iron will, like a wise woman plugged into an electric current. Clément was convivial and laid-back while Francine was super organised and dynamic. They made a powerful combination.

'*Très bien!* All the better for seeing you!' I said as I hugged Francine. It was four years since we had visited their vineyard in Alsace.

Clément took off to fetch another load from the car.

'What was the argument about?' I said to Francine as we unpacked wines.

'Oh, something about how we'll build our new wood house,' said Francine. 'We're planning to move out so our old house can become apartments. Nothing at all. We were squabbling over nothing. As usual.' She laughed.

'Sounds familiar – just like Seán and I do,' I said.

'Men can be so *têtu*! So stubborn!' said Francine. '*Allez hop!* It doesn't look like I'll have time for a coffee.'

A *caviste*, a wine-shop owner and client of theirs, presented himself at the stand. The show hadn't even officially started and they already had a client. The Klur stand was always buzzing with action. Their family vineyard had been in business for more than 400 years. It was about the same size as ours but with significantly higher density – that is, more vines per hectare. In addition, the grape types grown in Alsace were more productive than ours so Alsace maximum yields were around 8,000 litres per hectare while for most of Bordeaux and Bergerac standard appellations they were 6,700 litres per hectare. For some commune appellations like Margaux the limit was 4,500 litres per hectare, and for our dessert wine appellation of Saussignac it was 2,500 litres per hectare. With Klur's larger volumes they did business with specialist wine shops and restaurants all over France as well as exporting to many countries. The clients kept pouring through.

'How's the *gîte* business going?' I said as we chatted during a brief lull.

'Good,' said Francine. 'Last year was a great year. How about you?'

'I've lost a few potential clients because they want a swimming pool.'

'We find the same thing. With global warming, clients want a swimming pool, even in Alsace,' said Francine. 'But how to do it ecologically? Last year we created a small dam, like a natural swimming pool, that our guests can use. We've filled it with plants that clean the water so we don't have to add chemicals.'

'Wow, Francine! You're always a step ahead! I've been looking at the natural swimming pools but they're so expensive and they say not to use sunscreen. We can't ask guests to go without sunscreen.'

'Hmm. Yes, it's complicated for that and for the bureaucracy too,' said Francine.

She explained the bureaucratic hoops they had to jump through for approval and promised to send me the details of their installation and links to their suppliers. I was in research mode for a swimming pool and hungry for information.

Another client had arrived and, after pouring for him, Clément offered me a taste of the Klur Gewürztraminer. It was an aroma bomb; an explosion of rose and lychee. I sniffed for a few moments, enjoying the aromas before taking a sip, swirling it around in my mouth for a few seconds and spitting into the spittoon. It was slightly sweet but with a lovely freshness; a brightness that was the signature of biodynamic wines.

'How are the new Lodge and tasting room working out?' said Francine.

'Great. They're paying for themselves but it's a lot of work. I'm stretched.'

'You need to find a good person to help you.'

'But, Francine, we're so scared of French employment law. It's a minefield.'

'It is. We've had some expensive experiences over the years,' said Francine.

She went on to describe their stories and those of neighbours and friends. It confirmed what I feared: for a small business one bad hire could be the end.

'You have to be very careful about who you select. It's difficult to find really good people. Try to keep the contract as flexible as possible until you're sure.'

'Thanks, Francine. I really appreciate your advice. What about you? Any new projects?' I asked.

'Of course! Always. We're building a new ecological house as our home – that's what we were arguing about when we arrived. Then our current house will be renovated and rented out like the other apartments.'

'A big project,' I said.

'Yes, with many, many decisions and that means some arguments,' she said and laughed again.

Two gentlemen presented themselves at my side of the stand.

'Excuse me, Francine,' I said. It felt strange to be the one calling the halt to our flood of exchanges for once.

'*Bonjour, messieurs*,' I said. 'Welcome. I usually start the tasting with our driest white wine, a pure Sauvignon Blanc that we call *Sincérité*. Is starting with the dry whites suitable for you?'

I asked this question because sometimes buyers tasted one specific type of wine at a time.

'*Beh oui*,' said the stockier of the two in an accent of the south-west.

'Château Feely is an organic and biodynamic vineyard based in Saussignac, near Bergerac,' I said as I poured the Sauvignon Blanc then held up the bottle for them to see the label and gave them a moment to taste.

'*Moi j'aime bien*. I like it,' said the other man in English-accented French. '*Et toi, Raymond?* What do you think?'

'Me also, I like it a lot. It's lively,' said Raymond. 'I like wines like this. Racy.'

'The *Sincérité* is from two small parcels of Sauvignon Blanc, one on the plateau and the other an east-facing vineyard that descends off the plateau,' I explained. 'They're middle-aged vines with their roots deep in the limestone. Farming organically and biodynamically on the limestone gives freshness and minerality.'

'I can see what you are saying,' said Raymond.

'Yes, me too,' said the other gentleman, writing in a small notebook as he spoke.

'Now a white that is smoother, rounder, more rich. *Générosité*, our barrel-aged Sémillon,' I said and poured into their outstretched glasses.

Another winegrower from Saussignac, Jean-Marie, waved as he approached my stand.

'Caro, can I interrupt?' he asked.

'*Bien sûr*,' I said.

'Monsieur Walker, please may I have a photo with you?' he said to the gentleman who was writing notes. 'My clients in Germany will be so impressed. I'm an organic winegrower in Saussignac, like Caro, but most of my export business is in Germany.'

'Of course,' said Monsieur Walker. 'Please excuse us for a minute, Madame.'

'Sorry to steal your tasters, Caro,' said Jean-Marie. 'Monsieur Walker is a famous author. His books are bestsellers in Germany.'

They disappeared while I digested the brief introduction. Not only was Monsieur Walker famous but he and his friend were totally charming. I hoped they would come back and not get caught up somewhere else, as sometimes happened at wine shows.

A few minutes later, I was delighted to see them back at my stand.

'Sorry, we should have introduced ourselves. I'm Martin,' said the famous author. 'This is my friend Raymond.'

'Caro. *Enchanté*,' I said, reaching out to shake Martin's hand then to Raymond to do the same.

He took my hand and kissed it in a gallant gesture. I blushed.

'Thanks for stopping to taste with me,' I said.

'It's our pleasure,' said Martin. 'Especially for lovely wines like this.'

I continued through the range, moving from whites to reds and explaining our story as I went.

'They're beautiful wines, but not only that – they're presented by a beautiful young girl as well,' said Raymond.

'I'm completely in accord with you, Raymond. Magnificent wines and a charming young hostess,' said Martin.

I giggled and blushed like a schoolgirl.

'And she lives not far from us. I think we'll have to visit the vineyard,' said Martin.

'Of course,' said Raymond. 'Next time we are in the Bergerac direction we will visit, if we are welcome.'

'Of course!' I said. 'With great pleasure. Where do you live?'

'Le Bugue,' said Martin.

'Where is that?' I said.

'Near Trémolat.'

'Oh, Trémolat. I've never been but there's a restaurant there that I would love our wines to be in – it's called Le Vieux Logis.'

'That's one of my favourites. It's a great restaurant and I agree it would be a good place for your wines,' said Martin.

I poured the last in the range, our Saussignac dessert wine.

'This is pure gold,' said Raymond.

'Absolutely,' said Martin.

'It won the gold medal in this show's blind-tasting competition,' I said, pointing to the medal sticker on the bottle.

We didn't usually enter competitions because we didn't have enough volume but this one did not require a minimum volume. Competitions cover some of their costs by selling the medals. It's not that they sell them to the highest bidder; they sell them only to those who legitimately win the blind-tasting competition, but they set minimum volumes because if the winning wine is only 1,000 bottles and not 100,000 then the income from the sale of those medal stickers is significantly lower.

'It won ahead of the other dessert wines, including *grand cru classés* from Sauternes,' I added proudly.

'Just what I said. Gold,' said Raymond. 'More proof that the Dordogne produces better wine than Gironde.'

'Best-kept secret in France,' said Martin.

We shared a conspiratorial laugh. I gave Martin a copy of *Grape Expectations*, feeling anxious about giving it to a world-famous author. We said farewell and they promised to visit us soon.

Their visit left me powered up like I had downed a caffeine-packed energy drink but without the heart palpitations. In the short encounter I felt like I had made two new friends. Perhaps they would visit in the summer as promised. I hoped they would. I didn't have their contact details but I did have Martin's name.

At the end of the show I said goodbye to Clément and Francine, feeling sad that we couldn't see each other more often. The two days had passed in a blur of exchanges.

'I'll send you the pool info. Call me if you need more advice,' said Francine. 'You need to find someone to help you. Why not take on an apprentice? That could be a good way to start. But, like with all hires, it depends on choosing the right person.'

With that thread thrown out, Francine raced off up the corridor after Clément. Alsace was far, far away. They had a ten-hour journey back to their home in Katzenthal.

That night I looked Martin up. He was famous for a detective series called *Bruno, Chief of Police*, set in the heart of the Dordogne. I downloaded one of his books and couldn't put it down. The story flowed like music; he played the joys of the Dordogne with a dose of the reality of rural life and a touch of thriller into a glorious, fulfilling symphony.

The following day, an email from Martin popped up in my inbox:

It was a pleasure to meet you yesterday. I was enchanted by *Générosité*, *Sincérité* and *La Source*. Congratulations to you and SF. But I was also moved and delighted by *Grape Expectations*. There were times I laughed aloud; other times I was almost in tears. It is a splendid book, which says a lot about wine, the passion of winemaking, family life and France. I shall be putting your wines on the recommended list on my website.

I was amazed that he had read my book in one night. His compliments filled me with joy. In addition, I realised that a recommendation from Martin would bring credibility and more visitors. The previous season I had skated along, pulling the strings together by good luck as much as good management. Or by good luck and a good husband, according to Seán, who had bailed me out for a double-booking. I hoped I would cope this season.

Spring gave way to summer and with it came streams of visitors. I felt myself drowning. I was looking forward to my parents' golden wedding anniversary; to seeing them but also to having help from my mum with the lunches, laundry and non-stop action. But that was a short-term plaster. I needed a longer-term solution.

Francine's recommendation echoed in my head and I looked up apprenticeship in France. It seemed a way to put a toe into the employment market without exposing ourselves to too much risk. I sent emails asking for advice on the subject from our accountant and from Isabelle, our friend Thierry's wife who was a teacher at a local agricultural college. We had to find a way to get to the next level with our growing business that didn't include me having a nervous breakdown and our family tearing apart.

CHAPTER 6

GOLDEN WEDDING

'To Lyn and Cliffie!' said Gyles, a tall elegant Zimbabwean with a ring of white hair circling his bald head. He lifted his glass to toast my mum and dad.

We leaned in and said cheers over the old pine table, ensuring we made eye contact as 'To Lyn and Cliff!' echoed round the room.

'That sparkling is delicious, Caro,' said Rosie, Gyles's wife. 'Can I have some more please?'

Laughter rippled among the people gathered. Rosie was a party girl with a naughty sense of humour. Soon happy chatter was ringing around the room. The house was filling up. Mum and Dad arrived from Canada, then Aunt Sally from South Africa, and Gyles and Rosie Dorward from Zimbabwe. Gyles was best man at my parents' wedding 50 years before and Sally matron of honour.

Gyles and Rosie had visited us before. Over the years they had painted shutters, tied down vines, painted our front door and left their positive mark on the physical place and on our morale. It was Sally's first visit to our farm; I hadn't seen her in two decades. At three years off 80 she still raced around like a forty-something and had shrugged off the long journey as if she had come from next door. Sally is my mum's aunt but almost the same age. For their first seven years she and Mum grew up like sisters, sharing the house that belonged to my great-grandmother because Grandmother Gigi had moved home while my grandfather was away for the Second World War. Sally had taken me under her wing when I moved to Cape Town for my first full-time job, filling me with figs from their garden and helping my transition to a new city. As I looked around the room I felt deep gratitude.

With toasts complete, Mum and Sally returned to aperitif preparations and I joined them on the other side of the table to cut slices of *saucisson*.

'Did you see Foo's photo of her night in Vancouver?' asked Mum.

'What a stunning pic,' I said.

Jacquie, my sister, nicknamed Foo, was visiting friends in Canada en route to the celebrations in Saussignac.

'She looks so happy. I can't wait to see her and to meet Wade,' I said.

Six months earlier Foo had moved to Palm Springs in California to marry Wade. The Vegas wedding photos showed a gorgeous couple in love. But Wade wasn't in the photo in Vancouver; he was still in Palm Springs and due to join us two days after she arrived.

Mum's tablet rang in the bedroom. She washed her hands and disappeared down the corridor. A minute later I passed her door to fetch plates from our side of the house and saw her face was white as a sheet. I felt a stab of fear. Speechless, she held the tablet up and I read the message.

113

Had to miss my flight to London last night and fly back to LA. At 4 p.m. I got a call to say that Wade had been in a serious car accident. He went into surgery last night to set his right leg which is pretty smashed. He is going to be OK but will remain in the hospital for a while. Wade needs me right now. I am not in a state to talk to anyone… Haven't slept. Forgive me for not calling. Sending love, Foo.

'Oh my God,' I said.

Mum had tears in her eyes.

'Don't worry, Mum. Wade will be OK. He's young and fit,' I said.

'I know, darling. I'm sure he will be OK. But I was so looking forward to seeing him and Foo; to being together.'

I wrapped my arms around my mum and hugged her tight, tears welling up in my eyes too.

'I am so sorry, Mum,' I said.

She felt so fragile. Usually my mum was a powerhouse. She was tall, beautiful and strong. Normally she was the one comforting me. Now the roles had reversed. I wished that I could make the bad news go away.

'We will still have a good time. Look at your wonderful friends that are here to celebrate,' I said, trying to ease the blow.

'I know. But it's our kids that we most want to share this with,' said Mum.

'I will have to make up for it,' I said.

Mum gave me a sad smile, tears swimming in her eyes. I pulled her closer for another hug.

'Everything will be all right. Like Foo says, everything happens for a reason, even if we don't understand it right now. We have to be strong,' I said, sounding more convincing than I felt.

We sat on the bed for a few moments, my arm tight around my mum.

'I'd better get a grip on myself so I can tell everyone,' she said and gave me a determined smile.

We went through to the kitchen where the noise level had risen in cadence with the descent in the celebratory sparkling.

'What's wrong, Lyn?' said Sally, seeing Mum's face.

'Oh, Sal.' Mum paused for a moment, as if trying to formulate the best way to share the message or perhaps to keep her composure. 'Wade has had a bad car accident and Foo has had to go back to Palm Springs. He's OK but neither of them is going to make it here.'

'Hell,' said Dad, overhearing and taking the tablet Mum passed over so he could read the message.

'Oh, Lyn,' said Sally, giving Mum a hug.

'What a bugger-up,' said Dad.

Dad's reaction was anger and frustration while Mum's was sadness. Whenever an accident happened growing up, Dad would get mad. Instead of comforting us he got angry about how we had let the accident happen and wanted to work out how we could avoid the same thing happening in the future. He had worked hard to provide for us, to ensure we didn't have a precarious childhood like he had. Dad had integrity and grit but he was strict and didn't like uncertainty or problems that could have been avoided. In our family I reacted the same way; I knew it was something I had to try to control.

'I'm so sorry, Lyn,' said Gyles.

The room was quiet for a few moments then Rosie grabbed her champagne flute.

'Well, that means more champagne for us!' she said, lifting her glass. 'I have to say, it is rather lovely. One of the best I've ever had. May I have a little more please?'

115

'*Bien sûr*, Rosie!' I said. 'We never run out of wine here. We couldn't drink all the wine we have on the property.'

'We'll have a good try,' said Gyles, holding out his glass.

I did a refill tour of the room.

'I'm still amazed at how you hooked such a good-looking and smart girl, Cliffie,' said Gyles.

Mum gave a smile as everyone laughed. There was constant banter between Dad and Gyles. With Gyles, Rosie and Sally on-site, my parents wouldn't be down for long. More friends were due to arrive the following day. Even without my sister and brother we would be a good crowd. That didn't take away the deep sadness I felt that they would not be with us or the nagging worry about Wade.

The next day Foo messaged that Wade was recovering well. At least worries about his health would not hang over the celebration. Her message was upbeat and we had no idea of the trauma she was going through on the other side of the yawning Atlantic. The accident had taken an even more serious turn as one of the passengers in the other car had died. It was not only Wade's health she was worried about but the wider implications of the accident on their lives.

Oblivious to that, my thoughts were consumed with decisions about food. What, how much, when, who? More friends had arrived hence there were more people to feed. I sent Mum and Sally into the garden to forage for vegetables and set a pot of basmati rice to cook.

Sally and Mum rounded up a team of sous-chefs to prepare the fresh garden vegetables for a stir-fry. With Rosie and friends from South Africa, they washed great mounds of spinach, carrots, wild leeks, onions and garlic. Then, armed with chopping boards, knives and glasses of wine, they settled on the Lodge terrace in the sun. Soon chopping was interspersed with chatter and laughter and the vegetable mountains were effortlessly transformed into shreds.

'My beautiful granddaughters!' said Mum, seeing Sophia and Ellie come round the corner. She introduced them to the newcomers.

'It looks like the chopping is under control,' I said. 'Why don't we get the extra tables and set the table? *Allez les filles.*'

The sun was still bright on the vibrant lime-green vines of early summer. We brought extra tables and chairs from the tasting-room terrace and set an extended table on the Lodge deck. By the time we had finished, the shadows had grown and the green had begun to fade with the lowering sun. The vineyard scene below us was like a great work of nature's art, an ever-changing vista through the hours and the seasons.

'This looks fantastic, Caro. Well done, girls,' said Sally as Sophia straightened up one of the settings.

It was simple but, with the weather and the scenery behind it, it was regal. Rosie placed a vase of wild flowers on the table.

'Perfect! Great teamwork!' I said, hearing footsteps on the terrace.

Seán had arrived in perfect time for aperitifs.

'Your garden is magnificent, SF,' said Sally.

'I do what I can,' he said modestly.

I refilled wine glasses for those already installed and gave Seán a glass. Rosie and Sally started stir-frying the vegetables.

More footsteps sounded on the tasting-room terrace; the last guests had arrived. We did a round of introductions and I poured more wine.

'Cheers to our hosts!' said Gyles.

The clink of glasses rippled through the hiss of the stir-fry.

I passed the rice around the table then the stir-fry as it arrived fresh off the stovetop.

'Caro, is this the starter? Have you forgotten the meat?' said Gyles.

We all laughed. He was winding me up. We ate a lot of vegetarian. Organic meat was expensive and we only ate organic so meat was a special dinner for us, not an everyday affair. With the organic rice, the mountain of stir-fried vegetables from the garden and a few bottles of our homegrown wine, we were well fed. Being together brought a deep sense of happiness. I missed not being able to have large family get-togethers like this more regularly. Our families were far flung across the globe and international travel was a luxury, something we had not been able to afford for lack of money and time.

After cheese and chocolate and fruit for dessert, the evening wound down. Guests staying off-site wandered back to their respective lodgings and Seán took Sophia and Ellie to bed.

Mum and I cleared the table while Sally and Rosie washed up. Being together made the task of cleaning up fun. We finished, said happy goodnights and I walked back across the courtyard with Mum.

'Thanks for sharing your lovely friends with us, Mum,' I said, giving her a hug.

'Thank you, Toots,' said Mum.

'The stir-fry worked so well.'

'Well, SF's garden is wonderful. The veggies taste so good fresh like that,' said Mum. 'But it is rather labour intensive, all that chopping.'

'But that was the best moment of the evening – you had such fun preparing the food together.'

'I suppose you're right – when everyone is together it *is* fun,' said Mum.

'It makes me think of a kitchen saying I saw recently: "More chopping, less shopping."'

'Ha ha, I like that,' said Mum.

'There's an English journalist and chef, Hugh Fearnley-Whittingstall. You know the guy who looks a bit like SF?'

Mum nodded.

'He's famous for his fights to stop battery-reared chicken and to raise awareness of where seafood comes from and so on. In one of his TV series he offered six people a transformation week to change their habits from instant packaged food to preparing it themselves. One of the women was retired but she still bought ready-made food from the supermarket even when she invited her friends around for dinner. At the end of the show she said something like, "For ten years I handed over the joy of cooking to the supermarkets. Now I remember how much fun it is, I feel like I've had ten years of enjoyment hijacked. I will never buy ready-made again." She had tears rolling down her cheeks.'

'Oh, Toots! But you're so lucky to have SF who cooks as well. I cook every night and it gets a bit tiring even though Dad washes the dishes.'

'I know. I agree. But I think it's because we aren't doing family food as a communal activity. If everyone is in the kitchen together it's fun. Plus advertisers present food preparation as drudgery and serving up smart packaged food presented as your own with a quick wink as clever. But the hours spent driving to the supermarket and shopping to buy ready-made food totals more than it takes to create things from scratch in your own garden and kitchen, plus it's an ecological disaster. All that packaging, the carbon dioxide, the food miles...'

'Oh, darling,' said Mum, a little exasperated.

There was no doubt I could be obsessive. I found myself feeling guilty for throwing a few crumbs from the breadboard into the bin instead of into the compost. In John Seymour's book about his self-sufficient farm, *The Fat of the Land*, they washed their crockery in pure hot water so the used water could be given to the pigs. There were no chemical washing products and the pigs enjoyed the flavoured water. It was a total closed circuit with no waste. Pure self-sufficiency. I loved it. But we couldn't turn back the clock on our modern city-centric ways. City living did not allow for raising pigs on leftovers and washing water. We had to find new and better ways to keep challenging the status quo.

'Now I'm reflecting on this, perhaps we should do the dinner for the party ourselves. It would be convivial,' I said.

We had handed the main dinner for the golden wedding over to Luc and Martine Merlin at the Lion D'Or. All I was planning to do at home were the cheese course, dessert and coffee.

'Oh no, Toots! Absolutely not! You're too busy to even consider doing that. Look at you. You don't have a spare second to rub together. Anyway we've confirmed with the Lion D'Or. No, darling!' said Mum with finality.

The following evening corks popped on our sparkling wine as guests gathered on the terrace of the Lion D'Or. Sue and Ian Cameron, friends from Saussignac who had recently moved to Cunèges, a village nearby, joined us.

'We'll have to come and see you, Sue,' I said. 'I know it's only a short way away but it feels like another country. I preferred having you right here in Saussignac.'

'We would love to see you for tea or drinks,' said Sue in her beautiful English accent. 'You know it isn't very far. You could even walk to us.'

'Now that's the kind of challenge I like to hear,' I said.

Sue and Ian were a wonderful, slightly eccentric couple. They had lived in India, Kenya, Zimbabwe and Cyprus doing many things, including coffee farming, then retired to France for a quieter life. Sue was a dynamo, a formidable force for good in our village, from the communal gardens to activities for the kids. Ian would walk their beloved Labrador across the bottom of our farm most days in the early years, a familiar figure clad in corduroys, flat cap and walking stick, followed by his blonde friend. We missed having them in our village.

I passed around the golden anniversary menu then ordered a whisky and soda for Dad and poured sparkling wine for Mum. As the guests perused the menu I explained what it meant to those unfamiliar with French cuisine. Rosie held up her glass for more and Gyles proposed a toast to the happy couple, then a toast to absent friends and family. I saw tears in Mum and Dad's eyes, felt them in mine and fought them back. We missed my sister and brother intensely in that moment.

Dad selected the *salade chèvre croustillant*, a roasted goat's cheese salad, and Mum the *nage d'escargots*, a snail and mushroom soup that was so good people talked about it for years after having it. Both were paired with Feely *Générosité*, our barrel-aged Sémillon, but Dad paired his with whisky. For the main Dad chose *suprême de pintade*, a guinea-fowl dish with cream sauce, and Mum chose *magret au Xérès*, duck breast in sherry reduction sauce. Both mains were served with *pommes de terres Sarladaise et haricots verts*, potatoes fried in duck fat, a local tradition, and green beans. Feely *La Source* red wine was suggested with both and again Dad chose whisky. Perhaps being opposites was part of the secret of a good partnership.

After an evening of banter and fine food, we walked home to do speeches like a real wedding. Gyles cracked jokes and gave a short speech while we served the cheese course. Mum said a few words then Dad spoke. He ended his heartfelt speech with a toast to Mum. After the toast he held up his glass and said, 'Don't leave me, Choekie' with tears in his eyes.

I felt a bolt of panic. Perhaps Dad knew something that we didn't know. Both of them were in good health but recently Mum had learned that one of her kidneys had shrivelled up and was no longer operational. Now she only had one she had to be extremely careful with the anti-inflammatory tablets she took for her arthritis. She seemed more fragile than before. I set that thought firmly aside and focused on serving the next course, *tarte aux abricots*, apricot tart, with Feely Saussignac dessert wine, a classic pairing that was always a hit.

'To Lyn and Cliff, fifty years of marriage. Here's to many more!' I said, holding up my dessert wine and wishing them one final toast, my eyes swimming with emotion. It was a great score. I read recently that more than half of French couples got divorced. Seán and I had come close to tearing apart many times and we were only at fifteen.

The days took on a timeless quality and blended into a series of joyful moments. We picnicked on the highest hill near Saussignac. We explored an unknown path to Cunèges to see if we could find Sue and Ian's new house. En route I hesitated at a stream that was flowing strong.

'Oh, come on, Caro,' said Sally, bending to take off her shoes and socks. Jeans folded to the knee, feet bare and walking shoes in hand, she waded in. 'It's delicious! Refreshing! Come on!'

After fording the stream we crossed a small forest and followed a farm road up into the village of Cunèges. I didn't know which house was Sue and Ian's so we walked around the village looking for the finest garden. Thinking I had found it, I knocked on the door.

'*J'arrive*,' came a voice of fine English-accented French. Bingo.

'How lovely to see you! Come in, come in!' said Sue.

'Oh no, Sue, with our muddy shoes we won't come inside. We dropped by to see where you are,' I said.

'Well, come and see the garden at least,' said Sue, leading us around to the back gate. 'What about water for everyone?' she asked, already heading inside for it.

The garden was a perfect blend of French chic and English cottage garden, with benches strategically placed for views of rambling roses and scenic plantings. An organised *potager* bursting with vegetables nestled towards the back and an old barrel for collecting rainwater hugged the stone wall. Sue returned with a tray of glasses and we slaked our thirst. They had transformed their house and garden in Saussignac and they were doing the same here. Given that Sue was over 70 and Ian over 80, it was even more awe-inspiring.

Halfway back to Saussignac, Mum said she wanted to be collected. It was unlike my mum to drop out – usually she was raring to go. I knew she was worried about Foo and Wade but this seemed a bit more. I felt another bolt of fear.

That evening Mum owned up to a terrible toothache. She had been keeping it quiet to avoid worrying everyone but it hadn't gone away. I called around for a dentist appointment. The best option I could find for an 'emergency' appointment was in a few weeks. They would be back in Canada by then. I knew dentist services in rural France were bad and now I realised just how bad. John and Morag, doctor friends from Canada, organised an antibiotic to control the infection and strong painkillers so Mum could tough it out until they got home. I felt awful that we could do nothing but John assured me it would be OK and perhaps better to have it dealt with by the dentist Mum knew. I was relieved that Mum's slowdown wasn't something more sinister.

While I had been with Mum, John and Morag talking about the options for Mum's tooth, Seán had come in from the vineyard and was catching up on his email on my computer.

He looked up with a frown.

'Did you know you have the fourth of July entered twice?'

'No,' I said.

'Well, you'd better check it out.'

He got out of the chair and I sat down to look at my booking sheet.

'Oh my God!' I said. 'I've booked a Médoc tour and Play Winemaker on the same day. What am I going to do?'

'You have to cancel one of them,' said Seán.

'But I can't – everything is booked. The Coopers are staying in Saussignac for two nights specially to do the winemaker day, and the Médoc day is all booked and has been for months – we'll never get appointments for another day at this stage in peak season,' I said. 'OMG. What am I going to do? Couldn't you do one of the days?'

'You know I can't. I don't have a day to spare this time of year and I wouldn't know where to start with giving a full-day tour. I can bail you out for a short visit but I can't do it for a long one.'

My stomach clenched with stress.

'What the heck am I going to do?'

Seán lifted his eyebrows in a gesture that said, 'I don't know but you're on your own with this one.'

I couldn't push either a day forward or back as the days were packed with bookings.

The Médoc was the left bank of the Bordeaux area, the long finger that follows the Gironde estuary up to the sea. I was due to accompany the group in their car to do scene-setting en route but the visits would be with the *châteaux*' own guides. I reasoned that the clients could still do the day as planned and booked but without me. It was the only way out of the mess.

I steeled my stomach, picked up the phone and explained my mistake, then offered to come over with details of the visits, maps and a guidebook to give the context to the visits that I would have done with them if I had been there on the day.

For the following hours I was consumed by my mistake.

'What's wrong, Toots?' asked my mum. 'You seem distracted.'

'Oh, Mum, I made a double booking. It's a bit of a disaster.'

'Oh, Toots, darling! I'm so sorry. You're so busy and all our guests have made things even more hectic for you.'

'No, Mum. It's a stupid mistake. I shouldn't have made it in the first place and in the second I should have picked it up ages ago.'

'Is there anything I can do?' said Mum.

'I need to sort it out myself... Actually, since I'll be out this evening perhaps you could do dinner?' I said.

'Of course,' said Mum.

'Thanks, Mum. Sorry to rope you into work on your holiday, especially when you're not feeling so good.'

Mum had been setting tables, washing linen, emptying my dishwasher in the tasting room, sewing buttons and helping in every direction. I had kept some days clear but we also needed to keep the revenue coming in. We had created a monster that needed constant feeding, loans, bottling costs, social charges, laboratory fees; a never-ending torrent that needed to be paid, and if we weren't actively working it wasn't.

'It's nothing. We're worried about you, Toots. You work so hard. There seems to be no end to your days. We see you working at six in the morning and eleven at night. We don't want you to get burnout.'

'He he,' I laughed nervously. 'It's better than being worried that we aren't getting the business. I know how hard it was to get the ball rolling in the first place.'

That evening I took a gift bottle of our *methode traditionelle* sparkling wine and a profusion of apologies and explained the itinerary in detail. I offered my pocket guides that went with the day and refunded the deposit in full. The clients tried to be understanding but their disappointment was obvious.

I needed to get a grip. I went through all my reservations with a fine toothcomb to be sure that I hadn't repeated the error. I hadn't but it didn't console me much. Managing the comings and goings in the accommodation, visits on the farm and beyond, and holding down the administration and marketing of our wine business at the same time as trying to be a wife, mother and daughter had me swamped.

Mum and Dad and their friends left, and the season spun into high gear. All my waking hours were consumed with work. My nightmares about dying continued and if a nightmare didn't wake me then a feverish hot sweat did. With the lack of sleep I felt like I couldn't cope and my temper flared at almost nothing. I put it down to the stress of the growing business and resolved to have an apprentice in place before the start of the following season.

CHAPTER 7

MOTHERING AND MEMORY

With high summer I took cold showers. They left me feeling awake and alive. My sister Foo sent intermittent updates about the progress of her husband Wade. A court case was brewing but it looked like it would take years. Foo posted bail and Wade was able to live a 'normal' life but the case was looming like a sword of Damocles over his head. Weeks turned into months. As summer drew to a close and autumn took hold, I felt grateful getting into a hot shower. It was a gift of energy that something and someone had to generate. Like a car and a phone, it was a luxury, not a right.

I found a natural sleeping remedy at my local pharmacy. It helped a little but I was still depressed, tired and irritable.

'I don't know what is wrong with me,' I said to Seán. 'I've been so ratty lately. I'm not sleeping well.'

He looked at me knowingly, as if to say, 'You think we hadn't noticed?'

'Maybe it's menopause,' he said. 'You should look it up on the internet.'

I did a search and found that the symptoms I had been feeling for almost a year were signs that I was in 'perimenopause', the phase before menopause that could last years. Perimenopause created physical and emotional imbalance due to hormonal changes. The joyful list included hot flushes, irritability, depression, disturbed sleep, loss of libido, incontinence, weight gain, tension, anxiety, hair loss, memory lapses, irregular heartbeat, thoughts of suicide, dreams of dying and more. Longer-term problems that resulted from it included osteoporosis. Almost all the glorious signs had manifested in me.

Since the start of menstruation I had wished it would end; now I wished it wouldn't. Thirty years before when it started, I thought I was dying. It was a time when we didn't talk about things like sex and menstruation. The day my period struck I was out with my dad. No matter how serious I thought it was, I would never have talked to my dad about bleeding in my fanny. I stuffed toilet paper into my undies and prayed that I wouldn't die. When I got home – fortunately still alive – I told my mum about the bleeding and she delved into the medicine cupboard. That the sanitary pads came from the place she went when we were sick served to confirm my hunch that it was a bad omen for my health. Before she could explain anything my mum was called away. Foo was home from boarding school for the weekend and explained what it was, along with her girls-only-boarding-school version of the birds and the bees.

With this new phase I felt a little like I had when menstruation started. Why had no one told me about it? My menopause journey was relatively early on the bell curve of womankind, like my menstruation had been. My sister hadn't been through menopause yet even though she was older than me; neither had most of my friends. I had heard about hot flushes – usually spoken of with a nervous laugh – but I hadn't heard about the monster that had taken hold of me.

The perimenopause had me so depressed and stressed I considered all manner of ways of getting away from the infernal pressure, even thinking I would be better off in jail away from the stress of my life or in one of our vats filled with carbon dioxide, in the peace of that long goodnight.

Now I knew there was a reason for my strange behaviour that went beyond stress. With that knowledge I could do things to help myself cope. Top of the list were exercise, eating healthily and limiting alcohol intake. With the manic schedule required by our growing business, I had let my usual running routine fall by the wayside. I was walking to school with my daughters but that wasn't enough. I needed to exercise more. Many websites suggested yoga. A friend offered to take me to her yoga class. I tried it and enjoyed it but it was too far and too time-consuming. I couldn't afford to take a whole morning out of my schedule. The yoga idea slipped away but we ate healthily and I stopped drinking coffee. I laughed at a quote sent by a friend, 'It doesn't matter if the glass is half full or half empty – there is always room for more wine', but I cut back all the same, realising the hot flushes were worse after a couple of glasses.

While I toughed it out with perimenopause, Seán was finding Zen in our second vegetable garden. Our first failed despite great effort. It was a patterned geometric wonder – 'worthy of Versailles' according to Sonia, our neighbour. Mental labour – mathematical triangulations for perfect proportions – preceded physical labour. We dug, added horse manure collected from a neighbour, redug. Regardless our vegetables were a disaster.

Thinking like Dubliners, we had set the garden in the sunniest spot of the farm. On the high Garrigue in south-west France, the sunniest spot was perfect for scrubby herbs: thyme, rosemary, lavender and sage; our rosemary bushes became so large and thick they were more like trees than shrubs. It was too hot and dry; the vegetables, especially softies like lettuces, didn't have a hope.

Seán moved the garden down to a half-shaded field relatively close to the house. It was full of thistles and didn't look good but the middle shade it offered and the proximity made it a sensible choice. He began with a small bed and grew a few veg. The following year he increased his garden and his yield. The following year he did it again. One foot at a time, the garden expanded into a glorious profusion. He was like Jean Giono's 'man who planted trees'.

When we started our adventure it was a high-five achievement when we had a dinner produced exclusively from our farm. Now there were times in the year when everything came from our garden and I felt slighted if I had to buy vegetables. There was something deeply satisfying about harvesting from the backyard.

Seán grew 50 kilograms of potatoes (almost enough for our year's supply), countless pumpkins, butternuts, beetroot, onions, garlic, chickpeas and the usual garden suspects of tomatoes, courgettes, lettuce and beans. He became possessive about his garden.

'Don't touch anything. Tell me what you want and I'll get it,' he said.

I was the idiot that would pull up lettuces that weren't fully ready or harvest tomatoes before they had reached their heavenly peak.

'As of today you can pick all the baby tomatoes you want,' he said. 'They're almost over. We need to eat them or preserve them.'

Ellie and I obeyed, pulling luscious baby tomatoes from the bushes and eating as we went.

'One for the basket, one for me,' I said, popping another into my mouth.

'It's like a big market where everything is free,' said Ellie.

'Except if you count Papa's work. He enjoys it so it's not really "work" but it does take muscles, brains and time. But you're right – it's free in the sense that we don't have to pay money for it. Also it's right here, and when we pick it and eat it straight away, the vitamins are higher and it tastes better.'

'And they store better out here than inside. We've been eating tomatoes since early summer and now it's autumn,' added Ellie.

'Good point,' I said. 'Usually they keep better on the plant than off but if we leave them too long they'll still rot.'

'And,' said Ellie, giving me a professorial look over her glasses, 'there's no transport, no carbon dioxide to bring them to us.'

'Good thinking, Ellie,' I said, surprised that she had thought of this aspect.

'You know we're doing the law project at school, trying to work out ways to decrease carbon dioxide emissions?' she said.

I nodded, realising her school project must have helped to spark this reflection. With the United Nations Climate Change Conference Talks in Paris looming, the subject of how to decrease carbon dioxide emissions was getting more airtime.

'We might even go to Paris if they choose our project. Then we'll visit parliament and we'll get to have the *goûter* at parliament.'

'I wonder if they have their own garden there,' I said.

'If we go I'll ask,' said Ellie.

'Sorry, Ellie, I have to go,' I said, feeling sad to leave.

I was so enjoying our chat but I had a large group arriving in a few minutes.

I finished washing the tomatoes as the minivan of guests arrived. I got through another packed day, nerves jangling. I worried that my stress was visible but the feedback forms were glowing. The only suggestion for improvement was to iron the tablecloths. Usually I could rely on drip-dry to leave them wrinkle-free but rain the day before had meant I had to use the drier.

When I came in that evening, Seán was in the kitchen chopping a mountain of fresh spinach from the garden. He didn't greet me or kiss me as we would have when I got home when we lived in the city. We were like passing ships in the night. I was lucky if he grunted at me in the morning when I took a cup of tea up for him. There was barely a connection.

'You need to take care of your daughters,' Seán said. 'Teach them how to take care of their hair. Ellie's hair is in a knot again.' He didn't even look up.

Ellie came through. The entire middle section of her hair, from neck level to lower shoulder blades, was a solid mat of dreadlocks.

'I recommend cutting the hair,' I said.

'But they love long hair,' said Seán.

'You love their long hair,' I said.

Seán loved the girls' long hair but I didn't want it. Long hair was a responsibility. It needed to be brushed morning and night and washed regularly. In winter they needed to blow-dry it and neither of them did. If I didn't dry it for them they went to bed with wet heads. But they were attached to it, perhaps from years of positive reinforcement by Seán. Sophia had a little less hair and was a little more responsible. Ellie needed supervision – if I didn't remind her she didn't brush her hair, and even with reminding she sometimes didn't do it; she could be a bit of a rebel. I had spent an hour and a half a bottle of conditioner teasing a smaller knotted section out a few weeks before. I really didn't want to go through that nightmare again. A wave of anger surged through me.

'If you like the long hair so much, you get the knots out,' I shouted at Seán.

I felt like hitting him. I did not have time for long hair. Violence rose inside me; frustration that I wasn't being the mother I should be thrashed up against the pressure I felt about getting ready for a group arriving in the Lodge that evening and another group for a tour the following day. I still hadn't got to the emails that had come in. I hadn't had time to respond to all the previous day's emails despite getting up at six and not stopping. Clients expected responses in 24 hours. I tried to do that and if the pressure was too much, like now, within 48 at the very worst. I slammed the door and went to find Ellie, who had disappeared back up the stairs.

She and I closed ourselves into the tiny shower room and I poured the other half of the bottle of conditioner on to the knot and began teasing the hair out section by section. I was as gentle as possible but Ellie started crying, partly because of the tugging and partly because she was upset about the knot and my anger.

'We're going to have to cut it out,' I said. 'This is way, way worse than last time. You have to brush your hair morning and night. You have to be responsible, Ellie. You can't have long hair if you aren't going to look after it.'

I felt furious – with myself, with Ellie, with Seán, with a world that said they needed long hair.

We braved it out for an hour. Eventually Ellie was freezing, and I felt like I had arthritis I had been bent over her in the shower for so long. The knot was almost as big as it had been at the start and we were both crying.

'I'm going to get the scissors. It's the only solution. The knot is too big,' I said.

Ellie cried even harder.

'It will grow back, Ellie, *ma chérie*,' I said.

'OK,' she said finally through her tears.

I wrapped her in a towel and went to fetch the shears.

I cut off the clump and tried to tidy it up around the edges then we sat on the bed exhausted. I hugged her small, towelled figure in a deep embrace and we stayed there, meditating, trying to find peace between us.

'I am so sorry, Ellie bug,' I said and held her closer.

Once we got a grip on ourselves, I dried what was left of her hair.

'It's not so bad,' she said, looking at herself in the mirror.

'No, you can barely see it,' I said. 'It will grow out in no time.' I gave her another tight hug.

'Neither of us wants this to happen again so you have to brush it morning and night. I can't go through this again. Not ever.'

She nodded.

I hugged her again and we descended the stairs for our spinach dinner.

Along with the visits at our farm, the accommodation and organic wine, we offered multi-day tours and vineyard walking tours that went beyond our estate. I had recently found a new route for a walking tour around the area of Monbazillac that included a stop at Michelin-starred restaurant La Tour des Vents for lunch, a visit to an organic winery and a walk around the grounds of Monbazillac Castle. I had done it a few times and it was becoming a favourite, but as I took off from the village of Monbazillac with my latest group we passed a farmer spraying herbicide on his vineyard and I wondered if it was such a good route after all. I led the group as far away as possible but we could still smell the weedkiller. I felt anger boiling inside me. It was wrong that this farmer could legally pollute the air we were breathing with a carcinogen. In time we will not believe that humankind could have been so stupid. Jane Goodall recently wrote (in *Harvest for Hope: A Guide to Mindful Eating*) about how future generations would look back on this dark era of agriculture and ask in disbelief, 'How could we have ever believed that it was a good idea to grow our food with poisons?'

Our route took us through light woods and vineyards. As we walked I explained the different plants and trees, especially those we used in biodynamics, like the nettle, willow and horsetail.

'There's a hazelnut,' I said, pointing to a coppiced tree in the hedgerow of the adjacent pasture.

'Sometimes it's hard to tell it from other trees with similar shaped leaves until you get up close and see it has slightly furry leaves,' said Royce, a tall North American.

'Interesting,' I said. 'I never stopped to feel the leaves. Giving leaves textural consideration makes a lot of sense – it's another identification point.'

Another machine was lashing spray on to a vineyard up ahead. I considered an alternative route that was longer but one of the group had owned up to a sore knee minutes before so I was hesitant. A little closer to the sprayer I recognised the winegrower.

'Phew! We can pass,' I said. 'That is Kilian of Château Kalian, an organic vineyard. We'll have a bottle of his organic wine with lunch.'

We kept walking for a while then I called a halt for a break. I laid out my waterproof jacket and sat down to serve home-made elderflower cordial and organic biscuits.

The group's happy chatter filled the air while I located myself on the map before closing it into my backpack.

We set off again, picking up the pace, and came to a familiar fork in the road. Despite having done the walk many times, I experienced a momentary doubt about which way to go. I knew the route so well. I took the right fork but a few minutes later didn't recognise where we were. The person with the sore knee didn't need to walk any extra miles. I stopped and took the map out of my bag and tried to orientate myself. I couldn't work out where we were or where we needed to go. My brain shut down. I felt panic rising. We walked back to the fork so I could look at the signs.

'I'll look us up on my phone,' said Royce.

'Thanks, Royce,' I said.

'How many times did you say you've done this route, Caro?' asked Joyce, the lady with the sore knee.

'So many. I think I got disorientated because the seasons have changed since I was here last,' I said, my face going red with embarrassment.

Royce's phone showed to go back the way we had come. But it showed we had such a long way to go to the restaurant that I was sure it wasn't right. I hesitated. Had I got us that lost? Were we so far off our target? I doubted myself. For a few minutes I looked at my paper map and at the phone. Part of me said, 'Trust the new technology – it has to be right', and the other part said, 'Stick with your gut instinct'. I had to make a call.

'We must stick with the way I originally took us. The seasonal change and the new paintwork on the house disorientated me,' I said, sounding more convincing than I felt.

Joyce looked dubious. I didn't blame her. I led us back up the road, my heart racing. This had never happened to me, even on a brand-new route. I was always sure of my direction and this one was a regular, familiar route for me. As we popped out of a small forest I saw the restaurant in the distance and felt light-headed relief sweep through me. The map on the phone had the restaurant address as a place completely different to the actual location of the restaurant.

I chalked another negative mark down to the awful transformation I was going through; perimenopause symptoms included memory lapses. Or perhaps it was nervous-system disruption from the chemicals being sprayed next to our path at the start of the walk. I would never know. I wondered how I would regain the confidence and satisfaction of my group although being on the right path had helped already.

At La Tour des Vents, after nibbles of potato and *aioli* (a garlic mayonnaise) and tiny wraps of smoked trout, we delighted in an amuse-bouche of *mousse de courgette et fausse terre Parmesan* (dark savoury Parmesan biscuit crushed to look like soil and crumbled over courgette mousse) then a starter of tomato soup laced with olives and *jambon de Bayonne* perfectly paired with a white wine from Brigitte Soulier of Château La Robertie, a feisty woman I had got to know through a Women in Wine group. We continued the feast with guinea-fowl fillet wrapped around a langoustine with a flamed whisky langoustine sauce, stuffed courgette flower and spinach with cream, paired with red wine from Château Kalian, the winegrower we had seen en route. With the fine wine flowing, my memory lapse faded like the wisps of mist on the river below us. By the end my guests seemed to have forgotten but I had not.

At home I checked in with one of our hazelnuts. The leaves had always looked flat but close up they were furry. I rubbed a leaf between my fingers. It smelt like hazelnut. Now I went around feeling and sniffing the leaves of other plants and took more notice of the texture.

137

My experience with Ellie's hair had shown I wasn't keeping it together on the family front, and the walk and my double booking showed I wasn't on the work front either, but I couldn't let the lapses destroy my confidence. I had a packed schedule through to the end of October and harvest was in full swing. We had harvested the Sauvignon Blanc and the Sémillon. The reds would be next. I wondered if I would make it through the week, let alone the next four – at which point things would slow down and winter would arrive. I had never relished winter; now I found myself desperately looking forward to it. I picked a lavender flower from the pot outside my tasting-room door and drew the calming aroma deep into my being.

CHAPTER 8

TAKE TEN DEEP BREATHS

A petite woman with jet-black hair and a tall, slim man with sandy-brown hair walked up the Gardonne platform with suitcases.

'You must be Caro. I'm Chris and this is Dave,' said the woman in a warm voice, introducing them both with a flourish. We shook hands.

'Welcome to Aquitaine,' I said. 'It's great to meet you.'

We chatted as we made our way to Château Feely. 'We have limited time to travel since Dave still works full-time. I don't think he will ever stop working,' Chris said and gave a delicious laugh that filled the car.

Her laughter set me at ease. With the intense week ahead, their easy manner and good humour were what I needed.

'I'll run through the itinerary so you know what is happening over the next few days,' I said. 'Tomorrow is the Wine Adventure at Château Feely so you'll spend the day learning about wine at our organic vineyard. Wednesday you go to Bergerac for the market and the cookery class with Stéphane at Table du Marché. Thursday we will be harvesting our Merlot everyday red so there will be noise in the courtyard from around five in the morning and lots to see. Then we go to St-Émilion for the *grand cru classés* tour. Friday is a rest day for you – phew. Perhaps you can take a relaxing walk up to the Lion D'Or for lunch. Saturday is our vine-shareholder harvest day with a picnic for lunch then the harvest dinner in Saussignac, and then Sunday is a vineyard walking tour with lunch. That takes us to Monday, when I'll bring you back to the station where you just arrived. How does that sound?'

'Perfect for us,' said Chris. 'But it sounds like quite a packed agenda for you, Caro.'

'No worries. I'm used to it,' I said, feeling a little increase in my pulse all the same.

The next day there were another six people on the Wine Adventure. The day Chris and Dave Drake were in Bergerac for the cookery school I had a different group booked for the day. Friday would be manic with preparation for our harvest weekend, when we were expecting around 60 people. It was going to be non-stop – the way I usually liked it. Now I wasn't so sure. The effects of perimenopause, my memory lapse and bad temper with my family had sapped my energy.

The following day other guests arrived and we gathered on the terrace of the tasting room for introductions.

'I can tell the difference between white and red,' said one person, and the deck reverberated with laughter.

'I practise wine-tasting every night,' said another, setting off another round of laughing.

When sparks of humour flashed during the introductions, I knew it was going to be a good day; that there was an energy and dynamic in the group. We set off for our walk around the vines. At one of the baby Cabernet Sauvignons I picked up two flints and rubbed them together then passed them to the nearest person.

'Rub them together then sniff the stone. You pick up a flinty character, like the smell after a gun has gone off; for some people it reminds them of the smell of crackers or fireworks. That flinty aroma is a classic giveaway of Chablis, Chardonnay grown on flinty soil in north-west Burgundy. Now when you smell that on a wine, you will know it grew in soil that had flint stone in it.'

'That is amazing. I smelt that aroma on a Chablis last week,' said one of the guests.

'You'll smell it on our *Silex* and *Générosité*, two wines you'll taste later,' I said. 'But the taste of *terroir* will not show up so clearly in all wine. The wine must be farmed naturally. Any ideas why?'

They shook their heads.

'At the rock level there are critters that break down rocks and turn them into soluble minerals for the plants to feed on. This life in the soil contributes to the taste of *terroir* but also to the nutrition. Recently I read that a basket of fruit and vegetables today has the same calories but fifty-four per cent less nutrition than the same basket in the 1950s.' Eyes widened. 'Modern intensive chemical farming has impoverished our farmland, and done for long enough it will turn it into a desert. We'll talk more about the different farming methods later.

'Hand-weeding this acre of Cabernet Sauvignon takes around three man days and needs to be done two or three times a season. For older vines we use a mechanical hoe on the tractor but for baby organic vines the only solution is by hand. We think it's worth it. I can say that since it's Seán doing most of the back-breaking hand-weeding.' I paused for the laughter to pass then continued.

'This phase of "growing up", the first fifteen years of the vine's life, is the most important to farm organically for long-term health and capacity to resist disease. The vine's life cycle follows similar phases to a person's life cycle and this is the phase of building its body. By not using herbicide we offer them the opportunity to grow up healthy plus it encourages the roots to go deeper.'

'Why is that, Caro?' asked Chris.

'Hoeing cuts the weeds out but also cuts the surface roots of the vines and encourages them to plunge deeper. Chemical farming does the opposite. Herbicide kills the plants on the surface, leaving the space open for the vine roots so they're not encouraged to go deep. The main weedkiller used is not only bad for the vines; it's bad for humans too, classed as a "probable" carcinogen by the World Health Organization. The second chemical activity that encourages shallow roots is chemical fertiliser which, when sprinkled at the foot of the vine, is a natural attraction. The roots sit on the surface where the easy food is. Like us when we're attracted to unhealthy fast food, the vine is taken in by this food that will make it fat and unhealthy.'

'Interesting,' said Dave.

'I never realised any of this,' said another guest.

'Not only that,' said I, on a roll with my audience's attention. 'Chemical fertiliser turns the vine's life upside down. The vine is naturally orientated to the sky. It wants to reach for the sun and the stars, forging upwards by all means possible. By pouring man-made fertiliser – the famous mix of NPK: nitrogen, potassium and phosphate – at its feet, we make it focus on the ground instead. The vine can make ninety-four per cent of its dry matter from what it gets from the sky. It can take gases from the air, energy from the sun. Giving it fast food on the ground is like saying to someone, "Sit on the couch and we'll send you fast food and salty snacks so you don't even have to get up to go to work." The mineral salt in the chemical fertiliser makes the vine thirsty so it takes up more water and holds more water in its cells – like we do when we have too much salt – which makes it get fungal disease and that leads to using systemic fungicides. Those fungicides kill the mycorrhizae, a magical relationship between fungi and plant-root systems that helps them access nutrients in the soil. The mycorrhizae not only stock and distribute water and nutrients to the plants in exchange for carbohydrates (sucrose and glucose from its photosynthesis) for the fungi; they also act as a communication network between plants. Research has shown that mycorrhizal networks transport carbon, phosphorus, nitrogen, water and defence compounds (compounds that combat attack) from plant to plant. They're especially beneficial for plants in nutrient-poor soils and the best wine grapes are grown on relatively poor soil.'

'Fascinating,' said Chris.

'And to finish off, a third thing that can keep the vine's roots on the surface is drip irrigation. The French AOC or *Appellation d'Origine Contrôlée*, what we call PDO or Protected Designation of Origin in English, includes a law of no irrigation, which means that doesn't happen much here.'

'Why no irrigation?' said Dave.

'Back in 1936, when France set up the first appellations based on the traditional wine areas we know – like Burgundy, Bordeaux, Bergerac – they wanted AOC to be something that reflected the *terroir*, the place the wine came from and the unique vintage conditions; they didn't want it to be adjusted. Today many of us natural winegrowers are leaving the AOC because we find it incoherent to say no irrigation for *terroir* and at the same time allow chemical fertilisers, herbicides and systemic pesticides.'

'Sorry, Caro, but can you explain what that word *terroir* means?' asked Chris.

'Sure, Chris. *Terroir* is the combination of soil, microclimate, plant and the human hand that give a unique flavour. These four elements are interrelated and can also influence each other. Take the soil of this Cabernet vineyard: it has an unusual mix of clay, limestone, flint stone and gravel. The hot sun on the flint stone and gravel creates more heat and those stones keep the heat for longer overnight than a vineyard of clay or one of clay and limestone. That flint and gravel are part of the heat secret of this zone – the stones influence the microclimate. This is the best plot on the farm for Cabernet Sauvignon because of that but also because it's a plateau so it gets good sun all day. In addition, because of its shape and inclination – almost flat – we were able to go north–south with our rows for best sun exposure; it gives us full morning sun on the east side and afternoon sun on the west side,' I said, holding my hand on either side of the vine row to show what I meant.

As I turned, I noticed a wild salad and stopped to point it out. 'That red-stemmed plant is wild purslane. It's beautiful to look at but also good to eat. It has great crunch and tang, a fantastic addition to any salad. Go ahead and taste if you like,' I said, snapping a piece off and popping it into my mouth.

Chris took a piece and crunched it. 'Very tasty,' she said.

'It's great that you can pick wild salads under your vines. I guess that's only possible because you farm organic?' asked another member of the group.

'You guessed right,' I said.

As we walked, I spotted a few missed bunches of white so the visitors could taste the characteristics of the different grapes we grew: Sauvignon Blanc with its zesty grapefruit character; Sémillon with its stone-fruit sweetness; then the ones still waiting to be picked, the Merlot like blackberry and plum, and the Cabernet Sauvignon redolent of cassis.

I ended the outside part of the tour with talking about the different farming methods. For me it was the most important part of what we did. Organic was not merely about stopping the pesticides and their terrible repercussions of cancer, nervous-system disruption and endocrine (reproductive) disruption; it was about better nutrition, about rebuilding our soil, about leaving a healthy planet for the next generation.

A short tasting course, the wine and food lunch, and an afternoon on winemaking followed. The visits had evolved over the years with our increasing knowledge and increasing range. We had our first no-sulphites-added wine, *Grâce*, which offered the opportunity to talk about natural wine and why 'no sulphites added' could be interesting for a wine lover.

'Thank you so much, Caro. That was a great day!' said Chris when we finished in the late afternoon. 'I hope you don't mind me saying this but with everything you have going on, you need to relax to be able to cope. You should try taking ten deep breaths. Breathing deeply has a calming effect.'

'Thanks, Chris. I'll try it,' I said, barely taking a breath before racing on to the next thing. 'So tomorrow I'll see you for breakfast at eight, then I'll take you down to the station at nine so you can head into Bergerac for your cookery class.'

'Perfect,' said Chris.

I could see that she thought, 'Like hell she's going to try that deep breathing. Did she even hear what I said?'

But as soon as she and Dave left me alone in the tasting room, I tried her trick. After ten deep breaths I felt more relaxed. With my body and spirit calmed, I started the clean-up.

Seán was making good progress with our white fermentations. The Sauvignon Blanc was looking like it could be the best we had ever made but yields were low. We had done an estimate of our capacity to produce wine that year and it was not good, particularly on the Merlot. The cold wet spring had hit us and everyone else badly. The flowers did not fertilise properly so the fruit set was meagre. Ironically bad fruit set could be good for quality as the grapes that are left get more attention from the vine and have better aeration. I consoled myself that our wine was about quality.

We had decided that hand-picking everything was a priority for the following year. I made contact with our CUMA (agricultural co-op) president to negotiate a stop to our machine-picking contract. If everything went well, Thursday would be the last time we would have a harvest machine in our courtyard. We could not wait to say *au revoir*.

Thursday morning dawned dry but overcast. The starry dome that usually provided the backdrop for our harvest dance was missing.

Seán and I moved through the steps mechanically and the harvest machine did the same. We finished in good time, well before I needed to leave for St-Émilion. I had provided Chris and Dave with breakfast supplies the night before so they could serve themselves in case I was in harvest crisis. As it was, I could have served their breakfast tranquilly. Despite the morning going smoothly I had so much in my head, so many different things juggling for my attention – what I had to do that day, things required for the harvest weekend – that I felt uneasy. I took ten deep breaths.

With the grapes safe in the winery, Chris, Dave and I waved goodbye to Seán and set off for St-Émilion. I parked the car between two low-level marker rocks on the free parking near the Porte Brunet and we walked into town through the medieval city gate. I loved coming into St-Émilion this way; I found the promise of the gateway to somewhere exciting. In spite of having done guided visits there for more than six years, I still found new alleyways and doorways when I had spare time to wander.

We made our way to the central square, stopping at different points to appreciate the vistas over the town. I pointed out some key landmarks.

'Château Ausone, the top estate in St-Émilion, is the grey roof you see at the edge of town. It was started by Ausonius in around AD 350. The bell tower you see is the monolithic church carved from the solid rock by Émilion, hermit monk and namesake of St-Émilion, who settled here in AD 750. The square tower to the left is the King's Tower, built in 1200 for an English king, John, one of Eleanor of Aquitaine's sons. The English rule, from 1152 to 1453, started when Eleanor, the heiress of our region, married a toy boy, Henry, who become King of England soon after. Have you heard about her?'

'A little. She has quite a racy history,' said Chris.

'Absolutely. She was married to Louis VII, King of France, in Bordeaux city when she was fifteen years old. Fourteen years later she convinced the Pope to annul the marriage on the count of consanguinity and she married Henry. She outlived eight of her ten children.'

We took a commune path through the vineyards to our first winery visit. On arrival the winegrower led us out into his vines. I spotted a wild spinach plant and pointed it out. Chris bent to pick a leaf so she could try it, like we had tasted some of the wild salads between our vines two days before, and the winegrower dived like Superman to stop her putting it into her mouth.

'I would prefer you didn't eat it. We sprayed the vineyard yesterday to stop fungal disease,' he said.

Chris dropped the leaf like it was a snake about to strike. After all I had said about pesticides, she knew this was not something to be messed with. Spraying had to stop at least four weeks before harvest. The fruit was safe from fungal disease once it did the *veraison* (changed colour), but some winegrowers like this one sprayed a systemic fungicide immediately after harvest so they could keep their foliage healthy for as long as possible, theoretically to allow the vines time to take back the nutrients before the winter sleep. Ironically that would mean that the natural breakdown of the leaves, and hence the health of their soil, would be damaged since fungus forms a key part of this natural composting cycle.

Later, over lunch on the main square, we chatted about the reaction we had seen at our first visit, about the harvest that morning and about life. After a couple of days together, Dave and Chris were becoming my friends. I checked the time on my phone and realised we had been chatting so much we were running late for our next visit. I paid the bill and we raced back up to the car. As I took off, the car hit something then lurched forward and wobbled down the road.

'That's the tyre gone,' said Dave.

'Heck,' I said, holding back the expletive that I wanted to use and pulling over on to the grass verge. 'A burst tyre is one of my tour nightmares. Thank goodness I'm with wonderful people like you!'

In my haste I had forgotten about the marker rock. In my recurring nightmare I was with difficult clients and we were under pressure to get to the airport for their flight home. I stood on the side of the road thinking, *What will I do? How do I even change a tyre?* I had no idea. Then I woke up in a cold sweat. Now here we were with a real puncture. We would be even later for our visit – and in a week where

I really couldn't afford any lost time – but at least I was with friends.

'Ten deep breaths, Caro,' said Chris.

We all laughed.

'Dave, do you know anything about changing tyres?' I said.

'A little,' said Dave. 'I'll give it a go.'

'Thank you! I'll call Antoine and let him know we'll be late.'

Antoine Mariau was the winemaker at Château Cadet-Bon, where we were due. He picked up.

'Antoine, I have burst my tyre.'

'I will come over and help you,' he said without hesitation. 'Where are you?'

I explained, and in minutes Antoine's small white van turned up the road snug between St-Émilion's ramparts and vineyards. He was a dark, good-looking twenty-something. We got on well. With my regular visits to his vineyard he had become a friend. I introduced him to Chris and Dave.

He and Dave reviewed the 'biscuit' replacement tyre Dave had found in the boot of my car and the car jack. They were in the process of installing the jack when a man in shorts and flip-flops sauntered past.

'I'll do it for you. I am a mechanic from Poland,' he said. 'I can do this in my sleep.'

Dave and Antoine happily handed the task over and we formed a committee of observation on the sideline.

'He knows what he's doing,' said Antoine.

'He sure does,' said Dave.

'You don't need me. I'll head back and see you at the vineyard in a few minutes,' said Antoine.

'Thank you so much, Antoine,' I said.

'It's my pleasure. But, in fact, I did nothing,' he said, laughing. He jumped into his *forgon* and sped off.

The Polish mechanic swiftly finished the job.

'You saved the day. I can't thank you enough,' I said, giving him a token of appreciation. I felt like hugging him.

'Oh, it was nothing. Like I said, I can do this in my sleep,' he said.

Dave and I carefully checked for marker stones and I cautiously took off again.

'And so I find that my wine tour nightmare turns out to be a great opportunity to meet people and chat with friends on the roadside in St-Émilion,' I said.

Dave and Chris laughed. I was trying to put humour on the situation but I was rattled – I didn't usually forget things like marker stones on the road in front of where I had parked.

At Château Cadet-Bon Antoine led us into the barrel *chai*, a semi-underground cellar carved into the limestone with a wood-panelled roof shaped in a sensuous curve. The ancient stone and modern, organic roundness finished in natural material were a perfect blend of old and new *and* it was filled with fabulous wine in beautiful French oak barrels.

Antoine explained how he made the wine, the ageing and his barrel selection process – a fine art. For each vineyard and each grape type he had preferred oak forests and preferred barrel makers based on years of careful selection.

Since our first year with a badly behaved Merlot that had us chewing our nails and me breaking out in eczema and insomnia, I knew that ageing in oak could truly change a wine. It helped soften the tannin through micro-oxygenation and made the wine weightier and a little creamier so it could match slightly heavier food. Aromas of barrel ageing can include vanilla, chocolate, toast, sweet spices and even coconut, depending on the origin of the wood, how it was dried and how much 'toasting' (the burning of the inside of the barrel) the wood has had.

As winegrowers we were aware that one kind of oak was different to another but, with the price of six new barrels equivalent to a new small car, Seán and I were not experts in the field. Here at Cadet-Bon, on the other hand, it was a high art. With his consultant, Antoine assessed the barrels they purchased each year, comparing barrel maker, toasting and forest with overall quality, taste and effect on the wine. With at least 30 new barrels each year, they had the luxury of comparison.

'Well, enough talk about barrels. What about some tasting?' said Antoine as he dipped his glass pipette, called a 'wine thief', into a honey-coloured barrel. It slowly filled with deep purple wine then he closed it with his thumb over the small hole in the top, lifted it and released a sample amount into my glass before stopping the flow with a deft thumb over the top and doing the same for Chris and Dave.

My nose descended into the glass; the aroma was deep and mineral with liveliness of fresh fruit and rich spiciness of plum pudding. When I tasted, there was a marked difference to their usual Merlot on limestone: the tannins formed two parallel lines on my tongue, more spicy and astringent than usual. I lifted my eyebrows then moved towards the spittoon at the end of the row of barrels.

'Delicious,' said Chris.

'Jupille forest,' said Antoine. He closed the bung and moved to another barrel.

'This barrel is the same wine, the same barrel maker, the same toasting as the other limestone Merlot, but the oak is from the Tronçais forest,' said Antoine, filling the barrel thief again and serving us.

'Incredible,' I said after sniffing and tasting the sample. 'The tannin is completely different. It's more integrated and less sappy.'

'I am blown away,' said Dave. 'I would never have thought the forest the barrel came from could make such a difference.'

'Yes, on the whole I prefer,' said Antoine, skipping the 'it' in the French way like he sometimes did. 'But I like to have a little Jupille. It adds to the blend.'

The Tronçais forest was close to Jupille – they were both in the central part of France. We could taste their *terroir* talking.

'It takes all the different parts, the different barrels, grapes and soils to make the final blend. Two Merlots planted just a few hundred metres apart can be totally different. The Merlot on limestone gives us a wine that is long and taut, filled with freshness and vivacity, while the Merlot on the deeper clay is round, full and rich but a little shorter. We need to use them all in the right combination to make a beautiful finished wine. So now we will taste two examples of the finished wine.'

He lifted an unmarked open bottle that had been left on the upturned barrel that served as the tasting table and poured.

'So how old do you think it is?' he asked after we had observed and tasted.

'I really don't know,' said Dave.

'Don't even look at me,' said Chris. 'I'm just here to enjoy the ride.'

'Six years old?' I asked.

Age would bring certain signs that help ascertain the vintage but telling two successive vintages apart many years later is often a matter of knowing the vintage conditions.

'Perhaps. It could be seven,' said Antoine. 'Mr Richard left it out and I am not sure what it is. I will go and check.'

'*Chapeau*,' he said on his return, a term that meant 'I lift my hat to you', and gave me a look of respect.

'How did you do that, Caro?' asked Chris.

'The colour and nose gave me an idea of the age range, then there was a clear fresh note to the wine I associate with the year of the early frost, the year we lost almost half our harvest,' I said. 'This year we had bad weather at flowering and lost almost half the Merlot. The weather gods like to shake it up a little.'

We all laughed. Antoine finished the visit with his favourite vintage, a beautiful wine that had won the *Coup de Cœur* award from the *Guide Hachette*, one of the most respected wine guides in France, alongside the hallowed Château Ausone, an estate that sold their top vintages for thousands of euro a bottle. Chris and Dave bought a couple of bottles and we said *au revoir* to Antoine before driving carefully home at under 80 kilometres per hour on the biscuit tyre.

A couple of days later, after a hectic but successful harvest weekend and a tyre change, I said goodbye to the Drakes with tears in my eyes. In a short and manic week we had become part of their lives and they had become part of ours.

On their return home, Chris sent me photos of their celebration for her mum's ninetieth birthday in Hawaii, of Dave preparing the hall with one of our T-shirts on. Over the months Chris sent intermittent emails. Each one came at the right moment with the right message. I did her ten deep breaths each time I felt stress overcoming me and thought of her. After the breaths I felt renewed, calm and at ease.

CHAPTER 9

CANCER UP CLOSE

I needed more than ten breaths to digest Seán's mum's news.

The radiation was the start. I need chemotherapy now. When life knocks you to your knees it's not a bad time to start praying, said Mum Feely in an email.

Mum Feely had been treated with radiation for a cancer spot on her lung. When she first told us about it, the cancer was an 'out there' idea, something like flu. It was bad but it would be fixed soon. Both our dads had had prostate cancer and both recovered after radiation. I hadn't even looked up the details of what it meant to be radiated. I was a wimp when it came to medical issues. This was serious cancer – it needed chemotherapy. I had heard people talk about it but never experienced it in my immediate circle.

Mum Feely's email included a link to a website with a two-page summary of what chemotherapy was and the side effects it could create. I read through half a page and felt so horrified I couldn't continue. I closed it down, tears in my eyes. I felt sick that anyone should have to experience what I read. The side effects sounded worse than anything I could imagine. It was torture, not treatment.

That night I explained what I had read to my mum, who trained as a nurse a lifetime before.

'Darling, they have to put all the side effects into documents like that. Not everyone will feel them,' said Mum.

She was trying to downplay it but I saw the look on the faces of chemotherapy survivors on documentaries I found online. It was a dark side of their lives that they could barely talk about. I didn't know enough about the 'treatment' but, as a medical simpleton, treating an illness with powerful poisons that also gave you cancer didn't seem to make sense.

Mum Feely started the treatment. She had swelling, exhaustion, pain in her joints, nausea – in fact, almost every side effect that had been outlined, and in spades. She put a brave face on it and tried to be positive.

When I first met Seán's mum, Peta-Lynne, we had a slightly uneasy relationship – often the case between a girlfriend and a mother. We were very different. Peta-Lynne had trained as a nurse, like my mum. When her four kids were growing up, she was a traditional stay-at-home mum for whom family was everything. Later she started a sideline business typing up recordings of court proceedings that allowed flexible hours and being at home for her family.

I was a career girl. I didn't even foresee myself having kids at that time. In spite of this discordance Peta-Lynne went out of her way to welcome me. I loved raw cabbage and she would buy it for me when I came to stay. She was mad about animals and cats in particular. I painted a cat for her and she gave it pride of place on the wall in the lounge.

In our first year on the farm Mum and Dad Feely visited us for six weeks. She and I started their long stay with a deep sense of unease. We hadn't seen each other in a while and I could tell that she didn't approve of how little attention our daughters got, how little cooking I did and the cleanliness of our house. I could see her and my dad shaking their heads in shared disgust at what he called the 'Corridor of Crisis', aka our house, a normal house for a couple working long hours, with two kids under three – even without changing country, career and language.

A few weeks into their visit Seán chopped a third of his finger off on the harvest trailer. After that everything changed. We pulled together. I felt like we were seeing each other more clearly; for what we were and what we were doing right rather than what we were doing 'wrong'. I felt very close to my parents-in-law after that baptism of fire.

Now Mum Feely was fighting for her life. The number of cancer lesions increased after the first go of chemo then reduced after the second. The oncologist felt it was worth it to continue. He upped the dose to a 'doublet therapy', a treatment of two chemicals, carboplatin and taxol. Even the names didn't sound good. They were administered by a slow drip that took five hours to feed into her body. Her hair started to fall out. She felt awful but she still sent upbeat messages to us and kept in regular touch with Sophia and Ellie, exchanging photos of cats and jokes. They found a wig maker.

'You should go for a visit,' I said to Seán. 'Perhaps waiting until next year is too long.'

We had been saving up for our family trip to South Africa and hoped to do it the following year for Mum and Dad Feely's fiftieth wedding anniversary.

'I think it's OK to wait,' said Seán. 'My mum is positive. She's going to get better.'

Seán's mum kept her emails coming. With the cancer lesions reducing, we began to feel upbeat about her progress.

For years we had been waiting for the final part of the financial aid for our tasting room and new Wine Lodge to be paid. I had jumped through so many administrative loops that I was ready to give up. For a period my nightmares were about deadlines for signed copies in triplicate and incomprehensible letters in French. The last letter required another special trip to the accountant because the summary spreadsheet had rounded off the cents on some of the invoices listed. Given that the original signed invoices included the cents and were included in the same signed-in-triplicate package and that the rounding had no impact on the total value, it was a step too far for me.

I was almost ready to cry, 'Mercy! Keep the f'ing money!' when it hit the bank account. It was the green light we needed for the swimming pool and the work on the exterior facades of the property to go ahead. We elected for a long rectangle that would almost look like a water feature rather than a classic swimming pool and for saltwater rather than chlorine. I enjoyed planning and dreaming about the pool so much I wondered if the reality could ever be as good as what I had imagined.

'Now staying at home in the summer will be like being on holiday,' said our pool constructor.

'Once our fourteen-hour work days are done,' I said and laughed.

'Oh, you'll find the time,' he said.

We had chipped a small section of the concrete off the house over the years so we knew there was stone underneath it; we just didn't know how much and in what state it was. Tomas, the mason that did the stonework on the Lodge, returned for this new restoration work. Each part uncovered whispered a little more of the history of our house. The oldest part of the main house was the central section with a rounded cornice below the roof, thought to be a 'lookout' built during the

English rule of Aquitaine. Rounded cornices carved from stone were replaced by *genoise*, small bricks that look like a row of orange teeth, around the sixteenth century. Most of the rest of the house was from the 1700s before the Revolution. We wished the stones could talk, although in a way they were, telling us via the methods they were cut and constructed the era they were from.

'I think this double-storey part is older than you thought,' said Tomas as the work progressed. 'The stonework suggests sixteenth century. It looks like a fortress house, the sort they built during the religious wars. I can't wait to do the rest.'

I couldn't wait either but we needed patience. We had to follow the cadence that time and budget allowed, and at that moment we could only do the first small section. Seán and I had decided that I couldn't go through another season without help and our reworked budget that included the cost of an apprentice salary meant the next phase had to take a back seat.

I waded through CVs and interviewed candidates, recalling Francine's advice on how important selecting the right person was. I asked two candidates to come back for second interviews and to do a few exercises to see how they handled some of the activities that were part of our daily fare. We made our selection, a young local woman who had done one year of university and wanted to change to tourism with an apprentice *alternance* contract. She accepted and we prepared for our first experience of hiring someone in France.

It was the 'hungry gap' time of year; a moment when creating good food despite the dearth of ingredients, and doing outdoor activity despite the miserable weather, were key. Christmas was long past and spring seemed far, far away. I formulated a few tricks to keep my sanity.

First, I ate kale. Years before when I tasted kale for the first time it was 'No thanks for me'. We had a rule in our house that Sophia and Ellie were not allowed to say 'That is disgusting' or similar about food so anything they didn't appreciate had become 'That's no thanks for me'. But kale cooked right could taste superb. Organic kale was also vitamin- and antioxidant-packed. Our *potager* was bursting with a purple cabbage kale that was delicious and helped us through the hungry gap.

Sophia, Ellie and I noticed that even when it wasn't Seán's night he was inspired to cook on Wednesdays. He would spend hours in the kitchen. We were served sculptured towers of vegetables, delicious combinations and imaginative impressions of single vegetables such as kale imagined three ways: as chips, with mashed potato and stir-fried. Wednesday couldn't come around quickly enough. We had spinach mousse, Jerusalem artichoke chips, hummus three ways – made with chickpeas in the classic way, with chickpeas and fists of fresh coriander leaves, and with beans instead of chickpeas. Seán's ideas seemed endless and his gourmet plates were Michelin-star quality in presentation and taste.

We discovered that Seán had found the French version of *Top Chef*, the professional chef competition reality TV series. The three-hour show on Tuesday night meant he spent most of Wednesday thinking about what he would create. We looked forward to that special day with our taste buds on high alert.

Sophia took to cooking. She turned out a round of potato soufflés worthy of a professional. Seán was impressed – and that was truly high praise. He was hard to please. Ellie started baking, making magnificent doughnuts, cheesecakes, hot cross buns. Seán was over the moon.

But no matter how high I set the bar on my cooking night, it wasn't good enough. I had to admit I didn't get to the heights that Seán reached at times but some nights I was pretty impressed with my efforts, as were Sophia and Ellie. Seán's constant criticism was a thorn in my side. The next time Seán went off the deep end about the failure I had created I let rip.

'SF, if you don't like my cooking and you don't like me any more, we should just call a halt. I'm working as hard as I can. Sorry I don't have time to spend hours in the kitchen turning out wonders,' I said crossly.

'Just because you're busy doesn't mean you can behave like a monster and serve up slop. We're all busy,' he threw back.

'I don't know what you're staying with me for – all you do is criticise. You don't greet me in the morning; you don't say goodnight to me. I've had enough. We have to fix this or I want out. I will not have it, SF,' I said, getting more furious and upset with each word.

'Don't you talk to me about criticism,' he said. 'All you ever do is criticise me. You can't just throw a few roast vegetables together and call it dinner.' Seán's eyes flickered with anger.

'Stop fighting!' said Sophia. 'I can't take it any more!' She started crying.

'Well, SF should think about that next time he lambasts me and my efforts in the kitchen. I have had enough.'

I got up, slammed the door and stormed out into the night, full of bitterness and angry tears. I wanted to run away and especially to get away from Seán. I didn't like who he was at that moment; I was losing respect for him. I felt like he was driving me away, that the wall between us grew daily.

I had to find ways to cope with my new angry, violent self. I had always found winter tough and that winter was worse.

We needed to get away. I found a last-minute special for four days at a spa in Ireland that was such a deal we could make it reality. We attached it to my planned marketing trip. Perhaps it would help plaster over the ever-widening fissures in our relationship.

I took to drugs, adding organic hemp seeds to my morning muesli and to my home-made bread. Maybe it was my imagination but it helped to make me happier.

'I love Dublin and I love Saussignac. They are so much better than Paris. There are no *gratte ciels* (skyscrapers),' said Ellie.

'It's so friendly. It's not polluted,' said Sophia.

'Yes, for a city it's really not polluted,' said Ellie.

'And I love the sea,' said Sophia.

'And especially these moving stairs are great. You can even rest your case on the step above,' said Ellie, gazing in wonder at the magical escalator. The last time she had been on one was five years before, on a visit to Ireland when she turned four. Like our friend Thierry, we were *ploucs*, country bumpkins, in awe of this high-tech cityscape.

'And laser water! *Mzzt, bzzt*,' said Sophia, referring to the sensor-operated water in the airport washroom we had just used.

Our tour of Ireland included some work but also play. We visited the people's park market in Dún Laoghaire. I spoke at a Grow It Yourself (GIY) group meeting. Markets and GIY were becoming more popular. Dublin fit like a well-worn glove. From there we took off into wild Ireland, with its layers of sea and sky and green pastures. It felt like home. Driving from friends in County Meath down to County Cork, I watched the pastures through the car windows. Hills like a cardigan strewn with silver and lime bobbles and white-dot sheep filled the frame. A flying visit with Colm McCann, sommelier at Ballymaloe House Hotel and Ballymaloe Cookery School, was inspirational; the place buzzed with action and energy. I did a five-minute talk on Château Feely and organic and biodynamic wine to the cookery-school class then we raced on to Cork city for a talk and tasting at a chic wine bar, L'Atitude 51.

Mary Pawle, our wine importer and friend, took me on a tour to meet the people that stocked our wines. She introduced me to a pal that was doing a PhD on the food and wine in James Joyce's *Ulysses* and living in a funky apartment in the heart of the city. I felt a flash of envy for the freedom of her single student life.

The swans near Clonakilty sat between sea and river on beach sand tufted with grass; a rugged, beautiful scene. The seascape was everywhere. Inchydoney Spa offered us aperitifs in a luxurious lounge area with wall-to-ceiling glass windows with panoramic views of the sea. We felt like royalty.

Our apartment's expansive windows looked on to infinite wild Atlantic. I opened the doors and felt the sound of it pouring through me. Sophia, Ellie and Seán went on to the balcony, leaned out and sucked in the salty sea air and crashing waves. Ellie was in my gold bowling shoes. I had a strange sensation like I was looking into my past and my future.

Then the rain was lashing so hard we closed the doors quickly and the glass became a mass of liquid dots moving in a crazy dance. In Cork city someone had recommended an app that predicted exactly when the next shower would come and go. The rain stopped in eight minutes and the sun came out. I moved from one side of the sofa to the other to escape the glare off the sea.

'It's such a beautiful day it's a crime not to be out there,' I said.

'We're going to the lounge for the Wi-Fi and then to the spa,' said Ellie.

'OK, Papa can go with you. I want to go for a long walk,' I said.

'I didn't say I wanted to go to the spa,' said Seán.

'OK, I'll go for a quick walk and be back to catch the last half hour of the kids' session in the spa,' I said.

'Good. See you at eleven thirty so,' said Seán.

'No, midday,' I said.

They scrummaged out of the door, electronic devices in hand, on a mission to find the library lounge where the heavenly Wi-Fi was.

A tiny chocolate-brown bird perched on the balcony railing for a second then flew off. I put the washing on and prepared to go. As I picked up the keys, the bright sun that had been blinding seconds before disappeared behind a black storm cloud. The wind thrashed, the rain lashed then it snowed. I took a photo of the cars covered in snow in case it was gone by the time my family emerged from the main hotel and they didn't believe me. I tidied my suitcase into neat piles of shirts and trousers. I took the rubbish out to the bins outside, my face stinging in the freezing rain. It was still too wet. I went back inside and stared out of the window, wishing the rain away. It went. I felt a sense of power commanding the weather like that.

Then I was out of the door in my runners and rain gear. I raced along the car park and down the long set of concrete stairs, passing one soul coming back well soaked. The beach was empty. High up the dune I could see his tracks filled with white snow. I ran down the beach, singing and laughing into the wind. The blue sky was clear save for a seagull crying lonesomely. Solid sand then soft sand. I began to recognise colour coding could help me avoid sinking and tracked along the hard sections. How long until the next storm?

At the end of the strand I felt the bracing wind pick up a notch and saw a black cloud in the distance. I turned and raced back, the wind carrying me, flying and singing with the sun bright in my face and the cold darkness rolling in behind me.

Faster and faster I ran. Almost out of breath, I raced up the steps two by two and back across the car park. The first splats hit my back as I took the corner on to the concrete pavement of the apartments. I scrambled to get the key in the door and was just inside gasping as the fury hit. It was so dark I needed all the lights on even though it was nearly midday. I did a few stretches to calm down and watched the grey waves swirling under the charcoal sky. Then I grabbed my swimsuit and ran the gauntlet to the main hotel to take Sophia and Ellie to the spa.

Our holiday was so good I swore we had to take more time off. But when we returned home we were back to long days and thoughts of holidays disappeared. I went back through the emails received while I was away. I had tried to reply on my tiny phone screen while we were at the spa but I hadn't got to everything. I waded back and back and saw an email from FranceAgriMer asking for an additional document over and above those already requested as part of our application for state aid for modernising parts of our winery. It ended with: '*Sans retour de votre part en date du 27/02, votre dossier se verra automatiquement rejeté*' ('Without your reply before 27/02 your file will be automatically rejected'). It was 29/02 and we had missed the deadline. I felt a cold sweat break out. The email had arrived 15 minutes after we left for our week away. It was Sunday morning, the last day of our 'holiday', and I spent it in angst.

'We must not apply for aid any more,' I said to Seán. 'I can't take the stress.'

'What?' he said. 'That would be madness. If everyone else is doing it and we don't, how can we compete?'

I called first thing on Monday and found my contact was herself away on holiday until Thursday. I asked for a colleague. She called me back the next day and within hours everything was resolved. The labyrinth of French and EU bureaucracy could not be understood. I had to be Zen about it but it was hard to do.

Despite our great holiday in Ireland, back at the grindstone Seán and I continued to drift apart, barely acknowledging each other except for action required for the business. I was short-tempered and edgy. My disrupted sleep and dreams of dying continued. The hot flushes got worse. Sometimes I felt like a fire was burning me up from the inside. It seemed there was no end to this perimenopause nightmare.

Worry about Mum Feely churned in the back of our minds. She appeared to be making progress but the chemo's side effects were terrible – at least as bad as the article I couldn't bear to finish. It was like voluntary torture but she hadn't been given any other options.

The geese passed over. There was a feeling of freedom in the cold air and blue sky. They honked way up high, so far up they were almost invisible. Black spots set in great Vs across the sky, V upon V, upon V, upon V. They announced the change of seasons, our connection to the earth, the power of instinct. I felt the earth turning, the return of the sun.

PART 3

WATER AND LEAVES

Let food be thy medicine and medicine be thy food.
Hippocrates

CHAPTER 10

LANGUAGE AND PHILOSOPHIC CHALLENGES

'Madame Feely?' said a voice on the phone.

'*Oui.*'

'Mr Vellami, Vellami *méthode traditionelle.*'

I was surprised to receive a phone call from him; I had only ever spoken to his salesperson. Over the years we had had great success with our *méthode traditionelle* (MT). It was a favourite with our clients and visitors, dry and crisp with floral and green apple aromas. Each year we made about 600 bottles. Once the fermentation was finished and the wine was stable we would give it to Vellami, a service provider that did the *méthode traditionelle* – the fermentation in the bottle, like with champagne – for us. Each year we sold out before the next batch arrived. We were considering making double to meet the demand. I had been chasing them for weeks for the delivery of our latest batch and to talk about the next vintage.

'I am very sorry but we have lost our organic label,' he said.

'What do you mean, lost the label?' I said, feeling a stream of panic. 'Where is our wine? We really need that wine. We've been sold out for months and I've promised it to many people.'

'We have your wine, don't worry. We can deliver to you next week. But we have to label without the organic logo.'

'Why?' I said, my brain trying to grasp what he was on about. 'What happened?'

'Our processes weren't controlled enough between when we bottled organic and not organic. When we changed from one to the other there was a chance that a tiny bit of not organic got into the lot,' Vellami said.

'But is it still our specific lot? Our wine?' I said.

'Absolutely,' he said.

'So it's just an administrative issue about your changeover controls?' I said.

'Yes,' he said.

I knew that the organic certification controls had been tightened. Our bakery had stopped doing organic baguettes because they were too strict. They had to completely clean the kitchen each time they did an organic lot in case a little chemically farmed flour got in via a floured surface. It wasn't economic for them given the hours of work involved in fully cleaning down the kitchen and the volume of organic they were proposing so they stopped offering it. In our local supermarket they had stopped cutting the organic loaves because the cutting machine had to be dedicated to organic to be sure that a few crumbs of chemical bread didn't get in. There was no way they were buying another professional cutter so the organic loaves went uncut. I could see where they were coming from but on the other hand I knew that it was decreasing supply and perhaps even demand for organic. Busy people preferred pre-sliced bread and perhaps some would select non-organic as a result. It sounded like this situation was a similar case of the tightening of the process rules.

Our sparkling was the only wine that left the property before it went into a bottle and with this crisis I saw the risks involved in that. With all the rest of our wines we knew every tiny step intimately. Every process from pruning to bottling had our fingerprints on it. I could see the value in our artisan processes that kept all the steps at a human scale so we knew them personally.

'What will you do for us? Not having the organic label decreases the value of the wine. It is a serious issue,' I said.

'We won't charge you anything more for the service. We'll keep your deposit but you won't have to pay the balance,' he said.

'OK,' I said, still digesting the news and too surprised by the whole affair to negotiate.

'We will deliver next week *alors*,' he said.

'Yes, please deliver as quickly as possible – we really need our wine.'

I felt gutted about our wine losing its label but also pleased that organic was so carefully protected that it was a guarantee in Europe. It was reassuring in a world where the crisis of horsemeat being sold as beef was still reverberating around the nation's radio stations, a classic example of industrial food production gone wrong.

The food industry was rife with loose terms. 'Irish smoked salmon' and 'smoked Irish salmon' were totally different. The first was merely smoked in Ireland; the second was Irish salmon. Terms like 'natural', 'farm-fresh' and 'sustainable' had been hijacked by the large-scale food industry and offered no meaning whatsoever. Someone shopping for their family needed to have hours to read each label in detail and a PhD in food science to be able to decipher them. It was part of the reason why, if we did have to go food shopping, we typically bought exclusively from local organic shops. Their ethos meant that I didn't need to read every label for its fine details; I didn't have time. Economic *and* organic was becoming possible in France. Our local organic shop offered bulk bins of core products that were our staples. They often had local, organic, in-season fruit at a lower cost than the same chemically farmed fruit in the supermarket.

As promised, a week later we took delivery of our MT. We were relieved it tasted like ours but we would not risk another batch with them. I started researching a new MT service provider, someone who specialised in organic rather than someone who did organic as a sideline.

As a result of tighter regulations our annual bottling was even more complicated than when we started. Our labels alone had to be checked by three different parties and we had nine references.

'I'm even dreaming about the bottling,' I said to Seán as we drank our morning tea.

'I know,' he replied. 'It's *déjà vu*. You rolled over and said "corks, labels, capsules" in a panicked voice in the middle of the night. You did the same thing a few years ago.'

It was a premonition. My email delivered a message that the labels still weren't right – there was yet another administrative rejection by Ecocert, our organic certifier. I called our label provider back for the fifth time and explained that the new law required the mention of Agriculture France below the sign Ecocert FR-BIO-01. He sent the new label back with it above. There wasn't a lot of difference between *dessus* and *dessous* – it was in the lips, and mine had failed.

It wasn't only language that I found disconcerting. I dropped a friend at Bordeaux airport and was stuck on the ring road of Bordeaux in what felt like a giant car park. It gave me time to reflect on many things, including how grateful I was that we did not face city traffic every day. It also gave me time to listen to the radio.

There were two key topics of discussion. The first was a ceiling on rents in Paris. The French government had set band limits for rents by *arrondissement* or district. For me the obvious negative effect was a slow pull to the bottom; there would be no incentive to renovate or invest. When that topic was exhausted the radio host moved on to a ferry company that was about to close because it was not making any profit. A Scandinavian company had offered to purchase it but the employees had voted against the purchase. In essence they preferred that the business closed and they lost their jobs than that they were purchased and helped to become more competitive, thereby securing their jobs.

I began to feel like I was Alice in Wonderland. When I reached home after three hours of driving, having listened to more radio than was good for me, there was barely time to shower before going to Thierry and Isabelle Daulhiac, winegrower friends in Razac-de-Saussignac, for dinner.

The table was set in their *cuisine d'été*, their summer kitchen. It was a traditional lean-to, with Roman tiles on the roof, a stone wall at the back, with the barbecue built into the wall and a counter running to the right providing preparation surface and a small sink. Thierry was good with his hands. Along with his day job of being a *vigneron*, he offered tool-engineering advice to a vineyard equipment manufacturer in Germany and could turn his skills to building work too. They had recently finished a major renovation of their house, transforming it into an ecological haven. In winter wood-fired heating ran under their tiled floor and the warmth was kept in by hemp insulation on the walls. They had created a large open-plan living, cooking, eating space rather than separate small rooms. The summer kitchen was a recent addition.

'We need one like this,' said Seán, admiring the set-up.

'It's true – in summer, we use it a lot. We live outside, in fact,' said Thierry. 'Especially when it's as hot as last summer.'

Isabelle arrived with aperitifs and a bottle of wine and we settled into outdoor sofas. Opposite us were two hammocks: one for lying in and one that was like a swing seat. Sophia and Ellie were attracted to them like magnets.

'Hey, girls, what about a drink?' said Isabelle. 'Coke? Fruit juice?'

'Coke,' they replied.

'Fruit juice,' I said, jumping in. I avoided sodas like the plague. They were bad for health and bad for the planet.

Sophia and Ellie glared at me.

'*Quoi de neuf?*' said Thierry. 'What's new *chez* Feely?'

'Ah, you know, twiddling our thumbs,' said Seán.

He and Thierry laughed. They were entering the busiest time for the vineyard. Vegetal growth was motoring towards its peak, creating the need for mowing, weeding and trimming. Potential dangers of pests and diseases were also gathering pace, so spray treatments were required even in organic winegrowing – but these were natural contact sprays rather than systemic.

'I was in Bordeaux today – that's why we're late,' I said. 'Traffic hell.'

'Me too!' said Isabelle. 'What a nightmare. An hour and a half for what should take ten minutes.'

'It gave me time to listen to the radio, which was more scary than the traffic. What are they thinking with fixing rents in Paris?' I said.

'Oh no, I find it a good thing. It's time they stopped the rents from going stratospheric. Normal people can't afford to live in the city any more,' said Isabelle.

'But, Isabelle, it means that people have no incentive to renovate their apartments. Everything will be pulled to the bottom. Bad areas with run-down apartments will stay run-down. Fewer investors will make apartments available for rent.'

'Oh no, I am not in agreement. We have to stop the rich owners from gouging normal people who need a place to live near their work.'

'But if we leave the market to be free then people can choose to renovate or not and can choose the price they want to charge and renters are free to choose. If it gets too expensive people will move to less expensive areas and so on. The rents reflect the cost of the property too; it's based on availability and demand. We can't legislate this – it's economic reality.'

'No, absolutely not. We cannot leave students and workers to be the ones to do the long-distance travel to their study or workplace. We need to have local places where they can afford to live.'

Isabelle was the economics teacher at the local agricultural college. It was a full-time job but she had a second job helping Thierry with their vineyard administration. I tried to see where Isabelle was coming from but I was too much of a free marketeer. I could see too many bad things coming out of too much legislation. We needed freedom of choice that enabled creativity and rejuvenation. The discussion was getting heated.

'I can see that Caro is coming from one side and Isabelle is coming from another. I think you're both right in some ways but I don't think we'll be able to get you to agree so let's eat and drink,' said Thierry, acting the diplomat.

We all laughed. We probably would never agree but hearing Isabelle's arguments did make me reflect on the other side of the story.

Thierry raised his glass in a toast. '*Santé!* To your health!'

We clinked glasses.

Isabelle's cooking prowess was legendary. She could turn out a gourmet dinner while organising their sons' homework, solving the business's marketing and administrative problems, and planning Thierry and his part-time employee's workdays. She was a superwoman. I knew Seán wished I was as gifted. We moved from a luscious salad with walnuts and feta to duck breast that Thierry had cooked on the outside barbecue.

'I am not good,' said Thierry.

'*Au contraire*, this is some of the best duck I've ever had,' I said after taking a forkful.

'How do you do it?' said Seán, eager to pick up new tricks.

'Well, Isabelle does it. I just put it on the barbecue,' said Thierry.

'In fact, it's really easy,' said Isabelle. 'I slice it and marinade it then Thierry puts it on to the barbecue for a very short time.'

'So the marinade is "*vin et aile*"?' I said.

Sophia and Ellie laughed, and I knew I had made a faux pas.

'*Vin et ail*,' corrected Isabelle.

'Wine and wing' wasn't quite the same as 'wine and garlic'. The cooking technique was one we hadn't tried and it worked a charm. This was one to add to our duck recipes. We loved to barbecue down near our hangar and Seán's prolific *potager*.

'So are you still running?' said Isabelle.

'No, I twisted my *chenille* a week or so ago,' I said.

Sophia and Ellie burst out laughing again. They tried to be discreet but there was no covering it up.

'*Cheville*,' corrected Isabelle, laughing too.

I was providing the entertainment for the night.

'*La chenille, la chenille, la chenille,*' chanted Thierry, overhearing and cutting away from his discussion with Seán. 'Do you know the tradition of dancing the caterpillar at French weddings?'

He started acting out the caterpillar dance.

We nodded, already laughing at his rendition.

'Isabelle didn't want it at ours. It was too *plouc* (country bumpkin) for her. She had a horror of it. We told the DJ that we categorically didn't want it; that the music he played must not even encourage thoughts of the caterpillar dance. But our friends bribed the DJ to play the caterpillar dance music and they all started dancing it at full speed. We were forced to join in. Sorry, my beloved Isabelle, what can I say? You married a *plouc.*'

Thierry was hilarious when he got going with his stories.

'Even more so now we are *bio, hé, ma chérie*?' he said. 'Isabelle is shocked. Why do our organic advisers have to look so organic? The long hair, the dreadlocks, the beards, clothes that haven't been washed in a few days. She is worried I will start to look like that. That will be even worse than dancing the *chenille, hé, chérie*?'

Isabelle was laughing so much she couldn't answer – she just nodded – and we all pictured Thierry transformed into a bearded dread-head.

'Now, on to more serious subjects,' she said, gaining control of herself. 'We're looking for extra people for my Thursday yoga class. Do you know of anyone that might want to join us?'

'I would love to try it,' I said. 'I've been looking for a yoga class that can fit my schedule. When is it?'

'Thursday evening. We can go together if you like. *Co-voiturage* is better for the planet and more fun. Meet me in front of the Relais de Monestier the first Thursday in September and you can try a session to see if you like it.'

'It's a date.'

With one chance exchange I found my yoga session. Perhaps it would help me get through my difficult passage of perimenopause.

I checked the weather forecast before washing clothes; for ecological and financial reasons I preferred to hang rather than use the drier. At first it seemed like a nasty chore then slowly my attitude changed. Now I enjoyed it. It was methodical, melodic. It was a service to those I loved.

'Peg one side on to the line. Take the other side and peg it on. Bend, take the next item, peg it with the same peg as the first, then take a new peg for the other side, and so on and so on,' I said, showing Ellie.

We worked steadily together, filling the four strands of wire that ran the 12-metre length of the *potager*. As we worked, the Dordogne Valley changed with the rising sun; the plum trees, vines and forests dressed in shimmering greens, their peak-season splendour. The Merlot vines closest to us were lime-green brilliant; in a few weeks their leaves would be dark green and the bunches of grapes would change from green to purple.

The last items were crocheted blankets made by my grandmothers. We watched the multicoloured squares dancing like stained-glass windows in the bright sun for a moment. Both my grandmothers had passed on but I felt their love in these beautiful things handcrafted from wool scraps so long ago. In the twenty-first century it was much easier to buy a synthetic blanket. Both my grans rarely sat with nothing to do. Whether chatting over tea or watching television, their hands were busy with something for family or friends.

We finished in time to walk up for Ellie's school bus, chatting and singing en route, enjoying being together. I loved our shared walks up and down each day; they were treasured moments. But Sophia and Ellie didn't take to the idea of walking or cycling to begin with. Even though it was only a kilometre it was easier to get into a lump of metal and be propelled there by fossil fuel, especially first thing in the morning. I bribed them with money, paying the equivalent of what we saved in fuel by not driving. It was the incentive required to start doing it grumpily, but we started. Now we walked even when there was a little rain and enjoyed it; it had become a habit.

That evening I walked up to meet Sophia, who had started high school and was on a different bus timetable to Ellie. I missed walking together as a threesome but going up and back to Saussignac with Sophia and with Ellie was good for my fitness and for Dora, plus it gave me an opportunity to talk to them individually.

'So what have you and Papa been up to?' asked Sophia.

'I'm finishing off a book about wine for my publisher,' I said.

'Oh, that's good. You know, I'm very proud of you for writing books,' she said.

'Thank you, Sophia. I appreciate your compliment,' I said.

'And Papa?' said Sophia.

'He's been working in the vineyard most of the day,' I said.

'It's a bit of a waste of his education,' said Sophia. 'You don't need to go to school to work in the vines.'

'*Au contraire*,' I said. 'Working with living things and creating great wine requires wisdom, art, instinct and finesse. Where did you get that idea?'

'At school.'

I explained that people following their passion and working creatively with their hands and nature had to be highly skilled and should be honoured and appreciated as much as bureaucrats, lawyers or engineers. Our urban world was getting further and further from nature. We had to find ways to reconnect.

In French school there was little encouragement to take risks; if the kids weren't sure their answer was correct they wouldn't try to answer. A significant school reform programme was announced, part of it an effort to correct this recognised problem. The teachers' unions took up strike action to counter it. The programme was a leap forward for the education system but any change was systematically rejected. We loved so many things about France – the history, the food, the culture, the strong connection to the seasons, the markets – things that ironically had been preserved by this very issue, the inability and unwillingness to change.

The following day it was barely light when Sophia tore round the corner on her bike and passed my office window. Her teachers were on strike, and she and her friend Julie wanted to do something useful with their day off so they were going to offer to help Olga, the chef at Saussignac school, our local primary establishment, which wasn't on strike that day. I was impressed with her idea and her motivation to get up and be in Saussignac for 7.30 a.m. when she could have been cosy in bed.

I ran outside and yelled, 'Put your hat on!'

'I don't want a hat,' shouted Sophia. She paused, looked back, then took off again.

'You have to wear a hat,' I shouted.

'No! I don't want to!' she shouted back.

'Stop!' I yelled.

'I'm going to be late. I'm going.'

'No, Sophia. You wait there. I'll get it for you.'

'I don't want it,' she shouted. She stopped then pedalled away again.

'Sophia! You stop right there! You do not speak to me like this!' I yelled. 'You're not going anywhere! You get off that bike! You're going in the naughty corner!'

In my angry perimenopausal mania I was resorting to techniques that would have worked when she was four years old, except I had never needed them. She was such an angel; she always listened. She stopped and looked at me aghast. I realised how stupid I sounded.

'Stop right there,' I said. 'You're not going anywhere without your helmet.'

I ran to the shed, found the helmet and raced back.

She grabbed it from me with a look of fury mingled with astonishment.

'I thought you meant my woolly hat. I didn't realise you were talking about a helmet. I didn't want to wear the woolly hat.'

She raced off. The broken telephone was at work again. Only this time in English.

Seán signed Sophia and Ellie up to a programme that would give them A-level English by the end of their French schooling and thereby offer them a wider choice in their post-school education. Perhaps it would help us to understand each other better too.

Spring was almost over. We had successfully bottled our latest vintages. Demand for our accommodation, wine school and visits kept growing and promised to stretch me to the outer boundaries of my capability. I could see 14-hour days shimmering in my future and hoped that our apprentice, due to start in a few weeks, and my planned yoga session with Isabelle would help me stay sane.

CHAPTER II

POWERFUL HERBS AND DANCING BEES

I looked to our garden for solutions to ease the ratty, sleep-deprived monster I had become. Most pharmaceuticals started out as medicines made from plants. Having a herb garden outside was like having a natural medicine chest available 24/7.

Lavender is a great soother. It calms, reduces stress, improves sleep and soothes inflammation in the body. I found that drinking a *tisane* (infusion) made of lavender calmed my nerves. Merely running my hand over lavender plants and inhaling the aroma lifted my mood. But I read that it wasn't a good idea to drink lavender tea for two weeks before surgery since it could slow down your central nervous system. It was well to remember that these were powerful plants to be treated with respect.

I often found the ancient song 'Parsley, Sage, Rosemary and Thyme' coming naturally to my lips as I picked herbs in the garden. The four famous herbs it speaks of are culinary but also medicinal. The first one, parsley, lifted a buttery scrambled egg on toast from a casual supper to a heavenly feast, especially when paired with Feely *Générosité* barrel-aged white. Our main *potager* parsley often went to seed in the summer heat but the parsley that had self-seeded into crevices along the north-facing winery wall thrived all year round. They knew where was best for them.

Another parsley classic we loved was tabbouleh, a couscous salad packed with this magic herb and other bits that had become a summer staple for us. Parsley provides vitamins K, C and A, folic acid and iron in good levels, is a great cleanser and has been popular for more than 2,000 years – in fact, it was used medicinally before being used in cooking.

The second herb in the song, sage, was another favourite. It grew like a weed in our first *potager* on the hot plateau where the swimming pool now had pride of place. After years of dreaming, it was a reality. Ad, our friend from Holland who, with his wife Lijda, had been part of our farm's story since the beginning, had arrived to build the iron fence for our new swimming pool. No ordinary fence would do; it would be a beautiful handmade fence. Ad, the bionic man, was as fit as ever. He lifted lengths of metal that I couldn't even drag and barely broke a sweat. At the end of a hard week of metalwork weight-lifting he rode his bike to Sainte-Foy-la-Grande to relax.

Before taking off on his cycle ride one evening, Ad helped me unload two boxes of live chickens. We had decided we couldn't wait any longer and had purchased a selection: two white, two brown and two with beautiful high-sheen black feathers. They were different breeds to our original chickens, which had been a classic French laying breed with bare necks. I was tired of explaining that bare necks did not mean they were sick so these new chickens had feathers thick and lustrous around theirs. The sun was shining bright; lime-green leaves created dappled shade from the afternoon sun. We let the chickens out in the run and they immediately started scratching like it was home.

'Chicken paradise,' said Ad.

'It is,' I replied. 'I love the black ones – that beautiful sheen.'

We made sure the chickens had settled and Ad went for his bike ride. Then we took a Friday night break to the pizzeria in Gardonne. When we returned the chickens were happily roosting in trees and not in the henhouse. Our previous chickens had roamed free; we didn't close them in at night and we never had a problem.

This time not so: the next morning we found chicken hell. A fox had got in and both black sheen hens and one of the whites were gone. The feisty brown chickens had made it – there was no messing with them. I felt sad and Seán felt culpable. We had never seen foxes close to the houses at the top of the hill. From then on we closed our chickens into the henhouse religiously.

Now the plateau sage was replaced by a pool but we had transferred some plants to the pots in the courtyard and to the new *potager* so we could continue to enjoy the herb. The official name of sage, *Salvia officinalis*, originates from the Latin word *salvare*, 'to be saved'. It is a miracle herb, preserving and helping memory (I needed to eat more), and aiding digestion. In winter I loved to pick it fresh and serve it with honey as a *tisane*. It is recommended as an anti-inflammatory and to combat arthritis, asthma and Alzheimer's. It is also an excellent source of vitamin K.

Before fridges sage was used to preserve meat as it is a powerful antioxidant. In the seventeenth century it was so sought after the Chinese traded three bushels of dried tea for one bushel of dried sage from the Dutch. I found that when it came to cooking, sage suited sweet and sour. It was fabulous with blue cheese and with pork. The sage and Saussignac jelly I made brought cold meats and cheeses to life. With Roquefort cheese it was heaven.

The third herb in the song, rosemary, was delicious in winter served with aubergines, potatoes, lamb, duck – actually, most things. I loved to throw sprigs into my jams to give them a hint of something unexpected. But I discovered it was useful beyond cooking; a branch at each end kept ants off my clothes line and the leaves offered calcium, iron and vitamin B6. It is also a medicinal herb for memory and concentration enhancement and has anti-cancer and anti-inflammatory properties. Chopped fine and mixed with garlic and a little salt, sprinkled and baked on polenta, it was a delicious snack.

Rosemary contains carnosol, a potential cancer-preventing chemical. Research shows it inhibits the growth of breast tumours in studies of rats. Rosemary also helps lift your morale, relieves pain (including migraines), aids digestion and has antibacterial properties. It can be used as breath freshener and to stimulate hair growth. Rosemary can do well in and out of pots, and in the right conditions will grow into a large shrub with flowers of cornflower blue. Researchers put the exceptional longevity of a small Italian seaside village, Acciaroli, down to rosemary, anchovies and outdoor living. I was pleased to see the researchers noted that these amazing people (in a village of 2,000 inhabitants, more than 300 were 100 years plus) were not shy of enjoying a glass of wine either.

The last in the song, thyme, was my favourite herb to kill a sore throat. The instant I felt one creeping up I put a great bunch of thyme in a cup and poured hot water over it. A few minutes later, when it had cooled and extracted the benefits from the herb, I added a large teaspoon of honey and a drop of organic lemon juice. It was a magic pick-me-up.

Thyme kills off bacterial throat infections and helps decrease the oxidation and degradation of everything from sunflower oil to cheese. It is also an excellent source of vitamin C, a very good source of vitamin A, and a good source of iron, manganese, fibre and copper. But most of all, it is delicious. I sprinkled thyme on fresh tomatoes with a little oil and vinegar for a taste sensation or grilled it on tomato and goat's cheese toasts. Like rosemary, thyme can do well in and out of pots in the right conditions.

The famous four were staples for us and we always had a good few thriving bushes. Growing herbs gave me cooking inspiration. It was also the best way to be sure the herbs had been grown in a healthy fashion. In the new half-shaded vegetable garden, herbs like borage, coriander and basil were thriving at last. They were a tonic for us but also for the pollinators. The borage hummed like a propeller aeroplane about to take off it was so packed with bees recently received from a local beekeeper, Mr Patriarcha.

'If you don't use the smoker the bees will take Seán from here to Monestier,' he said, his greying head bent over his *forgon* (utility vehicle) parked in our courtyard.

'We were hoping to work more naturally and to avoid smoking the bees,' I said.

He laughed heartily. 'You must respect the bees but smoking doesn't harm them. Look at this beautiful mix – it is lavandin granules, lavender and pine needles,' he said, lifting the lid off a metal container in the back of his van.

I dipped my head inside and felt like I was stepping into a warm, relaxing bath.

Mr Patriarcha closed his eyes and leaned back like he was going into a trance.

'You see, that's what it does to the bees too – it calms them, relaxes them – so we can do the work we need to do,' he said dreamily.

Mr Patriarcha had delivered our hives earlier in the spring. At the Christmas market five months earlier, he announced that he was winding down his activity to retire and looking to sell most of his hives. We had bought two.

The bees appeared to have settled into their new home. On this, his second visit, he checked on them and offered advice on how to manage them. As the months progressed, we learned about the bees and I felt a whole new level of respect for each teaspoon of honey I ate. They tapped around 4,400 flowers and flew about 175 kilometres to make 1 gram of honey.

The bees were giving a clear early warning to the human race. They were dying in hordes, with 'colony collapse disorder' sounding the alarm about the environmental degradation caused by pesticides. In places like California, the almond and fruit farmers paid fortunes to bring bees from the other side of the USA and even flew them in from Australia because their own populations had been so decimated.

Bees have a sophisticated society and work together for the good of the hive; they are the ultimate socialists. They do a dance at the hive entrance to tell the other bees where to find the best flowers, giving the GPS coordinates in bee-speak and saving time on searching and unnecessary flying. This was where the systemic pesticides, particularly a new type called nicotinoids, were most dangerous. They worked on the bees' nervous system and impacted the bees' ability to remember where flowers were located and how to find their way home. Some were shown to not kill bees directly but, by impacting their ability to forage for nectar, to remember where flowers were located, and to find their way home, they destroyed the bees even if they didn't die instantly.

With research showing a direct impact on the bees' nervous system, these kinds of insecticides were probably also the reason for massive increases in nervous system disorders like Alzheimer's (up 500 per cent according to a recent study) and Parkinson's among humans. It is not possible to wash systemic pesticides off so certified organic or healthily homegrown are the only ways to avoid carcinogenic, nervous-system- and endocrine-disrupting chemicals getting into your body.

We learned that a key difference between organic and biodynamic honey was that organic beekeepers could still take all the honey as long as they provided the bees with an organic certified version of the sugar syrup offered as replacement. With biodynamic you had to leave the bees enough of their honey for them to survive the winter. The bees' honey was packed with immunity boosters, making it worth far more than just the calorie value. With their real honey the hive avoided many of the health problems that were damaging bee populations. But it was a lot more expensive than the honey – even the organic one – I found on the shelf in the supermarket. Now we knew the work that went into the honey – for the bees, let alone the beekeeper – we knew the price was justified.

Things were changing in other parts of the farm thanks to the bees. We left the ivy in the vineyard because along with biodiversity, the ivy offered bees flowers and hence pollen in early winter – one of the few plants that did. Ivy isn't a parasite – it climbs, so it doesn't harm the vine.

Through the beekeeping experience we learned that all honey, like wine, was not the same. They both reflected their *terroir*. We tasted honey from bees collecting pollen from lavender, sunflowers, spring flowers, summer flowers, forests like chestnut, and found they all had their unique flavour, a real sense of where they were from. Like wine, some honeys were not as wholesome as you might think. Some jars marketed as honey had even been found to contain no honey at all, just corn syrup.

Our apprentice Sandrine started her trial period with us. I asked her if she wanted to taste the honey from Mr Patriarcha.

'No thanks. I don't like honey,' she said.

'Why not try a little? This local honey might be different to what you have had,' I said.

She tasted.

'Hmmm. You are right. That is great. It doesn't taste like the honey I have had before. I really like it,' she said.

'I read that three quarters of the "honey" sold in the world is not honey,' I said. 'It's corn syrup dressed up as honey, or honey laced with corn syrup.'

Sometimes canny labelling led to misunderstanding by the consumer and at other times it was plain fraud. Neither was good since the health-giving properties of honey are legendary and research points to the health dangers of corn syrup.

'I saw a television show about that,' she said. 'That must be why I didn't like the honey I had before. I will send you the link.'

'Thanks, Sandrine, I would appreciate that,' I said.

Sandrine was keen and appeared to be embracing our organic perspective even though she had not arrived with that philosophy. Training her with the season already in full swing added to my stress although I knew it was necessary. I shoehorned training time into already long days. At the end of another long day, I ran out of the tasting room to cross the courtyard and flew across the gravel again. This time it was worse. My toes, knees, hands and chin were bleeding and I had a bump on my forehead I had come down so hard. I washed and disinfected my grazes then sat down, my head spinning. I had to slow down and get a grip. I felt like I was on the cusp of a nervous breakdown.

But as the days progressed things got better. The initial extra stress was worth it and Sandrine became a lifesaver for me. She needed guidance but she was keen. Wine sales were going well and growing; more wine lovers visited the property each season and our mailing list grew. Sandrine learned to sell wine at the *château* door and to fulfil internet orders. She followed me on visits and we set a target for her to be comfortable doing the half-day visits at our farm on her own by the end of the season. The time invested would really pay off the following summer when she would know the ropes and be able to make a serious contribution. Our first foray into the French employment market was working out.

While direct sales were flying, trade sales were limping along. The price of our wines had gone up in line with the increasing quality and constant cost increases. Trade clients were more price-sensitive than direct clients, who tasted and bought based on the quality not the price. We had to develop our trade sales and particularly those that would help us to sell more direct from the farm. I made a list of the top restaurants in the region, the ones we most wanted to be in, and talked them through with Sandrine. I hoped that having a French person to represent us would help with restaurant sales and that would in turn bring us more clients in the season.

'We must target these places with our wines, especially the Michelin-star restaurants,' I said. 'We're already on La Tour des Vents' wine list. I also really want to be on the wine list of Le Vieux Logis in Trémolat. I've read that it's the best restaurant in the Dordogne.'

'How will we do it?' asked Sandrine.

'We'll have to research as much as we can about them online then see if we can meet the sommelier. We're too busy now. It's a project for winter.'

Our restaurant list was put on the back-burner. With the tourist season well under way we couldn't spend time away from the property. We had reached a point where we regularly sold out of our whites and our top reds before the next bottling but we still had extra volume of our everyday Merlot red wine. We joined a newly conceived grouping of organic growers set up to sell the growing volume of bulk organic wine available in the region, hoping it would be a channel to sell our excess. France had gone from 1 per cent of the vineyards being organic when we arrived ten years before to almost 8 per cent.

More organic farmers represented potential for the region. State aid was promised for the grouping, enough to fund a salesperson, stands at wine fairs and the development of a brand. As a foreigner and relative newcomer, I sat quietly on the side watching the meetings and reading the emails. An uneasy feeling grew with each exchange.

The president of the management body and the newly appointed salesperson postulated that we shouldn't communicate about organic because their research said, 'No one wants organic wine.' I knew that wasn't true. Almost every day I had visitors who said, 'We want organic wine but we can't find it on the shelves.' I also knew that no one wanted cancer and if they hadn't made the connection between systemic pesticides and cancer yet then they were walking around with their eyes closed. I deleted their summary presentation in fury. Perhaps I should have kept it and put together a counter-presentation but I had the impression their views were fixed and I had no time to waste.

We found a *negociant* (a wine merchant) who offered us a better price than the producers' group and promised collection before harvest thus freeing up important tank space. It would give us a cash-flow injection but even at this higher price we had sold at a loss – the devastating reality of the bulk market. Meanwhile the producers' group sold no organic wine and dissolved. It was like watching an Astérix and Obélix village brawl except I wasn't laughing.

I had completed the details for the bulk sale with the *courtier* who acted between us and the *negociant* and was feeling depressed when a smart silver four-by-four with French plates drove up and parked outside the tasting room. A slim young man stepped out. I met him on the terrace and we introduced ourselves.

'I read your book *Grape Expectations* – in fact, I couldn't put it down. I had to come and visit,' he said.

'Welcome,' I said. 'Thanks for buying my book. I can do a tasting now. Actually, I could do a quick visit if you like.'

'That would be great,' he said. 'A quick visit then I'll buy some wine.'

'That's what I'm here for,' I said.

As we walked the vines it became clear he knew something about the subject. He was very interested in the biodynamic sprays that had helped us solve our downy mildew problem.

Back in the tasting room I took him through the range.

'I love your wines,' he said. 'They more than live up to my expectations after reading the book.'

We laughed at the unintended pun.

'Thank you. I'll let Seán know,' I said, hoping he would put his money where his mouth was.

'I should probably tell you I work for one of the big agrochemical companies.' He looked me in the eye for my reaction.

I felt a little shocked but tried not to show it. I hadn't pulled any punches against systemic chemicals as I took him on the visit of the vineyard. Was he about to announce that he would be suing me for my denouncement of the kind of products his company produced?

'I'm head of a research department. I know that what you are doing with biodynamics is the way we have to go. We have to make it easy for the big players to do what you're doing.'

'But you know biodynamics is about understanding your farm and being in it. It doesn't work by a simple recipe. It can't work as effectively as it has for us working by rote with no intimate understanding of the *terroir*.'

'I know. I got that from your book. But there have to be active properties in these solutions that could replace the systemic chemicals being used today.'

'Perhaps. But then it won't be biodynamics – it will be plant-based solutions. Still very interesting,' I said.

'It's the only way forward. The systemics will be stopped eventually and we have to have products to replace them,' he said.

He ordered ten cases. It was my biggest single end-client sale from the tasting-room door. I was stunned that I had made an impact on a key researcher in an agrochemical company. My first book was having an effect on our wine sales but also on a wider scale. His visit lifted my spirits and helped salve the loss-making *negociant* sale.

My second book, *Saving Our Skins*, launched in the UK and *Grape Expectations* was released worldwide in anglophone countries. We hosted a small launch event with Martin Walker, author of the *Bruno, Chief of Police* series, and his friend Raymond, who I met at Vinexpo, as guests of honour. They were as charming and tonic as they had been in Bordeaux.

I began to receive uplifting letters from across the globe: a young woman who bought *Grape Expectations* at her local post office in a tiny village in New Zealand; an Australian who had found it at her local bookshop; and an octogenarian who had borrowed it from his local library and then bought wine and *Saving Our Skins* direct from us. What really motivated me to keep writing and helped lift me from my perimenopausal depressed funk were the letters that said, 'Your book made me think about the provenance of my food and wine. It changed my habits.'

Our bees were doing well, we were selling books and wine, but the *negociant* still hadn't collected the bulk wine. I followed up and followed up again. With the contract signed we couldn't sell our wine to anyone else but it was clear that they would not fetch the wine in the given time frame. It was a classic *negociant* tactic to wait until harvest when growers needed the tank space then offer a price below the market rate. At that moment cash-strapped growers would take anything since they couldn't afford more tanks. I got the feeling the *negociant* on the other side of our deal might be hoping to negotiate the contract down. There was no way we were doing that. Thierry regularly had us rolling with laughter at his renditions of the smartly dressed *negociant* with pointy Italian leather shoes arriving in his latest model Mercedes to squeeze another few centimes out of the farmer in his tatty clothes and bashed-up *forgon*. We had to laugh or we would cry.

I had to be patient. I made myself a calming cup of lavender tea. The experience with the producer group and the *negociant* made me even more resolved to keep our focus on high-quality wine and to sell everything in the bottle rather than in bulk.

Mum Feely went back and forth with the chemo treatments. She had months of hellish side effects, pain and fatigue. We thought the war was being won and began to look forward to our trip for the golden wedding anniversary the following year. Our savings for the trip to South Africa were almost there: we had enough for two fares, now we needed to save for another two.

Mum's positive emails and photos of cute animals for Sophia and Ellie came through regularly and we chatted every couple of weeks. We were sure she was through the worst of it. Then her medical team did a scan to check progress and discovered that the lesions on her lung had increased significantly. The initial success of the chemo was a false message. It wasn't working despite the increased doses and horrific side effects.

I felt like I had been punched in the stomach. Mum had been so positive that she would beat the cancer and that going through hell would mean she would become well. The oncologist said there was one more treatment that could be tried but it would depend on 'the histology lump compatibility with the agent' and that would take three weeks to check. We had been given little real information about Mum's cancer and its dangers. We were in a deep fog.

CHAPTER 12

BLOSSOM AND HONEY

I read more about cancer and more particularly about chemotherapy treatment. I found documentaries and some studies that seemed to show that people who had cancer and rejected chemotherapy lived longer than those who took chemotherapy – there was clearly a lot of uncertainty about this treatment.

The hope of another treatment flickered for a moment then came back negative. Mum was relieved that she wouldn't have to go through any more terrible side effects. With no more treatments, Mum and Dad Feely began to think of plans for the future, perhaps some travel. We discussed when they might visit us again. Mum started to walk a little, to try to get her mobility back, but she was worn out. Despite having stopped the chemo many of the side effects continued and she needed more medication to cope with them.

We were experiencing cancer first-hand in our family and outside the cancer epidemic was growing. A vineyard worker in the Médoc region who lost her brother to cancer started a blog called *The Sewn-up Mouth*. Her brother had been the employee responsible for the sprays for a large property in the region. When she asked for the records of the molecules he had sprayed over the 20 years prior to his premature death she got no response.

She campaigned for greater awareness. In partnership with Générations Futur, a French association founded in 1996 to raise awareness of the dangers of pesticides, she organised the analysis of pesticide residues in the hair of workers in conventional vineyards, people living near conventional vineyards and people 300 kilometres from where vineyards were being sprayed. The level of pesticides was highest in the vineyard workers but also very high for those living near vineyards.

We knew it. When a conventional farmer sprayed even several kilometres away I could sometimes smell it, which showed that it spread well beyond the target. Seán told me only certain sprays gave off a bad smell; many lulled you into a false sense of security with little odour. The agrochemical companies had spent millions to find ways to make the chemicals odourless so we didn't suspect they were poison.

There was a lack of action by political players and lack of knowledge for the majority of people. A local school in the Sauternes region of Bordeaux had a level of cancer that was five times the national average. It was no surprise that the school was surrounded by conventional vineyards. When the *Telegraph* did an article on it they quoted a former mayor saying there was a 'law of silence' because if they stopped the pesticides the next day the local economy of Sauternes wine would collapse. They quoted the current mayor as saying: 'One cannot say there is a problem.'

The key point the article missed was that it is possible to farm and make beautiful wine without using carcinogenic chemicals. We had been doing it for ten years and I knew a number of Sauternes winegrowers that did too. It was possible to make a living and not give people cancer. It was not necessary to create excessive yields that generated the need for carcinogenic chemicals. The global market had 20 per cent too much wine at the time so ironically if everyone went organic the market would be in equilibrium.

I received an email from a couple that had read *Grape Expectations*. They were on the hunt for a house in France. Sally worked for Neal's Yard Remedies and they were very aware of the dangers of pesticide exposure. They wanted to have a holiday house in rural France where they would eventually move. They had already visited the only 100 per cent organic wine commune appellation in France, but had found it too expensive. Prices had increased significantly as it was seen by those who were aware of the dangers of pesticides as one of the few vineyard areas where it was safe to raise a family. That commune had nine *vignerons* (winemakers), all organic. We had around 30, of which more than half were organic.

I dreamed that one day Saussignac would be 100 per cent organic. We had recently earned the official status of *territoire bio engagé*, a 'territory engaged in organic'. It sounded good but I still ran the gauntlet with pesticide spray machines when I ran or cycled with Sophia and Ellie. While 60 per cent of the number of winegrowers was organic, only about 26 per cent of the farmed surface area was organic. The big players were generally the ones that were not organic – the ones that needed to be turned around.

Around that time a large estate in the Saussignac commune went organic and biodynamic, the conversion hot on the heels of losing a court case to a worker who had been sent to do handwork in the vineyard less than 24 hours after an insecticide spray was done. Since the exposure the worker had experienced serious nervous-system disruption:

headaches and dizzy spells so bad that they could not work or drive. The estate's owner and method of agriculture had changed. It would not turn back the damage to the health of the individual but for future employees and for us as a commune it was good news. There was growing awareness among farmers. Where personal experience and conviction weren't forcing the change, the financial and reputation implications of a court case like this one could make large businesses think twice.

France put in place a two-day course called *Certiphyto*, mandatory for all people responsible for using chemical sprays. Seán attended. At the start of the course two burly farmers were laughing like schoolboys in the back of the class, bemoaning the waste of time the course represented. They were uninterested in and unaware of the dangers of the poisons they routinely sprayed on their farms. By the midday break they weren't laughing. The statistics shared on the dangers of the products and the dramatic effect they were having on the wider environment had left them silent.

It was ironic that organisations spraying systemic chemicals were not allowed to send employees into the zone that had been sprayed for the required 24 or 48 hours but there was no requirement to notify walkers, clients or schools in the area of the no-go period. I felt more determined than ever to spread the word about why it was so important to support a healthy, no pesticide, organic agriculture. I knew the scourge of cancer was a direct result of what we were doing to the earth and particularly what we were doing in agriculture.

As author Michael Pollan said, each of us votes for the future we want three times a day: at each meal. With every purchase we encourage the kind of production it encompasses and hence the kind of world we want. Organic farming delivers relatively more expensive food on the face of it but it is the true cost as opposed to chemically farmed food where you are only seeing a small part of the real cost. The pollution and health implications of the cheap chemical solutions are 'externalised' and not shown in the price – things like treating cancer and nervous-system disruption and cleaning polluted water. They are left out, set aside for someone else to pay.

Mum Feely put on a brave face when we spoke but Dad told us she needed an oxygen machine to help her breathe at night.

'I think you should plan a trip,' I said to Seán when we hung up from the call.

'And who would look after the vineyard? You know I can't get away in the peak growing season,' he said.

It was true: no one could do the vineyard work that he did. If we missed a beat or hit a crisis while he was away we could lose our crop.

'I read that people with this cancer can live for years,' said Seán. 'We'll wait for our family trip next year for their golden wedding anniversary.'

In a whirlwind of visitors, summer passed and harvest was almost upon us. We planned to hand-pick everything. Through contacts I sought potential pickers and learned how to do the associated paperwork. Our apprentice Sandrine, who had been a significant help through the summer, would be a key part of the team. She had energy and was keen to learn.

Feeling confident we could leave the vineyard with Sandrine for a few days, we booked a last-minute getaway to an ecological campsite, mere steps from a beach near St-Jean-de-Luz, four hours away on the Atlantic coast near the Spanish border. I had confirmed a large group for the Monday long before we thought of the idea so Seán and the girls left on Saturday and I was to follow on Tuesday by train.

The day they left, Sandrine took a message down for me saying Clément from Bio Logis had called and could I call him back. I had no idea who Bio Logis was and a quick internet search offered up nothing.

I called the number.

'Le Vieux Logis,' said an elegant voice on the other side. 'How may I help you?'

'*Bonjour*,' I said. 'I am looking for Clément – he left a message for me to call him back.'

'Oh, Monsieur Clément,' she said. 'He is the master of the hotel.'

My heart upped its pace. Clément from Bio Logis was, in fact, the *maître d'hôtel* of our dream client Le Vieux Logis, one of the most hallowed restaurants in the Dordogne.

'Oh, thank you. That must be it. May I speak to Monsieur Clément?' I said, feeling super excited.

'I will see if I can find him.'

'*Bonjour*, Madame,' said the suave voice of Monsieur Clément a few minutes later.

'*Bonjour*, Monsieur Clément. It's Caro Feely from Château Feely. I think you left a message yesterday asking for me to call you back.'

'Oh yes, Madame Feely. I would like to visit to try your wines. A wine critic visited us this week and said that of the wines he discovered in Bergerac yours were some of the best. He said I had to come and taste your wines.'

'Thank you. I didn't know we had had a visit from a wine critic this week,' I said.

'He stopped incognito. It's my day off on Monday so I was thinking of coming to see you.'

We agreed a time and I hung up then danced round the room, singing hallelujah.

On Monday he visited as promised and bought several cases of two wines for his Michelin-star restaurant list. Alone that night I raised a glass in celebration. Clients were coming to us without us having to 'sell'. Seán's hard graft in the vineyard was bearing fruit. A few weeks before, a Dutch importer had emailed to ask if he could import our wines. He paid for a box of samples to be shipped to him and ordered 10 boxes, then 20.

The next day I trained down to join my family near St-Jean-de-Luz. That beach holiday I found deep joy being with Sophia, Ellie and Seán, reading on the beach, swimming, walking. I considered how much we had sacrificed of this time together over the years of incessant work and felt sad. I knew that we needed to change something. I had escaped for three days and it felt like Christmas. Having an apprentice was a start but I wondered if it was enough.

On our return it was a headlong rush into harvest and back to school for Sophia and Ellie. Harvest looked like it would be early. I booked the team for the following Monday. It would be our first fully hand-picked vintage and we were excited but anxious. It was a different way of doing things. We didn't know how long it would take, particularly on the vineyards we had never picked by hand, and we didn't know what pace to expect from paid pickers. All our hand-picking to date had been done by friends and clients.

We were chatting about this and Seán was drawing out each vineyard and its quantity estimate while I prepared dinner when

Ian, Seán's brother who lived near his mum and dad, rang. He never called so I knew something was up. I handed the phone to Seán.

As they spoke Seán's face clouded over. Ian said Mum Feely was not doing well; that Seán needed to come and see her. It felt like days since we had chatted with her. With the chaos of our tourist season and our escape to the beach, we had missed the signals.

The following day Seán went through the motions of his work like he was in a trance. He was in shock from the news and not sure what to do. Going from rural France to rural South Africa was a 24-hour journey. Our harvest was ready and we couldn't harvest without him. If he did go, he would get there and have to come straight back. He checked flights. His mum wasn't getting any better – it sounded like she wouldn't hang on until their golden wedding or even until after harvest – but it seemed crazy to go for a single day.

Bruce, Seán's sister's husband, called.

'It's really important that you go and see your mum even if it's only for twenty-four hours. It's not how long that matters. It's the fact of being there.'

His advice helped clear our harvest-pressure-addled brains. Seán found a flight leaving the following day, Friday, and returning on Monday. While he packed his case, I called our picking team to delay the start by a day. I felt like organising harvest was wrong, like we shouldn't be doing it, like we should be focused on our family, that Seán should be going for longer, that we should all be going – but nature would not wait for us.

Seán joined his siblings and dad at his mum's bedside, cherishing the brief moments with her and them. He crossed the world, changed seasons and continents, and returned in three days.

'Her eyes flickered recognition when I showed her the fresh figs I had packed for her but she couldn't eat them,' said Seán. 'She's on liquid food and a drip now.'

His mum loved figs and she knew our tree. We started harvest with heavy hearts.

Mum Feely passed on two days later. Even though we knew it was coming, tears poured out of me. I recalled shared moments, especially their visit over our first harvest. We raised a toast that night and wished her well on her way. I passed the tissues around the table. I loved the Irish wake idea; that everyone gets together to celebrate your life when you pass on. That's what I want when I go to the next place, a big party to celebrate and share memories. Seán was missing that. He was missing being with his family at this critical time of grieving and celebrating Mum Feely's life.

In the days that followed, Seán focused on harvest with quiet determination. He went through the motions but he was in shock. Missing his mum's funeral and the shared time with his family made it difficult to close the circle.

Seán's sister Glynis stayed on for a few weeks with their dad then he was alone. The shock of Mum Feely's passing after almost 50 years together, especially after the intense nursing of the last few weeks, hit him hard.

For the following month Seán had a constant upset stomach. Eventually he agreed to go and see our doctor, who said it was because Seán hadn't had the time to grieve, to assimilate the passing of his mum. Our hard taskmaster, the vineyard and its associated business, did not let up – there was no getting away, no escaping. Seán needed to go back and to see his dad, as much for himself as for Dad Feely. He booked a two-week trip in November when the key winemaking activity would be complete.

Hand-harvesting was different to machine-harvesting. It was convivial and slow. Whereas machine-harvesting all our whites had taken one short morning, now it took five mornings for a team of six. We started at dawn and slowly proceeded across the vineyards. It was better for us and for the grapes; the human scale and pace of it were peaceful and joyful, and the grapes were handled gently rather than thrashed. It was hard work but it was worth it: the grapes arrived sorted, whole and perfect into the winery.

I noticed that Sandrine was slower than the rest. She kept standing up to stretch her back. Slim and young, she should have been one of the swiftest of the group. I asked if she was all right and she said yes. Seán noticed too. We decided I needed to have a chat with her when she returned from the next few weeks at school.

Between harvesting our whites and reds, Seán, Sophia and Ellie harvested honey from the beehives and processed it for the first time. I returned home from a day of touring in St-Émilion and found them deep in sweetness. My feet stuck to a floor decorated with a mass of sticky spots and the fragrance of honey and beeswax engulfed me. They used a stainless steel centrifuge to separate the honey from the wax and were starting the next step of pouring the honey into glass jars. The thick liquid squeezed out in a lazy river of gold, catching reflections of the setting sun. Seán, Sophia and Ellie were working as a perfect team. I wanted to stay but I had pre-booked visitors that had arrived for a one-hour visit.

It was almost dark when I returned. Boxes of honey jars were stacked on the bench. All the stainless steel trays and pans we owned were dispersed around the kitchen coated in golden honey. The kitchen floor hadn't escaped either; instead of spots it was an almost continuous layer of stickiness.

'Get out and leave me to clean up this mess,' said Seán. 'Take these and lick them. Out, out!'

Sophia, Ellie and I took slices of bread from our bread tin and scurried out. We scraped honey in great slow sticky waves. The aroma was rich and deep like an intense field of wild flowers but more concentrated. It was the best honey I had ever tasted. We swished and lavished honey on to bread and ourselves. I felt like I was taking a honey bath. By the end there was honey everywhere, even in our hair. We licked our fingers, our lips and finally the pans themselves. By the time we had finished the pans almost didn't need to be washed.

Seán had read that the best way to clean the honey racks and any other honey utensils was to put them outside the hive. He did this and the bees took every last sticky drop. The harvest of blossom-rich honey was especially poignant; Seán's mum's nickname was Blossom.

CHAPTER 13

GROWING PAINS

Seán left to see his dad in South Africa. With him away I was so engrossed in keeping the business afloat and being a single mum that I didn't have time to think about Sandrine's slowdown. Before we knew it, Seán was back, looking more at peace for having made the trip. The Friday evening before her return from a few weeks at school, Sandrine called.

'I have some news,' she said. 'I am pregnant. I will be on maternity leave from May to September.'

I felt a shot of panic. We had taken an apprentice so I would have help in the summer. The rest of the year we didn't need the help. Sandrine was on a two-year apprentice contract, the time her tourism diploma would take to complete. In term time she had two weeks with us then two weeks at school. It didn't make economic sense to have an apprentice unless you had the benefit of their full-time summer.

'I know this is happy news,' I said. 'But I am a little upset since we took you on specifically for the summer. What will you do about your studies?'

'I will continue until I go on maternity leave and then go back after the maternity leave,' she said.

A moment of silence passed where I didn't know what to say. I decided to say as little as possible to avoid saying something I would regret.

'Thanks for letting us know. We can talk about next steps on Monday when you're back,' I said. 'Congratulations. Have a good weekend.'

A whole summer of training had gone up in smoke. Despite Sandrine's assurances that she would continue after the maternity leave, I wondered if she would. In the meantime we were stuck, contracted for another 18 months. I could not cope on my own but we couldn't afford two apprentices. I felt trapped. My new hormone-driven aggression came out in full force and I hit the countertop then leapt back, hopping in pain and holding my hand.

I recalled a friend in Dublin who owned his own small business saying he only hired men because they didn't go on maternity leave. Now I completely understood. In his shoes I could see what it meant for a small business. A third of our manpower would be gone but the costs would keep coming. I ran to find Seán, my heart racing. He was pruning in the Hillside Sauvignon Blanc. He looked up in surprise.

'The mystery of the slowdown since September is solved. Sandrine is pregnant. She's tired and no wonder,' I said.

'Feck,' said Seán.

'She'll be on maternity leave for the whole summer.'

'Double feck,' said Seán.

'Exactly. What are we going to do? Already we've seen the effect of maternity on her motivation. It will only get worse. It's as good as not having an apprentice at all.'

'We should have seen it coming,' said Seán.

'All the signs were there,' I said.

'But it's not as if we haven't had our minds on other things,' said Seán. 'No wonder we didn't cop on.'

I thought of Mum Feely, felt tears and swallowed them back.
'We are where we are,' I said. 'We have to find a solution.'

'Have you looked up what happens with maternity leave? Do we have to keep paying the full salary?' said Seán.

'I had a quick look but it only confused me,' I said. 'She called after office hours so I won't be able to get any answers until Monday.'

I felt like a bomb waiting to explode. That night the sheets wrapped round me in a sleepless dance. On Monday I called our accountant for advice and information.

'Don't worry, the state will pay the apprentice salary while she is on maternity leave,' he said.

I felt relieved – at least for the maternity-leave months we would have a small budget to put towards getting a replacement – but I didn't want to put in the training again only to have them leave when our apprentice came back. I reminded myself of my sister Jacquie's words: 'challenge is opportunity'. What we were experiencing was necessary to our future; it was making way for something better.

Christmas was a couple of days away. We buried ourselves in preparations although there wasn't much to do since we would be having Christmas as our small family of four. Seán's brother Neal and family had cancelled their plans to be with us to go to South Africa to be with Seán's dad instead. We went to Bordeaux for the day before Christmas Eve. It felt great to be together doing something completely different to our everyday activities.

Compared to our first visit 15 years before on a holiday from Ireland, Bordeaux city was transformed. Quiet silver trams slid on green carpets – mostly living grass – through organised clean streets. A core of the central part of the city had been pedestrianised and was bliss to walk around. From the tram stop at the Place de la Bourse we walked up to the Grand Théâtre, whose restaurant Le Quatrième Mur was the new stomping ground for *Top Chef* judge and '*meilleur ouvrier de France*' ('best worker in France') Philippe Etchebest, directly opposite Le Grand Hôtel, where Gordon Ramsay held sway.

St Catherine Street stretched from there into the distance, the longest shopping street in Europe. We walked its entirety, Sophia and Ellie in heaven. At the largest bookshop in south-west France, Librairie Mollat, we found copies of *Grape Expectations* and *Saving Our Skins* next to the full set of *Harry Potter* books. I felt like I had arrived.

We found an organic restaurant down a small side street in the old town and revelled in delicious fresh salads and quiche. Like the holiday on the coast, it felt like pure luxury to have a day off. But our apprentice dilemma nagged in the back of my mind. That night we tucked the girls into bed then Seán and I finished the tidying up.

'I can't take the uncertainty of this apprentice thing,' I said. 'We have to find a solution. I think we have to bite the bullet and take a second apprentice.'

'But the same thing could happen. I looked it up online. There are special forums to discuss how to organise and get the most out of summer maternity leave as an apprentice. It seems like a popular thing to do.'

'I will only hire men,' I said.

Seán guffawed, remembering my outburst to our friend so many years before.

'A French *man* cleaning *gîtes*, setting tables, serving lunches? I don't think so,' he said.

'You're right, it's a long shot,' I said, biting my lower lip.

France was still chauvinist, decades behind the UK and Ireland, and even further behind places like Canada and New Zealand.

'But even if you find the right person can we afford two?' Seán asked.

'We will be financially strained,' I said. 'But I don't think Sandrine will come back.'

'But we won't know until the end of her maternity leave after the summer,' said Seán.

'We'll have to play Russian roulette,' I said.

'I'm not sure,' said Seán. 'I think you should look into finding someone just for the summer. Maybe search for both and see which candidates are best.'

With that decided, we enjoyed our quiet Christmas *en famille*. Friends Pierre and Laurence de St Viance and Thierry and Isabelle Daulhiac joined us for New Year. We usually had New Year with Pierre and Laurence in the great hall of Château Saussignac that was their living room but that year I announced that the party was *chez nous*; a fancy-dress party with the themes of the colour pink and pointy shoes. Seán had a tradition of ragging Thierry about his pink sweaters and Pierre about his pointy shoes. Pierre generated hearty laughter attired in bright-pink pointy shoes, pink cape and pink underpants, his solid frame and receding ginger hair perfectly offset by his rose-coloured Superman outfit.

After the break I put a job specification on the internet, contacted schools specialising in wine tourism and started the process of sorting through résumés again. It was time to move on.

A couple of years before, I was waiting for a friend in Bordeaux airport when the automatic glass doors of the arrivals hall opened and a slight man, with greying brown hair and spectacles, clad in a tweed jacket, stepped out and stopped in the sensor zone, suspending them open.

He announced in English-accented French, 'Can someone lend me a portable phone? Mine is in my suitcase in the hold and I need to get in touch with someone urgently.'

He didn't dare step out for fear of being shut out and not being able to get back for his luggage but he was desperate for a phone.

I came forward.

'Thank you!' he said, exuding relief. 'Our flight was so delayed. I should already be at an event.'

As he talked I realised he looked familiar. By the time he finished I thought I had it.

'Are you Steven Spurrier?' I asked.

'Yes, as a matter of fact I am.'

In front of me was one of the most renowned wine journalists in the world. He was a columnist for *Decanter* magazine, *the* wine magazine in the UK, and in fame probably second only to Jancis Robinson. Steven was a household name in wine circles across the globe, perhaps even more so since the screening of *Bottle Shock*, a film about a wine competition he had organised in Paris in the seventies when he owned a wine shop and school there. The despair of some of the scenes in the movie captured the angst of being a winemaker so perfectly I found it truly artful. We knew those feelings only too well.

'I'm here as guest speaker for a wine dinner,' said Steven. 'Thanks to you at least they know I'm on my way. May I ask who you are?'

'Caro Feely. *Enchanté*,' I said, using the French term but holding out my hand to shake his in the English way rather than leaning over to give him a kiss on each cheek. 'We're organic winegrowers in Saussignac.'

'Oh, very interesting. I regularly visit friends near there. Do you have a card? I will come and visit you next time I'm in the area.'

I dug into my bag and handed over a bent and lipstick-smeared home-printed business card, the only one I had, kicking myself for being so ill prepared and unprofessional. Steven didn't seem bothered.

'Well, it's been a pleasure to meet you. Thank you for lending me your phone,' he said and disappeared behind the glass doors with a wave.

I was enveloped by a warm feeling of unexpected good fortune.

Since then Steven had fulfilled his promise and visited us at the farm and I had seen him at Vinexpo.

'You will have no trouble selling these,' he said on tasting our wines.

His prediction was turning out to be true. We were turning wine buyers away instead of chasing them. I kicked myself for not taking a photo of him in the tasting room. I had missed the opportunity with two famous Irish personalities that had visited too. Our wall of fame could have been growing and with it our social media following. Taking photos had not entered my head.

Anne Twist, mum of Harry Styles of One Direction, visited incognito. She enjoyed a tasting and a cheese platter on our deck with friends that were regular visitors. I wouldn't have recognised Harry, let alone his mum, so I was blissfully oblivious. She posted a photo of a glass of wine and our tasting-room deck and vines on Instagram. Chiara Wilson, a friend of ours and a Harry fan, spotted it. By the time I looked, the photo already had 470,000 likes but alas no Feely branding. My daughters berated me for not recognising fame when it slapped me in the face and I berated myself for another lost photo opportunity.

Soon after, Martin Moran visited en route to a master of wine bash in Bordeaux. It was a while since we had seen him.

'God, I can't believe how much this place has changed. You have been working hard,' he said.

'The buildings have changed, the tasting room and Lodge are new since your visit, but the biggest fundamental change is the vineyard,' I said. 'Perhaps it's harder to see on the face of it but every year we see an improvement, a change in the health of the farm. Claude Bourguignon, a top soil scientist in France, reckons if it has been farmed chemically for thirty years it will take thirty years to get full health back.'

'That will take some stamina,' said Martin drily.

'Indeed,' I said and laughed, picturing us in twenty years. 'But already after three years of organic conversion we saw a big difference: the chemical residues were gone; the wild orchids came back. Every year the disease resistance of the vines increases; more of the natural clover and other beneficial plants install themselves; the biodiversity increases.'

I pointed to the clover thick around our feet as we made our way back up from the vineyard.

In the tasting room I placed two glasses and a spittoon on the table and we tasted through the range.

'Your wines have changed too. They're good – I mean, really good,' said Martin.

He wasn't one to mince his words or to give unearned compliments.

I poured the last wine.

'I think it's worth getting a Riedel glass for these reds if you have one,' said Martin. 'I sense another layer that isn't coming through.'

Riedel is a brand of crystal wine glass and it's considered one of the best because of the quality of their glass and their varietal-specific shapes. I found our two Riedel glasses that were kept for special occasions and poured the pure Cabernet Sauvignon, a new *cuvée* recently christened *Vérité*.

We compared the two different glasses of the same wine.

'Incredible,' I said.

'I was at a Riedel tasting a couple of weeks ago and it reminded me just how much difference it can make. *This* is the *Vérité*,' he said, holding up the Riedel glass.

We laughed.

'Wow,' I said, shaking my head in disbelief. 'It has far more fruit. The barrel aromas are still there but they're playing a support role rather than being in front like they are in the other glass.'

We tried it with the other reds. There was a difference but nothing as dramatic as with the *Vérité*.

We finished tasting and took our glasses inside to delight hungrily in Seán's duck breast in a red wine reduction sauce with homegrown potatoes and spinach paired with our no-sulphite-added *Grâce*. It was the perfect match; a dense, rich and mineral blend made for duck. Intense chat about Ireland and wine sparked. We proceeded on to a selection of organic cheeses, revelling in Valérie's *tarin*.

'I know it's a weekday for you so I won't keep you up,' said Martin. 'I might take a glass of that *Vérité* with me – I have some writing to do and it will be a good companion. Thanks for a great dinner.'

I filled his Riedel glass and he set off to write in the Wine Lodge.

The following morning I knocked on the door with the offer of coffee and muesli in our kitchen.

'Sorry to hurry you, Martin, but I need to turn the room around before the tour guests arrive,' I said after settling him in with a strong brew.

'No problem. I'll be fine here now I have coffee and Wi-Fi.'

I tore across to the Lodge, removed the sheets, raced round to put them on to wash, then returned with fresh sheets, vacuum and cleaning equipment. As I finished making the bed, Martin returned to fetch his suitcase.

'Ready to go?' I said.

'Another hard day of wine-tasting ahead of me,' he said and laughed. 'By God, you work hard. Another role you have to play: chambermaid.'

I laughed. 'Yep! I'm really sorry to rush you but I have to get this ready for clients this afternoon and I have wine-school guests arriving at ten.'

'No problem at all. It was fantastic to see you again and to see the progress you've made. You can be proud of yourselves. I know it isn't easy. Look at my friend Charles Martin. He worked hard, made great wine and still had to sell up.'

When Charles was forced to sell I felt desperate. He was one of the iconic estates in the region. Looking at the backdrop of him and others that had closed their doors reminded me how fortunate we were to be surviving as a small farm business.

We said our goodbyes and I raced on with the rest of my day. A few weeks later Martin covered no-sulphites-added Feely *Grâce* as his wine of the week and wrote about how we were back on '*terroir firma*' and had turned our farm around. As I looked at the article I slapped my head. Martin was a celebrity wine journalist regularly featured on the radio and in print in Ireland, and I had missed another photo opportunity.

I waded through countless CVs and interviewed four candidates in person. None of them fit what we were looking for. Spring had arrived, the pace was gathering, and I felt like an Olympic sprinter limbering up for the spurt required to get through the six months of manic that was our season. I didn't want it to include falls, memory lapses or 14-hour days every day. It wasn't good for me or the rest of my family. We had to find someone – and soon.

Seán came up from the vineyard with wild leeks, purslane and kale from the garden. He took off his boots, washed his hands and started chopping. We had passed each other that morning but still hadn't actually greeted each other.

'I've been looking through more CVs. I still haven't found anyone,' I said, diving into a work discussion. 'I don't want to settle for someone who isn't passionate about organic and about wine.'

'You made that mistake the first time,' said Seán.

'Exactly,' I said.

I didn't need reminding. Even before Sandrine's pregnancy, it had become clear that she was losing interest in wine – a serious problem for a business that was all about wine. It had been hard to judge with someone almost straight out of school. I had picked up that wine was part of her parents' culture and she *was* interested at the start, but as the months progressed it was clear the interest was waning.

'This time we need the right person or we'll cost ourselves more time, money and angst than if we have no one,' I said.

'But you have to have someone. You can't cope on your own,' said Seán definitively, sensing that I was about to lay down arms and surrender.

Our local organic association, AgroBio Périgord, suggested listing our job description on two agricultural job networks, and a promising email arrived a few weeks later. The applicant looked like our dream come true: a landscape engineer interested in all things ecological. Cécile had worked as a volunteer and *au pair* in Ireland and loved the place. She was a part-time beekeeper planning to sign up for a one-year *alternance* work-and-study wine tourism degree at a school about one hour from us in Bordeaux. I interviewed her online then organised for Seán and I to chat with her again. She was available from June, when we needed her, and could be with us for two summers plus some of the time in between during her year of school. As I sipped sage-leaf tea I reflected on our interviews. Cécile appeared dynamic and steeped in our ethos. Her CV showed useful work experience and strong organisational ability. She looked like a good fit, someone who could make a difference to our business at this critical moment in our evolution and in the process help bring a little more balance to our lives.

PART 4

EARTH AND ROOTS

We consider the best wine is one that can be aged without any preservative; nothing must be mixed with it which might obscure its natural taste.
Columella

CHAPTER 19

ORANGE WINE AND A NEW ERA

Cécile arrived for a trial month, an opportunity to see if she got on with us and to iron out the administrative aspects for her contract with us and her school. My admin folder was filled with paperwork about how apprenticeship worked, the cost formulas and details like the obligatory doctor's visit required for any new hire.

With our first hire the obligatory doctor's visit had created chaos. The school said they would organise it for all the students for economics of scale then they decided not to because the social services organisations were split by county so there were different doctors for different students depending on where their employer was based – only they didn't tell the employers that the plan had changed.

Six months into the contract and a couple of weeks before we received Sandrine's maternity news, our accountant called in a panic to say we were being hit with the charges of a full-time worker and associated social charges because the apprentice contract had not been registered because the doctor's visit had not taken place. The MSA (the social security service for farmers) bill for thousands of euro arrived to reinforce the message.

I tried calling the MSA and got no answer. They were shut during the hours I was not in front of clients, and for one full day every week their phone lines were closed. A farmer friend had had all his bank accounts frozen for a late payment. I wasn't going to pay a bill that was incorrect but I didn't want our accounts frozen.

Seán and I visited Vinitech, a machinery and technical show for winegrowers, to investigate alternatives to our heat exchanger and other necessary winery investments, and found one of the head honchos of MSA at their stand. Within days I had a doctor's appointment and the crisis was over. This time I would not let that particular problem happen. The doctor's visit would be organised well in advance no matter what the school said. I had kept the contact details garnered from my first mission since this information was nowhere to be found online.

From the first day Cécile was a joy to be with. She was eager to learn and had a great sense of humour. I felt a weight lifting off my shoulders. She picked sprigs of vines and placed them artfully in a decanter in the tasting room, bringing a touch of nature and elegance. She began working on our wine list, aiming to present it in a more pleasing and easy-to-understand format.

'What do you think of this shit?' she said, presenting me with her latest version.

We both cracked up. With her French accent 'sheet' came out sounding just like, well, 'shit'.

'What do you think of this sheeeet?' she said after regaining her composure.

From then on when we spoke about sheets – whether for the beds in the accommodation or sheets of paper – she would carefully stretch the word out and both of us would have a good laugh. She was a tonic.

Her course director arrived to finalise the *alternance* contract. All was going well until we discussed the statutory rate of pay. Cécile had already been on an *alternance* contract so she didn't fit the costing scenario I had on file and on which I had based our budget calculations. Given that Cécile had already been on a contract like this, her contract had to be set at almost 50 per cent more than I had estimated. We still didn't know if Sandrine would come back. With her and Cécile on the payroll we would be in too deep and even deeper with this new higher wage. I felt a little nauseous; in three short weeks I had become attached to Cécile. The school representative looked worried and so did Cécile.

'I will have to talk to Seán. It's a significant difference. I hope we can come up with a solution,' I said.

That evening Seán and I talked through the new hurdle.

'How come you didn't know before?' said Seán. 'How did you get this far without realising?'

'I had no idea there was a special clause for someone who had already done an *alternance* contract – it wasn't in the costing scenarios I had from the school that I thought worked for all applicants,' I said.

'Well, another lesson learned the hard way,' said Seán. 'Cécile seems worth it but you've worked closer with her than I have these past three weeks.'

'I think she's worth it. But can we afford it? We have hefty loans in progress. We're going to take the hit of the low yields from the bad flowering. I think she will contribute. She'll definitely bring us more business, especially in the season when we know we lose sales if I'm not here.'

'Exactly,' said Seán.

'Cécile is already making a real contribution. She isn't like an "employee"; she's part of the team. I feel like we're working together for a common purpose. Before I think of something that needs attention she's on to it. She's been working on new marketing cards for the business and has already captured the essence of what we are better than I have in ten years. She's a dynamo.'

'She's proactive,' said Seán.

'Yes. We have to find a way to pay her. She'll be worth it,' I said, almost thinking out loud.

'There you go,' said Seán.

'Not only that, but the *alternance* contracts are usually half of the term time at school and with her school it's only a third.'

'So you do know what to do,' said Seán.

I realised he had been acting like my business consultant. He had made me work out what I already knew but hadn't articulated.

With the budget discussion concluded we moved on to the naming and blending decisions for our upcoming bottling. We were in the thick of our annual reflection, a time when we spent hours trying different blends. My notebook became a spider's web of notes on different wines, barrel samples and potential combinations. Seán poured a wine into my glass.

'Look at that colour,' he said.

It was bright orange, a most beautiful but unusual tint for a dry white wine.

'I love it,' I said. 'What is it?'

'It's our first no-sulphite-added white, Sémillon that has been in barrels for more than a year. It's so stable I'm happy to bottle it without sulphites added,' said Seán.

Sulphites are added as a preservative during winemaking to protect wine from oxidation and to stop things like re-fermentation and the development of bacteria.

I lifted the glass to my nose.

'It smells so good. Honeysuckle, oranges, *tarte Tatin*.'

'Honeycomb. Perhaps a hint of quince,' said Seán.

'And a touch of ginger.'

I took a sip. It was dry but it tasted like honey, flower nectar and oranges. It was not like any white wine Seán had made – in fact, it was like no white wine I had experienced.

'Delicious and so original,' I said. 'But will our clients accept it? It's so different.'

'I don't think we can sell it to professionals for resale unless they specialise in natural wine, like Yanflorijn Wijn in Amsterdam. You'll have to explain it on the website and make sure that people understand what it is when they're here in the tasting room.'

'What are we going to call it?'

'Honeycomb? Blossom? *Fleur de* something?' said Seán.

'What about *Mille Fleurs* or *Champ des Fleurs*?' I said.

'*Mille Fleurs* has a good ring to it,' said Seán.

I saw tears in Seán's eyes. Both of us were thinking of his mum and her nickname Blossom. This first no-sulphite white would be a homage to her.

'That's decided then. *Mille Fleurs*,' I said.

No-sulphite-added wines had become a key part of our range. We had progressed from deep fear of them to confidence. The first time we tried doing no sulphite-added wine it went wrong and the volatile acidity – a sign that the wine was starting its journey to vinegar – went through the roof. We added sulphites and stabilised it but it wasn't a wine we were going to sell under our brand. Fortunately it wasn't a significant volume and it was still within the appellation norms so we sold it as bulk wine to a *negociant* who blended it with scores of other wines and sold it to supermarkets. In the process we learned that natural wine, with no additives at all, was not for the faint-hearted. We trod cautiously after that false start. The following year Seán's no-sulphite-added red was magnificent. It was my favourite red of all the wines we had made. We preferred to drink wine with low and no sulphites ourselves so it was logical that we were making our wines this way. Sulphites cause inflammation so it's better from a health point of view if wines contain lower levels. Organic wine guarantees lower sulphites than conventional wine and biodynamic wine offers less again. With *Mille Fleurs* and our other no-sulphite-added wines we were moving into a category called 'natural wine'.

Seán's confidence with no-sulphite-added wine had grown, as had the resistance of our wine. With natural farming the level of antioxidants like resveratrol grew. The level of natural acidity was also higher and that helped to protect the wine. With hand-picking the fruit stayed whole until it was in the winery protected by inert gas, further reducing the need for sulphites. We had increased to three no-sulphite-added natural wines in the range: wines made with grapes and nothing but grapes. For the rest of the range we were certified organic and biodynamic: our wines were made with grapes and a few sulphites at bottling but no other 'ingredients', unlike most industrial wine.

We moved on to the red samples. I lifted the *Résonance* Merlot to my nose.

'Hmm. Dark fruit, a hint of truffle. The deep cool of the limestone.'

'Plum and blackberry,' said Seán.

'It's incredible that this is from the same vineyard as our first few years of *Résonance*. It's yummy,' I said.

I had never been able to say 'yummy' before about our plain Merlot from the north-facing Garrigue parcel. It was my least favourite of our reds but now it was surprising me. I could see a net progression over the years that proved the wisdom of going organic and biodynamic. Our yields were low but our quality went up every year. It was a long, long game.

'What's the sulphite level?' I asked.

'It will be around sixty milligrams per litre at bottling. It's low, not "no". The next vintage of *Résonance* is no sulphite added, but I'm not sure we should risk going no sulphite on all of it,' said Seán. 'We'll see when the time comes to bottle it next year. I didn't bring a sample but it's even better than this one.'

Seán was not one to sing his own praises so it had to be good.

'The next few barrel samples are no sulphite added,' said Seán. 'This one is hand-picked Merlot from Hillside vineyard.'

'Very smooth,' I said after sniffing, taking a sip and spitting. 'Lovely notes of dark and red fruit with a hint of chocolate.'

I wrote furiously, trying to capture our perceptions of the different wines. Seán did what the French call *aviner*: poured a little of the next wine he was about to pour into the glasses and threw it out. This rinsing of the glasses with the wine before pouring the sample ensured an accurate reading of the wine.

'This one is thick with *cassis*, dark cocoa and bitter orange. It's lovely and smooth,' I said.

'It's the hand-picked Cabernet Sauvignon, also no sulphite,' said Seán. 'Let's try those two together in the proportions we have.'

He poured into a beaker then into my outstretched glass.

'That tastes like it should be *Grâce*. Delicious. I love it. These wines are so good, SF. There's depth of flavour and harmony like a magnificent symphony. You can pat yourself on the back.'

'But I don't like doing the heavy work of the winemaking – I don't want to do it any more,' he said.

I felt like I had been punched.

'What?' I said, then sat in stunned silence for a second. The wines were finally showing the potential of our hill farm and

Seán was saying he didn't want to do it. 'But you're so good at it – these wines are magnificent.'

'I like growing the grapes, I love gardening, but I don't like doing all the pipe-work and barrel-work in the winery,' said Seán.

'Shoot, SF,' I said, although I couldn't blame him. Our winery was so far from automated it was a nightmare to work in. I wouldn't want to do it. 'What will we do?'

'Maybe we can get someone to do the winemaking.'

'But what would you do for work at that time of year?' I asked.

'Go travelling.'

I laughed heartily. 'We can't afford to pay someone to do it and we sure as heck can't afford for you to go travelling,' I said. 'Anyway, in France we definitely couldn't get a flexible contract for that. If we were in California or Australia I bet it would be easy. But even then, these are great wines because you made them. It isn't just the vineyard and the growing. You don't realise how much experience you've built up in this kind of winemaking.'

'I know.'

With that bombshell stored away, I tried to concentrate on the rest of the samples, then with getting on with the season that was hitting us. It was hard to focus with this new curveball. I felt deep stress knowing that Seán was no longer happy doing this key part of his daily grind but we were like the pole that got stuck in the harvest machine – so far in we couldn't get out.

We bottled the new wines, including the no-sulphite-added *Mille Fleurs* white and the *Grâce* and *La Source* reds. I confirmed with Cécile and her school that we wanted to go ahead. We would find a way to meet the commitment. But adding another person to do the winemaking was completely out of the question.

On the other hand, Seán needed to be happy or we would have to sell up. I felt like I was in a catch-22. I told myself to keep calm and carry on.

Cécile and I attended Expressions Bio at Vinexpo together. It was great to be there but my friends Clément and Francine Klur were not attending and I missed them. We had a good position on a corner stand. Our only neighbour to our right was from a large inherited family estate and he had 'people' doing all the work for him. He was certified organic but not organic in spirit. He lived in the city and visited his estate a couple of days a week. He was an absentee farmer. I missed the Klurs even more.

Steven Spurrier, the world-famous wine journalist I had met in the airport, visited our stand. Cécile dived with gusto into the wine sessions that were available as part of the show and attended a session on Georgian wines offered by Steven.

'Caro, he was so good. Compared to the other presenters he was amazing.' She was impressed by him but also impressed that such a wine guru had made the time to visit our stand. As we packed up I realised I had missed yet another photo opportunity.

We caught a lift back to Saussignac with Gaby and Julien Cuisset, two young locals in the process of taking over the family vineyard business from their father. Cécile made friends easily and by the end of the trip was exchanging contact details with them. In a few short weeks I felt like she was part of the farm, part of Saussignac.

Late spring temperatures hit 35 degrees. It was the hottest month on record of what turned out to be the hottest year on record. On a day that was designated 'fruit' on our biodynamic calendar, I walked alongside our fig tree on my way back up from the vineyard. It was radiating such a strong smell of fig that I felt like lying down in its shade and drinking in the scent but I needed to get to school for Ellie. Once there I stood under the fig tree that grew along the fence line of Natalie's garden. Natalie had been Ellie and Sophia's teacher at one time and she lived across the road from the school. I loved the feeling of knowing these good people around me; there was a sense of security in it. I sniffed a leaf hanging close to me and was engulfed in the scent of the fig, cool and deep. It had positioned itself alongside Natalie's old well, a clever fig that had its roots deep in limestone and a water source. The fruits were still hard and scent-free but the leaves respired dense figginess.

At home Ellie and I picked cherries in the heat of the evening, swaying in the tree like sloths – one for the basket, one for me. Filled with cherries, I walked Dora down to the bottom of Garrigue Merlot. The sunset across the hills to our west was a profusion of golden glory. Cut grass, rows of trees, wheat ears undulating in the soft warm breeze. The hills drifted away like dunes alternating gold and green. As I passed a walnut tree I stopped and reached for a luminescent lime-green leaf. It was smooth and satiny. I inhaled above the leaf and was engulfed in the smell of walnut oil. Like the fig, its entire being was respiring, radiating its fruit aromas. I felt so happy, so filled with gratitude and joy for this beautiful place, for the wonders of the nature that surrounded me.

Cécile was proving to be a gem. She was on the ball and I soon discovered that we shared a passion for figs. We moved from spring to late summer in a whirl of guests. With the figs now ripe, Cécile made it her mission to pick fresh figs every day for the lunch served as part of our visits. Clients loved it and so did we.

The luscious purple fruits were sweet and plump. We ate and ate. Each day there were some left and I took them inside, finishing my day with a few, and then starting the next with a few more. The season was extremely long; the ripe figs ran and ran. Then Cécile discovered the green figs at the southern end of the farm. Fully ripe they were even more heavenly than the purple ones and we gorged on figs once more.

The following day I woke up with my palate transformed and not in a good way. Nothing tasted right, not my tea, nor – more importantly – the wine we served in the tasting room. What had caused it? Had I done permanent damage? Given that my job involved tasting wine every day it would be a catastrophe on a professional level, not to mention on a personal one for my own eating and drinking pleasure. Food was bland, tea was horrible and wine was worse.

I visited Antoine at Cadet-Bon in St-Émilion, the winemaker who had come to my aid when I had the puncture. As we walked down to taste the grapes in his vineyard, he pointed to a fig tree filled with bounty.

'They look good but don't eat them. When I first started with Derenoncourt Consultants I remember Stéphane saying to me, "Never eat figs when you are tasting grapes. They mess up your tasting capability."'

'Holy smokes, Antoine,' I said. 'I have that exact problem. I never heard this before and now you tell me the very week when I'm wishing I copied Robert Parker and insured my palate for a million bucks. My taste buds are banjaxed and now I know why: too many figs!'

'No way. For real?' said Antoine.

'Yes,' I said, laughing a little crazily.

I was worried. When would my palate come back?

Cécile had a similar feeling but less pronounced, and in two days hers was gone while mine was worse. I went searching on the internet for more information. Figs could attack the lining on your mouth, a bit like tannins. The white of the skin of the fig, much more pronounced on green figs, was responsible. The effect was far worse in and after menopause – which was why mine had persisted and Cécile's was gone. I had thought that I had almost licked that unpleasant phase of my life, that I had got the upper hand over its violent and suicidal effects, but now it had hit me with a nasty sting in the tail. I faked it through the wine-tasting classes, talking based on what I knew about the wines but unable to taste; my mouth was like sandpaper.

Just when I thought my mouth would never be the same again, my taste buds returned. I hadn't touched figs for a week. I didn't touch them for a few more days then I gingerly started again, peeling each one carefully before eating it, avoiding the green ones and vowing to eat the rest in moderation. Menopause had had the last laugh on this figaholic.

Sandrine was due back soon. I followed up with emails and phone calls over the weeks, asking about her baby and when she would be back. Eventually, a couple of days before she was supposed to be back with us, she emailed to say she was sorry but she would not be returning after all. We paid the required notice period and closed the chapter with relief.

Cécile was already doing half-day visits on her own, handling small groups with skill. By the following summer she would have experienced a full growing cycle and be able to talk even more knowledgeably about our organic vineyard. She researched new organic producers, slowly changing our lunch and cheese platter suppliers from large-scale organic producers to small local organic producers that we knew first-hand, then created pairing sheets to make it easier for our visitors to follow the wine and food pairing.

The ferocious heat meant an early start to harvest. We arrived back from a few days at the campsite near St-Jean-de-Luz and realised that our whites were more than ready. We booked the team and harvested ten days earlier than ever but our Sauvignon Blanc juice still displayed a hefty 14 degrees of potential alcohol. I worried that we had missed that elusive balance, the perfect harmony between alcohol and acidity.

'Perhaps we should have picked earlier?' I said to Seán.

'We went as fast as we could,' he replied. 'Anyway, if we had, it would have been too acidic and we would have had green notes. Look at the lime and grapefruit character it has as it is, and the level of acidity. We couldn't have gone any earlier. As the vintages get hotter we'll be walking a tightrope.'

'More than we are already?' I said, eyebrows raised.

Then it was the waiting game for the red grapes and we debated 'Will we harvest or won't we?' With each splatter of rain I felt butterflies in my stomach. Then it poured. I visited St-Émilion with clients and Antoine said they had had no rain. I felt jealous. Perhaps we should have picked before the deluge.

On Thursday I collected more clients from the station. There was so much rain that the road from Gardonne was like a small river. I could barely concentrate on our guests' questions. The amount of rain we were having could damage our red grapes and make picking a nightmare.

'What will this mean for the quality?' said Mary, one of the new arrivals.

'Oh, we hope it will be OK for us since we're up on the hill,' I said, thinking meanwhile, *We're toast.*

That evening I attended my first yoga session with my friend Isabelle. The yoga room was spacious and peaceful, with large windows looking on to a starry sky. At first I felt a little out of place; some of the French words for specific body parts were not familiar to me, like *clavicule* or collarbone. Most of the moves were unfamiliar and I lagged behind but the teacher quickly put us all at ease: 'It doesn't matter what the others are doing. What is important is that you feel comfortable, listen to your body, take your time.' It was totally unlike a city gym studio: there were no mirrors, no music; there was calm. We ended with ten minutes of relaxation. I realised that the classes would offer more than yoga. I had not sat consciously doing nothing in so long it was strange, but at the end of the session I felt relaxed – truly relaxed – an unusual sensation in the midst of harvest time.

The following days I toured St-Émilion with my guests and did the day visit at our farm. More rain fell. What had promised to be a good vintage was looking like it could be a failure. Seán walked the vineyards again and assured me there was no problem. Between deluges I had another set of clients for the Wine Adventure day.

'When it comes to winemaking, how we pick and when we pick are key. It's a time of great joy and community but also of great angst. Our whole year's work hangs in the balance,' I said as we started the afternoon part on the winemaking.

'Isn't that right,' said Karen. 'My family have a vineyard in New Zealand. We checked a parcel of Shiraz and it was perfect. Three days later when the pickers arrived, two thirds of it were rotten. It was that fast. I couldn't believe it.'

I felt a twist of fear. I don't know how I continued the rest of the afternoon but I did. At the end of the session I took a walk with my friend Laurence to find perspective. En route I checked the Merlot where the hail had hit hardest three years before and realised that Seán was right: the grapes still looked good. My long walk and talk with Laurence helped to ease my stress. Afterwards we sat in the courtyard of Saussignac Castle enjoying the last rays of sun and I felt a sense of peace.

I was always a little edgy at harvest and perimenopause made it worse. I needed to calm down. Back home I decided to do some brainless chores, starting with moving the packed-up boxes from the Cottage to our side of the house. The Cottage was due to undergo a renovation that winter and we were emptying it of its contents. As I carried a box of linen I noticed the duvet cover bought decades before when Seán and I first moved in together. For ten years it had been in service in the Wine Cottage and we had survived with my old sleeping bag thrown over darned sheets.

I pulled the cover out of the box. The cream linen with a simple embossed border almost looked like new. It would look great on our bed. The find was a catalyst to tidy the tiny bedroom Seán and I shared. Our room had some shelf space but no hanging space and our shoes were stacked neatly on the floor in Château Feely boxes. I cleared the surfaces then shook my old sleeping bag into the cream cover. The small gesture of taking back the cover was liberating; it felt like freedom, like I was taking a little of our life back from our all-consuming enterprise. It felt like a grand moment, a realisation. We could not sacrifice everything to follow this dream. We had to find a better balance. I put the matching pillow covers on to our pillows and then placed a cushion with lavender sprigs embroidered by Mum Feely on top. I thought of her for a moment then wiped my tears away. With the new covers and the cushion, our tiny bedroom looked beautiful and cared for, like it had had a makeover.

Back in the Cottage I measured up the walls of the end room for the new kitchen and a memory washed over me. Two tiny girls propped up in a double bed against the back wall, wrapped in winter clothes and blankets for a bedtime story. Sophia was three and Ellie one. The four of us had lived in this end room for almost a year as we renovated the first part of the house so we could rent it out as a self-catering cottage. That was a decade before; now they were like young women.

Sophia wasn't quite a teenager but she behaved like a reliable adult. She would wake at 5.45 a.m. and then wake the rest of the house at their requested times. She made her own breakfast, her homework was done, her bag was packed for the day and there was never a rush. She called me when it was time to go to school so I didn't have to clock-watch. Ellie was also top of her class or close to the top, but when it came to the morning she was grumpy and in need of prodding. They had both become fashionistas. They helped with the lunches and cleaning the accommodation to earn money for clothes.

I still wore clothes bought with one of my first pay cheques nearly 30 years before. Now I hit the high street of Bergerac with my fashion-conscious daughters and found it was fun.

The following day as Ellie and I walked to school she recited a poem about vines. It was beautiful, lyric and sensory. Dressed in new black skinny jeans, grey boots and her bright red coat, a hand-me-down from our friend Chiara Wilson, she looked so chic and grown up, like she could have walked out of a *Vogue* magazine. She took my breath away.

We picked the red grapes and my worries proved unfounded. The juice was beautiful and the subsequent wine looked like it could be another grand *millesime*, the French word for 'vintage'. By November the light and the mist were like nothing I had ever seen. The unusual heat gave a quality to the scenery reminiscent of Chinese etchings.

With the UN Climate Change Conference in Paris I read more about the out-of-control train coming down the track. It seemed insurmountable. I was struck by how little the journalists talked about what each of us could do to contribute to the solution. It was all about the big picture: talks about what governments could do with carbon trading; massive, complex solutions. There was a lot of 'we hope to' in the final agreement and not a lot of consequence for those who didn't. The consequences would be for all of us but worse for those already living precariously, close to sea level, in semi-desert and in storm belts. I was surprised that the talks didn't include much on how agriculture could contribute to the solution. Organic natural farming sequesters (captures and stores away) carbon dioxide, while chemical farming generates carbon dioxide and toxic nitrate gas.

My yoga sessions with Isabelle were becoming a sacred part of my week. She offered wisdom on school in France, the age of adolescence – her sons were a couple of years ahead of our daughters – and administrative challenges. En route we chatted non-stop; I enjoyed the time to chat with a girlfriend almost as much as the yoga. We signed up for a special extra session that was being proposed, a full Sunday of yoga. I wondered if my mind and body would be able to handle it but went ahead anyway.

CHAPTER 15

ONE YOGI AND FIVE TIBETANS

'In this silent moment of "now", of being fully present, we feel a great sense of peace,' said Xu Yen.

His round face radiated happiness and belied his age. Yoga was clearly doing something for his longevity, health and state of mind. He chatted warmly, initiating the session with words of wisdom.

'Enjoy every moment of life. In the depths of the ordinary moments we find the extraordinary.'

Every few minutes his discourse lightened up and he exploded with mirth. It was so infectious I laughed, even without understanding all of what he was saying in his heavily accented French. Then, almost without us noticing, he started a sequence of yoga moves and we followed.

'You see, we are doing nothing here. Nothing,' he said.

It felt like nothing the way he presented it but I knew it was something. He was a master yogi. As the day progressed we realised our concerns had been misplaced; instead of not coping physically or mentally, I felt energy building within me. Even after a luxurious lunch in the tradition of *auberge espagnole*, the French saying for 'bring and share', I felt energised. We feasted: a large vegetable soup made by Michèle, the founder of the Eveil du Souffle Yoga Association; quiches, breads, cheeses and salads; then fruit and sweet tarts to finish. To ease our digestion we took a walk around the farm lake, looking in on the dairy cows and vines of Michèle's organic family farm. Her 20-year-old son joined us for part of the day. At lunch he displayed the healthy appetite of a young farmer.

'So we will start slowly,' said Xu Yen. 'I will give your stomachs time to digest. For some of us that is more necessary than others.'

He gave Michèle's son a knowing look and then reverberated with mirth. 'Yes, I see everything. He he he.'

As the sun began to set, I felt a lightness of being, a joy in my core. We had done yoga all day but there was no pain and no stiffness. I was a yoga convert. I made it my mission to do a couple of yoga moves at home a few times a week in addition to my evening of co-voiturage with Isabelle for the one-hour session at Eveil du Souffle. Xu Yen's state of health and happiness was proof of what yoga could do but it was more than that. I had less backache; I was more supple. I felt better than I had in a long time and I was sleeping better. Yoga felt right. It felt like part of what we were about.

Our network of like-minded people was growing. Sandra and Santi Bontisane of Simply Permaculture and Simply Canvas joined us for soup and a sandwich the day our brother-in-law Bruce arrived for the Christmas holidays. Sandra, originally Dutch, and Santi, French Sri Lankan, had met at Plum Village, a Buddhist monastery founded by Thích Nhất Hạnh less than ten minutes from our farm. They followed the life of a Buddhist monk and nun for years and independently decided to return to secular life. Later they met up in Ireland, where Santi had settled, fell in love and decided to come back to France to set up a smallholding in the same region as Plum Village.

Their glamping holidays smallholding had recently added a permaculture garden open to visitors. We always met in winter to exchange ideas on self-sufficiency and tourism. As usual, they were bursting with new initiatives.

Bruce Bristow had arrived from Mauritius that morning. His children and Glynis, Seán's sister, would follow a few days later. We hadn't seen him in eight years. I recalled that when we met 20 years before, he had assured me that glyphosate (the most widely used chemical herbicide) was non-toxic – so lovely, in fact, that I could drink a glass of it no problem. Now Bruce had barely stepped through the door for his Christmas holiday and we were already in a heated discussion about whether organic agriculture could feed the world. I knew it could and that the chemical option would starve the world by leaving land unfit for agriculture and desertified after a couple of decades.

'Fight, fight, fight!' chanted Santi, like kids would in a playground.

We all cracked up. He defused the situation with a hilarious gesture.

By the time we said goodbye to Santi and Sandra, we were crackling with excitement about a permaculture vineyard and Bruce and I had steered clear of any more heated arguments. But it was the start of the *vacances de Noël* and I wondered if we would find more 'fight fight fight' situations. He was a strict disciplinarian but deeply loyal and loving. At just over 50 he was ahead of us in age but the first out running in the morning even after a few glasses of wine the evening before.

The following morning, Bruce opened my office door and peered in as the dawn was breaking.

'Have you heard of the Five Tibetans?' he asked, his breath billowing out like plumes of smoke in the cold air.

'No, who are they?' I said.

'A set of exercises a neighbour does on the beach every morning,' he said. 'He swears by it. He's fifty and you wouldn't know it. I'll show you when I get back from my run.'

Bruce lived a few paces from the beach in Mauritius. For a few years his work had taken him there and he had been juggling life between his family in the UK and the island.

'I'm in – anything to get you to close that door!' I said.

We both laughed. He closed it and took off.

When he returned we rolled out yoga mats in the tasting room and he showed me the routine. It was simple and quick and I felt good after doing it. I needed something to make me feel good since I was in the thick of a new task that French bureaucracy had thrown at us.

'You have to join a voluntary compulsory health scheme on behalf of your employees,' explained the accountant on the phone. 'It's the new law and you must have it in place by January.'

I was a little surprised by the idea of this new scheme being both voluntary and compulsory but it was an oxymoron I had already encountered so I knew that questioning this aspect would be futile.

'Do you have any suggestions of who we should sign up with?' I said, hoping she would make it easy for me.

'We're not allowed to make recommendations. You can sign up with the company you like. Look online and I'm sure you'll find one that fits,' she said.

I heard an advert on the radio for an international health insurance company, then received a cold call and found them online. They offered a package at half the price of the one proposed by the partner of our local bank plus they were friendly on the phone and I could do everything online. It seemed too good to be true. After a quick search online for other alternatives, I decided it was the one and signed up. Everything was smooth and super easy.

The following day I received an email inviting me to go and add my employees to the policy I had created. I went online with Cécile's details, hoping to get this task off my list. The time it had taken in investigation and administration was already way out of line, another victory for French bureaucracy.

I got to the second page after filling in Cécile's details down to her great-aunt's favourite pet and then it asked me for her *centre RO*, *caisse RO*, *code grand regime* and *rang de naissance*. I was stuck. I looked through the papers I had and found nothing of this order. I tried calling. All the lines were busy. I waited patiently in the queue and my call was dropped about ten minutes later. I tried again and had the same experience.

Then it was past business hours and the helpline closed. The page I had been working on closed me out with a session timeout. I logged in to see if it had kept the details from the first page that I had validated and found it had saved nothing. I walked outside and howled into the wild winter night.

The following day I contacted the administrator that helped us with payslips and asked if she knew what these codes were.

'*Ah mince*. You can't sign up with that company. The agricultural unions in Dordogne have done a deal with a single company. That's the only company you can sign up with.'

Now the new voluntary compulsory scheme was also a monopoly scheme.

'If they did that why didn't they pass the administration directly through the MSA and charge it as part of all the other voluntary compulsory payments?'

'You could ask that,' she said.

'It's the same company that was proposed by our bank. It's almost double the price of the one that I've signed up to,' I said.

'I know,' she said.

'It seems like a commercial gift for the company,' I said.

'You could say that,' she said.

I hung up feeling beaten. French bureaucracy had me crushed; I didn't even have the energy to howl a second time.

Bruce gave me a one-page outline of the 'rites' often shortened to 'The Five Tibetans' by those in the know. Over the following days I went through them either alone or with Bruce. After three times I remembered them without needing to look at the page. Each time I did it I felt good.

I found a moment in business hours to call the company I had signed up with. After ten minutes of queuing I explained my dilemma to the call centre representative. She said the only way to unsubscribe was to handwrite a letter to the company headquarters and rattled off the address.

Then I went to the voluntary compulsory monopoly company's website hoping that signing up with them would be as easy as with the people I had just had to un-sign from. There was no information about the product I needed, no way of getting in touch easily, no email address or direct phone number for a local agency. I filled in a contact form and waited for a response. I waited two days then sent a reminder. Still there was no response. I took ten deep breaths. I was trapped in a devastating, time-wasting loop. I could not have written a better imaginary skit on French bureaucracy than this reality. The next day I went back on to the website and sent another request. I emailed my bank that had originally told me about this company's offer. I heard nothing. I had spent several days researching and trying to implement something that had been decided for me but that was now proving impossible to put in place.

'How can you soar like an eagle?' I moaned out loud.

'When you're a turkey,' said Ellie, looking in the door.

'He he he,' I laughed.

My emails and calls disappeared into a black hole like my howl into the night; months later I was still waiting. Everyone knows from Economics 101 that monopoly is not an optimal solution for efficiency or for the good of the economic participants. Now I knew it was not good for my karma either. I rolled out the yoga mat and did the Five Tibetans to bring order to my disturbed spirit.

There was something about doing these five exercises that restored balance – perhaps even hormonal balance – inside me. Perhaps I was naturally reaching the end of perimenopause or perhaps there was some magic to them. The backache and stiffness I experienced when I spent too much time at the computer vanished; I felt more energised. The great swathe of grey developing in my hair even seemed to be disappearing.

The outline of the leafless oak next to the winery was stark against the winter sky. I sat on the bistro chair outside the kitchen door and pulled on my wellies then made my way to the Sémillon vines. Pulling wood was therapeutic. The sounds of winter birds and the rhythmic twang of the wires mingled. Each vine was like a movement in a dance. Grab the canes, yank downwards, drop the freed wood into the middle of the row, bend to gather up the canes that dropped at the foot of the vine, throw them into the middle of the row, pull away any remaining bits. Stretch up tall. Step across to the next vine. Start the dance again.

It was like a yoga movement, a meditation, especially if the sun was out and we weren't under pressure. Bruce joined me and we worked together, chatting, sharing experiences from the years since we had seen each other. He created a motivational force to get things done. During our second French summer he and his children, Duncan and Emma, came to camp with us and we mowed down projects like they were skittles. This time was no different.

We decided to bite the bullet and grub up a large section of ancient vines that were no longer paying their way. After cutting the vines off the wires and pulling the wood we had to dismantle the trellis wires then take out the poles. It was possible to rent or purchase a wire winder that worked on the tractor's power take-off (PTO) but we found horror stories on the internet of people being strangled. Thierry Daulhiac passed by and we asked his advice.

'Oh. Yes, it can be dangerous or, he he, funny. Joel's father-in-law was helping him roll up the wire and it grabbed on to a hook on his pants and ripped them off. There he was standing in the vineyard in his underpants. He he he.'

I found it strange how winegrowers talked and even laughed about the dangers of our *métier* as if it were normal to risk life and limb every day as part of your job. We weren't into strangulation or losing our pants so we decided to use our hand-operated roller, preferring a little extra work to potentially losing our lives. Over the next few days, Bruce, Seán and I rolled up two tons of wire and stacked a mountain of old wood trellis poles.

It was the start of a new phase of the vineyard, a phase of plantings that would be original individual vines from massal selection, each cutting taken from a different vine, rather than from the same clone. We were bucking the system and it would cost us almost triple what a standard planting would in terms of foregone aid and extra cost but we knew it was the right choice. With the latest aid rules, farmers had to use a specific clone from a specific varietal to avail of replanting aid. The state dictating the clone and varietal that had to be used was wrong: it created uniformity, took away the freedom of choice from the farmer who knew their conditions better than a bureaucrat, and made the plants of the region identical and weak. It would devastate biodiversity, the importance of which was a high point of conversation in the media that year. I wondered how many people understood what it meant. We decided that the long-term benefits of our decision would mean it was the right one despite the immediate financial pain. As a client said earlier that year, 'It's like me with my woodwork. You buy the best wood and cry once.'

We took a morning off from clearing trellising and Sophia, Ellie, Bruce and I cycled to Gardonne for the Sunday market. We bought a chicken from a local producer and organic supplies from a newcomer to the market, a lady in a *roulotte* (a wagon), who offered dry organic products *en vrac* (in bulk). Christmas carols warbled through the speakers strung around town; there was a general feeling of good cheer in the air. Stocked up with our supplies, we settled down on a low wall on the square to enjoy crusty *croissants* and *pains aux raisins* and bask in the clear winter sun, taking in the chatter, colours and aromas of the market. It was magic, a reminder of what we loved about France – the markets, the food, time to chat – things we had been missing of late in our frenetic lives.

After coercing ourselves back into the saddle we headed for home. Bruce and Sophia streaked ahead and Ellie and I lingered a few hundred metres behind. We crossed the train track and passed a hunter walking back into the village in combat gear with his shotgun hanging over his shoulders. About 50 metres on Ellie stopped. I pulled in alongside her. She was white as a sheet and wide-eyed.

'What's wrong, *mignonne*?' I said.

'Who is that man?' she asked.

'It's just a hunter like we see every Sunday,' I said.

'But what is he doing going into Gardonne like that?' she said, her voice shaky.

'He's walking home after hunting,' I said.

'I was worried he was going to shoot the people at the market. I was so scared, Mummy,' said Ellie.

In the past Ellie would never have had that reaction to a hunter walking on the road. Her reaction was a stark reminder that the 2015 terrorist attacks in Paris had affected us even deep in rural France. The ripples in the psyche of her generation were perhaps greater than we had realised.

'I'm so sorry, my lovely,' I said and gave her a squeeze.

'I was so scared, Mummy,' she repeated.

'Oh, my lovely,' I said, giving her another squeeze and holding her bike stable. 'Are you OK to carry on?'

'Yes, but I feel so tired,' she said.

'It's exhaustion after the adrenalin of being scared and getting a shock,' I said. 'We'll take it slowly but we'd better get on and try to catch up with Bruce and Sophia or they'll worry.'

We took off again. Ellie stopped every couple of hundred metres to check in with me and catch her breath.

Duncan, Emma and Glynis arrived and we got outside into the vines. It was fun working together and catching up on years missed. Soon we were singing and working. Duncan and Emma had beautiful singing voices. Duncan was part of an a cappella group at St Andrews University called The Other Guys, one of the top groups of their kind in the UK, with professional CDs and videos, the proceeds of which went to charity and with the bonus of helping marketing for St Andrews. Not that St Andrews needed help for recruitment: it was famous as a matchmaking university since Prince William met Kate Middleton there.

'You know, a couple of days ago I was at Bonny's and Jean-François, another winegrower, came in with a huge smile on his face,' said Seán. 'Mr Bonny asked why he was so happy. He said, "I have two Portuguese people pruning for me, and they are singing and working. It's two decades since I heard people singing like that in the vineyard. It brings joy to my heart." I can say the same thing here.'

We were having fun but also munching through the work. What would have taken me months on my own had taken a couple of days for our large family group.

That evening we wandered up to Saussignac for dinner. Glynis and Bruce walked ahead holding hands like young lovers.

'Why don't you and Papa ever hold hands like that?' asked Sophia.

I could have said, 'Because we've lost touch with each other. Because we're working too hard. Because, because…' But I didn't because I didn't know the answer. Instead I caught up with Seán and took his rough hand in mine. It felt good. I wondered why we didn't do it.

On Christmas Day the sun was shining. We did a polar swim after breaking the ice on the pool. I felt alive. As I prepared scrambled eggs I asked Emma if she could recognise parsley and to fetch me some. She nodded and instead of heading for the garden she opened the fridge. I realised how differently we were living to the majority of the world's urban population. We were connected to nature, earth and sky every day. As a global community we had to find a way to reconnect with nature. It would change people's thinking and it would change the world.

If we all grew some of our own food we would store carbon through those plants and prevent the carbon dioxide emissions generated by transport required to bring food to us. Small local farms were key to this renaissance, but making a living as a small farmer was tough.

The Wine Cottage renovations were gaining pace. The timing had already been pushed out two months and each day took us closer to when clients were due to arrive.

Tomas, our mason, appeared at the door.

'We are short of a few tiles,' he said.

'What? I ordered an extra ten per cent,' I said.

'I know but with all the cuts we have lost quite a bit,' he said.

'I'll phone the supplier to see what they can do,' I said.

I had searched Bergerac and Sainte-Foy-la-Grande for the perfect tiles. In the end I had done a special order based on a catalogue photo, a test of my renovation mettle. Each time I thought of it between order and arrival I felt a little spike of adrenalin. When the order arrived the tiles were beautiful, exactly what I was looking for. The risk had paid off. I called the supplier.

'Ah no, that was a special order. We don't have it in stock,' he said. 'I have a single display tile that I could give you.'

'I'm not sure one will do it. We need two or three,' I said.

'Then we're really cornered. I can't put in a special order for two or three tiles – it needs to be a good volume for us to do a special order. Anyway, even if we did order like last time, it would take about six weeks to arrive.'

'*Mince*. Please keep the display tile for us *alors*. We'll collect it today,' I said, praying it would be enough.

Tomas collected the tile and they carefully sorted the cut pieces and made up what was missing. They finished the floor so perfectly it was complete to my eye, but for them the last section would have been better if they had had that extra tile.

I took ten deep breaths. I had learned another lesson: when doing a special order, add 15 per cent. I would be 'building wise' when Château Feely was finished but 'finished' was a relative term. We would never be finished. Already the Lodge needed to be touched up. A living business and farm was an ongoing circle of renewal.

The Bristow family went home, leaving feelings of joy and gratitude in their wake. I had learned the Five Tibetans and with their help our farm work was so advanced we could look forward to our long-awaited trip to South Africa.

I had a dawn call with potential house-sitters Margherita, an Italian writer who preferred writing in English, and Nick, an Aussie photographer, who ran *The Crowded Planet*, a travel blog about their non-stop travel lives. They were looking forward to touching down in France for a few weeks to catch up on months of material from travelling. As I flicked through their blog I felt envious of their footloose lifestyle. Despite the bad reception of the call from their hotel in Indonesia, the tone of their blog and the brief conversation were enough to know we had found a match. I ticked 'confirm house-sitters' off my list. It would be a first for us to leave our precious farm for longer than a week but with Cécile on-site most workdays and this responsible pair we were feeling as sure about it as we could be.

CHAPTER 16

BACK TO OUR ROOTS

Our flight from Bordeaux to Paris was smooth but the line-up at Charles de Gaulle customs was a 200-metre snake seething with worried or plain impatient people. There was one booth open and three international flights to process. A 'jump the queue' feeder for first- and business class passengers ensured that the rest of us moved at a wounded snail's pace. French citizens had a special automated queue that worked intermittently.

An Asian lady raced past us, saying politely, 'I am sorry but I am very late. I am going to miss my connection.'

We happily let her through – we had been there before. The airport official controlling the entrance clicked over, heels tapping officiously.

'Do the queue,' she said, her arm blocking the lady's way.

'But I will miss my flight.'

'I don't care. Do the line. I will call you.'

The woman went to the back, cowed, anxiety written all over her face and in her movements.

I felt like smacking the control freak. She clearly hadn't been notified that an angry perimenopausal monster woman was passing through. Violence seemed to come naturally to me as opposed to the expected *sagesse* of ageing.

Two minutes later, the official shouted, 'Anyone for Seoul, Korea?'

The anxious lady stepped forward, relief flooding her features. I felt myself relax.

After 12 hours in the air, our Cape Town airport experience could not have been more different. All the booths were working and the queue flew through. Perhaps they had got the notification.

The customs official welcomed us warmly, took our passports and noticed we were born in South Africa.

'Do you have South African passports?' he asked.

'No,' we replied. We had let them lapse when we lived in Dublin and never had the need to renew.

'Do you still have family here?' he asked.

'Yes, we're going to Durban to see family and friends and then back to Cape Town to do the same.'

I felt tears as I said it. A sense of homesickness and a deep sadness that I hadn't been back in time to see Mum Feely swelled up.

'Welcome back,' he said, giving me an empathetic look.

I swallowed the tears. I had been holding back the longing and deep memories of Africa for more than 20 years. I felt homesickness like physical pain along with a note of sadness that our daughters had not experienced growing up here.

'This will be the first passport stamp for Sophia and Ellie,' said Seán.

'Oh, the stamps aren't for children's passports; only for adults',' said the customs official. He gave them a wink, lightening the moment. 'But for this special case I will make an exception.' He stamped the passports with a flourish.

'Thank you,' I said, smile wide despite swimming eyes.

This generous spirit made Sophia and Ellie's first experience of Africa great, a place of kind heart and good humour.

We collected our bags and rolled on. We had to find the mobile-phone shop, food, our next flight and deodorant – pronto, as the effects of almost 24 hours of transit were becoming obvious. At the phone shop the counter staff were inundated with clients, some super agitated. The staff kept their cool, their good humour eventually getting the better of grumpy travellers and their impatience. It was time to get on to African time and chill.

Phone in hand, we found a pharmacy for Mission Critical Deodorant. I waited with the bags while Seán went in with Sophia and Ellie.

A sixty-something white man walked into the pharmacy behind them.

'Have you got any ticks here?' he asked the lady on the counter.

'Huh?' said the young lady, looking uncertain of what he was on about.

'Have you got any ticks here?' he asked a little louder.

I could see her mind wondering if he was asking to buy ticks from the pharmacy. Or was he asking for some product she didn't know about? Or perhaps he was asking if there were ticks in the airport.

She shook her head. Her face said that she couldn't fathom how he could ask such a question. Of course there were no ticks here. If he was asking about South Africa in general then he was crazy too since, of course, in the *veld* (the bush) there were ticks all over Africa.

I imagined he was asking if he should buy a tick repellent but, given his manner, I could also see why the teller couldn't understand. I felt like helping translate but my attention was taken by Seán approaching the counter with sinister-looking canisters.

'No antiperspirant!' I shouted. 'Breast cancer in a can.'

Seán lifted his eyebrows and went back to the shelf. A few minutes later he exited the pharmacy.

'You had better go and look. I can't find any that aren't antiperspirant.'

I left Seán with the bags. Inside were rows and rows of deodorant that were all antiperspirant. I asked one of the advisers and she looked perplexed. We toothcombed the shelves and eventually found a roll-on that didn't contain antiperspirant for women but none for men. Seán risked a canister of antiperspirant deodorant for men. For someone who wouldn't let us use any cosmetics in the house and absolutely no perfume, it was a strange but necessary about-turn.

He sprayed himself liberally then sneezed.

Sophia approached and took a deep sniff.

'Hmmm,' she said. 'The *true* scent of a man.'

We all laughed.

It felt so good to be on holiday; I could feel the stress and responsibility of our everyday reality falling away like weights being taken off my shoulders. As we passed out of the international section of the airport a human-size sign announced, *Welcome to the Mother City*. A tsunami of missing this place – my original homeland, its familiar words and people – engulfed me, and tears flooded down my cheeks.

A few hours later we were in KwaZulu-Natal. We visited friends at their beach shack for a couple of days then went to Dad Feely in Howick. It was my first visit to the small house that he and Mum had built after selling the family house where I got to know the Feelys almost three decades before.

We revelled in being together. We visited Mum Feely's place, where her ashes were spread, a small river near Howick surrounded by fields and nature. Dad and Seán cleared the protea planted in her memory and Sophia and Ellie combed the river and surrounds for litter. We sat on a rock listening to the murmur of the river. It felt peaceful and good to be there.

We planted herbs – parsley, rosemary, thyme – and celery in Dad Feely's garden. We felt wonder at herds of impala, red hides against green scrub, at the twisted horns of kudu reaching to the sky. Our brief escape to a game farm was more than the riot of buck (gemsbok, blesbok, waterbuck, hartebeesbok, duiker, steenbok, blue wildebeest, black wildebeest, eland) and four of the big five (lion, rhino, elephant and buffalo); it was a precious shared moment. Sophia and Ellie seemed more outgoing here, more willing to take risks. We canoed a river and flew down zip lines strung across the largest indigenous forest in KwaZulu-Natal.

We left for Cape Town resolved to get back to see Dad Feely more often.

'Your South African accent is much stronger here,' said Sophia.

'That's funny. Everyone keeps asking "so where are you guys from?" as if we're foreigners,' I said.

We were on our way to visit two biodynamic vineyards. A trip to a winegrowing area was an opportunity to research ideas for where to take our wine estate.

The Waterkloof wine estate's glass-fronted restaurant was suspended over their winery and vine-covered hillsides, looking on to a panorama of mountains and sea. It was worth the visit for the views but with their food and wine it was an unmissable sublime experience. I took notes and photos feeling inspired by everything they were doing, from their horses in the vineyard to their winemaking facilities and restaurant. It was a large operation powered by a significant workforce and massive investment, in many ways a world away from our small vineyard in France, but their Circumstance Sauvignon Blanc, despite the different soil (granite and sandstone; very different to our limestone and flint stone), was the closest we had ever tasted to our pure Sauvignon Blanc *Sincérité*.

Our next visit was a little more our scale. Johan Reyneke was a wiry, tanned surfer and wine farmer based between Somerset West and Stellenbosch. Seán's grandparents' wine farm, sold decades before, was minutes away. After introductions in the tasting room, chat came easily.

'You know, when I was studying philosophy at Stellenbosch I couldn't get a job at a local restaurant because of my dreadlocks, so I got a job as a vineyard labourer instead,' Johan said. 'That was how I started. But let's go for a walk and look at the cows rather than just talking. I almost love them more than the vines now.'

We stepped outside.

'Look at that,' said Johan, pointing to a window lying on the grass in front of the building. 'I had a group of visitors this morning. One lady asked if she could let some air in and *pow*! She pushed the whole window out. I've never seen anything like it.' He laughed.

A monster dog came loping up and Johan took the cue.

'A word of warning,' he said. 'He has big chops and he's a farm dog. He slobbers, and it's not just the saliva – it's saliva and chicken shit and cowpat and a bit of hay thrown in. So watch out. Also, girls,' he said to Sophia and Ellie, who were stroking him, missing their animals at home. 'Just be careful with him. We've never had a problem but last week we had a lady that said she was a dog whisperer and she tried that on him and he went nuts.'

BACK TO OUR ROOTS

He laughed again – an easy, relaxed laugh – then led us down a dusty red track towards the cattle *kraal* (enclosure).

'There they come. You see the dust cloud? That's the cows coming in for their sweets. They've had a day of eating tough boring grass; now they'll come and eat some of the post-pressing leftover grapes. They love it. It's like candy after dinner.'

The view across the vineyards to the mountains of Stellenbosch changed colour as we walked, the sky progressing from bright blue to cornflower as the sun dropped lower in the sky.

'When I started farming we farmed with chemicals like everyone said you should. But using weedkiller and pesticides on your back in a backpack is not pleasant. So I decided we would stop using them. But it was bad. We had all the bugs and disease that you can imagine in our vines.'

'That was our experience too,' I said. 'The first two years of organic conversion were hell – I call it "the valley of despair".'

'Just so. *Jislaaik*. Anyway luckily I got talking to a lady in Wellington that was doing biodynamics. I tried the solutions she proposed and they worked.'

'That is exactly how we started biodynamics,' I said. 'We needed to solve our downy mildew. The organic wasn't working and biodynamics helped us solve a practical problem. Then we found it brought so much more. It impacts every part of our life, not just our farming.'

'Yes, it's about the balance. You see the vineyard over there?' Johan pointed to the opposite hillside. 'The one that's red? It's a vineyard attacked by the leaf-roll virus. It's a sickness that is spread by the mielie bug.'

'Aphid?' I said.

'Yes, exactly,' he said.

'That sounds like it's transmitted in a similar way to the *flavescence dorée* virus we have in France,' said Seán.

'We saw a lot of the leaf-roll virus in Franschhoek a few days ago.'

'Yes, it's a real problem in the Cape. But you know it's all about the balance. So, like I said, we used to weedkill all the stuff on the ground but in fact this aphid prefers dandelions to vines so if we leave the weeds there's no more leaf-roll virus. Of course, we have to control the weeds or our vineyard would be a wilderness. Those sick vineyards aren't ours by the way.' Johan laughed. He sounded like me when I disowned the chemically farmed vineyards below us.

'Anyway,' continued Johan, 'for me vine-growing is about fertilising the soil, controlling the weeds, managing the insects and pests, and preventing disease.'

I felt a smile breaking out on my face at how similar our discourses on the vineyard were.

'So when it comes to the fertiliser part, we used to spend about ten thousand euro a year on fertiliser; now we don't spend a cent. We have our cows instead and they generate income for us too. In the low period of the year the sale of an ox or two fills the gap. We use their dung, our wine waste and grass from old thatched roofs to make our compost – you can see the heaps over there,' he said, pointing across the cattle pasture. 'We feed the soil in autumn with the compost, spreading it by hand. Then in late spring we bring the ducks into the vineyard to eat the pests, and to attract the ducks we place a small dose of compost next to each vine. The ducks don't eat vines but they do eat grapes so we have to watch out. To break down heavy kitchen waste we use Australian red wrigglers in old vine barrels. We have researchers coming to study us now. The life in our soil isn't twenty per cent better than the chemical farmers'; it's nine hundred per cent. That's not my estimate by the way – that's what a recent group of academics found.'

He was passionate about his farm and proud that his tenacity had paid off.

'How many cows?' I asked.

'About forty at the moment for thirty-seven hectares.'

As I noted Johan's numbers on a scrap of paper from my purse, I felt a drop on my foot. I looked down. The chop monster was standing over me, gobs of sticky saliva drooling off his massive lips. I stepped back.

'For me it's about good farming. I try to get the balance. It's a tussle between building the soil and getting yield. One year I might farm for yield because I need it but then the following year I need to give back to the soil to bring back the balance,' said Johan. 'We'll check in on the winery on our way to the tasting room.'

The track to the winery hugged a vineyard full of bright-green happiness and verve, very different to some of the conventional vines we had seen. Johan waved to a crew member, sporting a Vine Hugger T-shirt, displaying the same easy manner he had with us.

'There used to be pressure between the picking team and the processing team. For the pickers it's all about speed and for the processors it's about precision. So we bought two refrigerated containers. Now when the fruit is picked we stack it in there and it waits. No problem. The guys can take as long as they need. Let's go and taste some wine.'

Back in the whitewashed room Johan poured us a sample of his Sauvignon Blanc.

'Johan, may I have a wine list so I can track the wines we taste?' I said.

'Sure,' he said. 'If I can find one. I don't often do the tastings these days.'

As he turned the back of his neck was like leather; it was clear he spent his days out there and not in here.

'Our wines are cheap,' he said.

'Never say "cheap"!' I said. 'They're great value.'

'Cheap. Too cheap. *Jislaaik! Lekker!*' he said, laughing and looking at the wine list before handing it over to me. 'The prices have changed again! They've gone up since yesterday. Soon they won't be cheap any more. Yeeeow. The Cabernet is eight hundred rand. I've never seen that wine or tasted it!' He was laughing hard.

'Good marketing,' said Seán. 'Sounds like something Caro would do.'

We all laughed; he was joking and so was Seán.

'What's this logo that I've seen on all the wine bottles in SA?' I asked, pointing to a sticker of a sugarbird on a protea that was placed over the screw cap.

'That's the biodiversity and wine initiative. It's a voluntary programme to promote conservation-minded farming practices that will protect nature. The seal above it is Sustainable Wine South Africa – it's the guarantee of IPW, Integrated Production of Wine. IPW is a "sustainability" label, a small step. You can still use herbicide but you have to think about it and lower your dose. It's not ideal but it's a start. It gets people who aren't organic thinking about their chemical usage. Each year they tighten the rules. Slowly, slowly, catchy monkey.'

'It sounds like *lutte raisonnée*, the reasoned fight, and the *Haute Valeur Environnementale* ('High Environmental Value') we have in France,' I said. 'I don't like it because it's confusing for the consumer. The lovely HVE label makes them think it's organic when it's not; it can still be packed with pesticide residues. But I see what you mean – it's making the bulk of the pack, those that might not have made any effort on ecology otherwise, move forward.'

'Yes, and of course all this certification is expensive. Demeter biodynamic certification want two per cent of our turnover to use their logo on our labels so we don't except for our top reserve wines. We do the South African organic CERES label then we do the EU organic label and even though there's reciprocity between the EU and the US on the organic standards we have to do it again for the US. It's so expensive.'

'We know. And it's crazy that those of us not using poisons have to pay the certification fees when it should be the ones polluting who have to pay,' I said.

'Just so,' said Johan. 'Now, I have a story for you. But first, something about this Sauvignon Blanc. It's wild yeast, barrel fermented, simple.'

I caught Seán's eye and we shared a smile at the word 'simple' that reminded us both of a hail-spattered afternoon in our tasting room that felt like aeons ago.

'No filtration, just a rock stopper to make sure the odd pair of forgotten secateurs doesn't get through,' continued Johan 'So anyway, back to my story. A lady solicitor from Amsterdam drove her car all the way down through Africa to Cape Town. She volunteered here for a while. She said to me, "Always employ people smarter than yourself otherwise you limit your business to the level of your ability." I took that as good advice rather than a slight on my intelligence and followed what she said.'

He waited for our laughter to subside.

'I have a great team. I once sent the wrong wine to Holland. Daniel, who manages our orders now, has never made a mistake like that.'

Johan poured his Syrah. It was gorgeous, smoky, sultry, dark fruit, liquorice and *fynbos* (wild herbal scrubland unique to South Africa).

'When we started the farm we did it with the team that had laboured with me in the vineyards when I was a student. My degree in philosophy taught me that empowering people meant giving them the "capability to choose" – it's more about that than about Maslow's hierarchy of needs. Regardless of whether these needs are met or not, we're only happy when we have choice. So I asked the guys what they wanted. I gave them choice. They said they wanted houses and education so we went all out for that. We still offer university education to all our staff and children but you have to stay ten years with the company to get a house. We burnt our fingers with people leaving after a year and selling the house.'

He poured Reyneke Cornerstone red. It was red fruit and bright, full of flavour.

'Anyway, back to the idea of choice and team. We know that the team is the cornerstone of our business hence the name of this wine to reflect that and our choice to offer choice to our people, especially education. So one of the original team who started with us is now our gardener; he's illiterate but his daughter Lizaan has a university degree and she runs the place. She's the one who has set the new prices and the price for the new Cabernet Sauvignon. With her in charge soon the wines won't be cheap but they will still be great value.' He caught my eye and we laughed.

'Back at the start I was sitting in this room, the place where we used to milk our cows. Things were really tough. We had bought houses for our staff but the wine business was rough. We were close to closing the doors. I really didn't know what to do. Then a lady walked in here and tasted our wines. She said she was from CNN and she wanted to buy all our wine for a big international event in Johannesburg. She followed through and I flew up for the event. Next thing I was being introduced to Madiba. Now, you know, it isn't good me being white, Afrikaans and a farmer given the history of South Africa, but President Mandela started a conversation smooth and in his stride, saying in Afrikaans, 'So how is it going with our farmers?' What an experience meeting him. But it also turned us around. From the precipice that lucky break in 2002 took us from strength to strength. We had already changed to farming without chemicals. We started the natural farming in 1999 but only started the biodynamic certification in 2006. At the start we had four families depending on the farm; now we have sixteen.'

'Impressive,' I said. But in the back of my mind I was also calculating, comparing our ten hectares with one full-time worker, Seán, to around four times our size with 16 people or more. They could hand-weed, hand-spray and have enough people in the winery for it to be relatively peaceful at harvest time. The minimum wage in South Africa was such that almost two days of work cost the same as one hour in France.

'It's intense right now, harvest time. I'm looking forward to going to the beach and surfing, not thinking, when it's finished,' said Johan.

'We know that feeling,' I said. 'Maybe we need to take up surfing.'

I could see from Seán's face he was thinking, 'And hire a few people if only we could afford it...'

'For me it's important to make good wine but also to enjoy my life,' said Johan.

As we took off back to Cape Town I reflected that we would benefit from following his philosophy. Our holiday offered a chance to do a little of that. In Cape Town Aunt Sally, who visited for my parents' golden wedding anniversary, organised a big family party. We talked, laughed, ate and played the racing demons like demons. It was good to be together, to experience intergenerational family contact. Despite having been away for so long, I felt a deep sense of belonging. The trip to South Africa reminded me how much we missed having time to relax, to be with friends and family – things we had sacrificed for ten years in order to turn our business around.

CHAPTER 17

SEEKING EQUILIBRIUM

When we returned home the daffodils were out but there was still a bite in the air. Our trip to South Africa had been a welcome break but things were not perfect between us and we both knew we had to find a better balance between our work and our personal life.

Seán and I were doing maintenance, cleaning and treating the tasting-room and Lodge decks with natural oil. The night before Seán had insulted my dinner again and I had cracked. We got into a roaring fight that left me and our daughters crying. I found myself wondering if this was the man I had fallen in love with so many years before.

'We have to stop fighting in front of the kids,' said Seán. 'They went to sleep after midnight they were so upset.'

'Then you should hold back before criticising my cooking,' I said. 'What's wrong? You seem so dissatisfied. We're no better than business partners. We have to change or call it quits.'

'That's the third time you've said you want a divorce,' he said.

'What?' I said.

'Yes, that's the third time you've said we have to call it quits,' said Seán. 'What do you expect me to do? Is that what you really want?'

I looked deeply into his eyes for what felt like the first time in years and was mute for a few moments, trying to compute what he had said. He was right. I had said it three times.

'No,' I said, feeling shocked as I realised exactly what I had been threatening.

'Neither do I, Mrs C. I love you. I want to stay together but I can't take this constant questioning and bickering.'

Seán's eyes filled with tears and I felt mine do the same. It felt like the first real conversation in ages – and it wasn't about labels, corks or sulphites.

'I don't want to keep doing the hard physical graft I do every day for another ten years,' said Seán, ignoring my comment about criticism. 'My body is telling me to slow down. I love being in the garden, growing things, tending the vines, and I don't mind that physical work, but when it comes to the pipe-work and the barrel-work in the winery I have had enough.'

'But we've just turned the corner: the wines are selling themselves, we don't have to kill ourselves to make sales, we know the ropes, everything is starting to roll a bit easier. With the investments over the last few years our cash flow going forward will be better. People love our wines and visits; the business is growing. We'd be mad to walk away. You're so good at winemaking. Look at the positive comments we get about our wines.'

'I still don't speak French well enough. I don't feel like it's home the way I felt in Ireland. I miss Ireland. I think I want to move back there.'

He left it hanging for a few minutes like a dare, as if he were waiting to see if I would say, 'Fine. Go!'

We had grown so far apart that, for a second, I saw that option. In that moment of consideration I felt like I had been hit by a wrecking ball; I saw our lives transformed, torn apart, as if my very being was split in two. Deep down I knew it was not the right choice for me or for anyone in our family. Then I felt a deep tenderness for this man I loved, for what was driving him to behave like he was under threat, driving us to the fights that we had been having. He was not happy doing the heavy winemaking, perhaps also tired of doing almost the same thing for ten years, and I had been a bad-tempered perimenopausal monster. That momentary flicker of 'then go' was my ego speaking.

When we let our spirits speak we were on another level. We hadn't given them time to be together. It felt like our egos were in charge and we had been going so hard to keep our boat afloat that our spirits had taken off in opposite directions. We had to find our connection again.

Before I said a word, Seán continued, 'I'm also concerned about France. The new labour law is supposed to help the unemployment situation, which is what we need, but people are out striking and burning cars. France doesn't like change. It doesn't adapt and that's dangerous.'

'Feck,' I said. 'Where did all this come from?'

'Look at us. We've given more than ten years of our lives to this place and where are we? We work non-stop, we've only just taken our first real holiday of more than a week – and even then you had to be online every forty-eight hours. What sort of life is that? I sometimes feel like we're slaves to the French Republic.'

'Holy smokes,' I said and stopped sweeping the deck to stare at Seán as I took it all in. 'I guess you're right. Johan Reyneke said, "It's important to make good wine but also to enjoy my life." He had the right balance. Perhaps we should track our hours and make sure we give ourselves the statutory minimum time off required in France. If we backdated that ten years I bet we'd be on holiday for years.'

'Yes, three years of solid paid holiday to be exact,' said Seán.

He had already done the calculation; this had been festering for a while.

'No one would pay us since we're self-employed so that's just theoretical. But you have a point. We have to be able to afford holidays, proper weekend time off, our daughters' studies and full-time help. But we're maxed out and you don't think we can charge more for our wines. What will we do?' I said as much to myself as to Seán. 'I enjoy what I'm doing and having an apprentice has made a difference. But the farm needs to grow and develop if we want full-time help and that means more work.'

'Well, I don't want to tend any more vines than I have already and I don't want to do the heavy work of the winemaking any more,' said Seán.

'Holy smokes,' I said, my brain scrambling with the potential implications of what Seán was saying.

We finished the deck and started collecting up our tools.

'I feel like I've been doused in a bucket of cold water,' I said. 'I love Ireland but I don't want to go back to being a project manager or strategy consultant. Anyway, I'm more than a decade out of date – no one would give me a job. And I won't go back to starting from the ground up like we did ten years ago. Do you remember how hard it was? I won't go back there, SF. I know we aren't living it up but we aren't on the precipice every month like we used to be.'

'I want a simpler life,' said Seán. 'Remember that when we came here it was to live a more self-sufficient life, to get away from the rat race. I feel like we're under more pressure now than we were then. The business is getting bigger and more complex all the time. I want to be more self-sufficient and have less administration, bureaucracy and stress.'

'But we have to grow to afford a full-time person. Think of all the projects we'd like to tackle: sheep and cheese, a biodynamic display garden, permaculture, more education, tourism and food pairing. What are we going to do?'

Until Seán's outburst I had been coasting along thinking we were into the 'plain sailing' in the life cycle of our business. We had offered Cécile a role with us once her apprenticeship was complete. She was going travelling for six months and we hoped would return after her trip. Our discussion was a swift reminder that there are no certainties in life or in business. Our fights were an explosive combination of my perimenopause and of Seán feeling unhappy, but perhaps there was an element of Johan Reyneke's philosophy of choice in our behaviour too. After what we had put in and considering how far we were into our vineyard dream, it felt like we didn't have any choice but to continue. We had lost our freedom.

'We won't solve this now,' said Seán. 'I'm just saying we need to consider our long-term well-being.'

We agreed that we needed to talk more.

I raced up to Saussignac to fetch Ellie. The sun was out at last after a slow start to spring. The late afternoon was too good to waste inside. Ellie and I decided to go for a knock on the Saussignac tennis court after she had finished her *goûter*. She and Sophia had started tennis at Pineuilh two years before; at first they didn't want to do it, but now they were enjoying it.

We walked up with the racquets and Dora on the lead. Saussignac village was quiet; no one was around except a few pigeons. The bell tower rang, echoing through the square and the budding trees.

We started with warm-up races bouncing a ball across the court. That always generated a laugh and did us good but when we started knocking Ellie wasn't playing well. She got mad. The madder she got the worse she played, and the worse she played the madder she got. It was an infernal circle and she became totally unpleasant, showing me an excellent example of what the French call *fait la tête*, 'to be in a bad mood'.

'We need to get back. Papa said we had to be home at quarter to seven at the latest,' I said. 'I'll collect the balls outside the court then we must go.'

As I did that Ellie served a few good balls but she was still in a foul temper. I walked ahead then waited near the Château de Saussignac for her to catch up. I had given her a few minutes to walk and calm down.

'You know, Ellie, one of the most important things about sport is to be a good sport. That means being nice when you lose and keeping a happy face even when you're not happy with how you're playing,' I said.

'Hurumph,' said Ellie.

'I know how you feel. I used to get really mad when I lost and I believed that I should have won, that I could play better than I had,' I said.

'Hurrrumph,' said Ellie again, but this time she lifted her head and looked me in the eye for the first time since she had got into her temper.

'And getting mad doesn't help you play any better, does it? In fact, it makes you play worse,' I said.

Ellie nodded.

'So next time just relax and try to enjoy playing even if you aren't playing your best. You need to be Zen if you want to play well.'

She seemed to have taken in what I said.

We reached our front door and Seán opened it from inside, his left hand held high in the air. It was wrapped in white tape that had ominous red smudges all over it.

'Don't worry, it's just a little cut. Nothing to get excited about,' he said, backing away into the kitchen. 'I've cleaned it out, run it under loads of clear water, put Betadine on and taped it up. No need to panic.'

I dropped the tennis bag and opened the cupboard to grab the car keys.

'You could just re-tape it with surgical tape,' Seán said. 'We don't even have to go to the clinic. It's just a little cut.'

Sophia was behind him, shaking her head wide-eyed.

'We're going to the hospital,' I said. 'Have you got your *carte vitale* and your phone? Girls, get yourselves some dinner and get ready for bed.'

'I'll make fried eggs,' said Sophia.

'No. I don't want you using the flame while we're out, especially with a crisis already on the go.'

'This isn't a crisis,' said Scán. 'It's just a little cut.'

It was *déjà vu* to ten years before, when Seán cut off a third of his finger on the same hand and I had raced him to Bergerac hospital. This time we knew that Sainte-Foy-la-Grande was slightly closer and for a cut like this would probably be faster.

In a quarter of an hour we were at the hospital. I pressed the buzzer on the intercom in the emergency waiting room and within minutes Seán had been whisked behind the plasterboard walls and I was left alone.

A blonde woman and her young son came in. Her husband had a crushed foot, a work accident that had happened half an hour before. He was already behind the plasterboard walls. His boss had brought him in and she had just arrived, hoping she could take him home.

We sat down on hard metal chairs. The tiny room had a coffee and soup vending machine, a few posters about hygiene, an empty table and the intercom. There was not a single magazine or book. The wait stretched out ahead of us. With each set of footsteps or voice on the other side of the door, I felt a flicker of hope that died as they disappeared again.

Half an hour. One hour. My partner in impatience organised for a friend to fetch her son and give him dinner. I got up and did some stretches.

'I'm so hungry,' she said. She rose and bought a cup of soup from the machine that had been humming intermittently at my side.

About 20 minutes later, I succumbed and bought a 50-cent tomato soup from the machine too. It was horrible but I was desperate. I hadn't thought to drink water after tennis and there was no sign of a water fountain in the A & E waiting room.

At one and a half hours, I got up and did more stretches. If I ever returned I would bring a book and a snack pack.

At two hours, I decided to go home and come back when he was ready.

I rang the intercom.

'It's Madame Feely, the wife of the man who cut his hand.'

'He's arriving,' said the nurse.

After another 15 minutes, my partner in impatience said, 'Well, he's arriving sometime tonight.'

We both laughed hard, the humour easing our worry.

'I hear a voice. I think it's my husband,' she said.

The door opened. It was Seán. She and I laughed again, and Seán looked at me quizzically, his left hand bandaged thick and held up like he was giving us a very large one-finger salute.

'Ah, bad luck for me,' said the blonde.

'I hope it isn't too long,' I said. 'Good luck to your husband for a fast recovery.'

'Thank you and to you too,' she said.

I held the door open for Seán. He passed through and we walked to the car.

'How many stitches?' I said.

'Seven.'

I guffawed. '"Just a little cut, nothing to worry about. We could just tape it closed."'

'I don't think he really needed to put the last one in,' said Seán defensively.

I laughed even harder; a little from euphoria that Seán was OK and a little from the absurdity of his comments.

'Still, as a way of getting out of doing the winemaking it's going a bit far,' I said.

Seán smiled.

Fortunately he had just finished all the winemaking steps that were required before bottling otherwise I would have been back in there like I was in our first year. I thanked my lucky stars. I wouldn't know which end of a barrel was up after years of Seán doing all of that part of the business on his own.

Then we were home. The girls had shared a jar of organic baked beans for supper. Seán went to lock up the chickens with Ellie helping since he only had one hand. Sophia let her friends know the latest in the drama via social media. It was way past their bedtime but on nights like this – that would go down in family memory – that didn't matter.

I decided to cook fried eggs, comfort food. Our chickens were well settled and we were back to enjoying the self-sufficiency they added to our lives. Sheep were still a way off.

I placed the eggs on rough slices of organic bread made from heritage wheat grown by an organic farmer up the road and a side of purslane and chicory – two salads that had made it through winter, with a dressing of local sunflower oil and cider vinegar. The bread was a find by Cécile that had quickly become a favourite with guests on our wine tours. It was nutty and satisfying, a world away from industrial bread.

We lifted our glasses and did cheers in the family way.

'To health,' I said.

'To health' echoed round the table.

'My friend Lauren's mum had a heart palpitation in her sleep,' said Sophia, following that train of thought. 'She could have died. She nearly died before when she had cancer on her kidneys. That's when you realise the most important thing is your health.'

'You are so right, Sophia,' I said.

'So when people complain that organic is too expensive they only need to think about that. Once you have cancer it is too late,' she added.

I could not have said it better myself.

'That egg is so good,' said Seán.

'A feast. So simple and such flavour,' I added.

'Well done for keeping calm, Sophia,' said Seán. 'You were so cool in the crisis.'

'I thought you said it wasn't a crisis?' I said.

We all laughed.

'When I came in I thought Papa was going to ask me to wash beetroot – the basin in the sink was so full of red,' said Sophia.

I pictured it and it took me back to when Seán slashed his arm on the vine trimmer, another accident that happened in our first year. There was so much blood trailed through the kitchen and in the sink that I kept having to sit down and put my head between my legs to stop myself from passing out.

'And well done to both of you for getting on and having your supper and getting ready for bed,' I said.

'Well done, Mum, for not having a TSA,' said Sophia.

TSA was her latest saying, as in 'Total Stress Attack' – what mums did when their kids forgot their school bag and they were already at the bus stop or when their husband chopped off his finger.

Aideen and Barry O'Brien, our friends from Dublin, arrived for their Easter holiday that coincided with helping with our annual bottling. With bottling complete, they moved my office out to the tasting room. It felt like freedom, like when I took my duvet cover back from the Cottage. Moving the office out of our living space to the business area gave us back a little of our personal life; part of finding balance. I bought an office chair, one that had proper back support, to replace the old wicker chair that had travelled the world with us.

Perimenopause had been akin to the phase of conversion to organic that I called the 'valley of despair'. When we started the organic conversion and stopped the chemicals it was like 'cold turkey' for the vines. They were weak and susceptible; the mycorrhizae had not had time to build in the soil and their immunity was weak. It took three years for them to make the transition. I was into my third year of transition and I was approaching the other side: my hormonal balance was coming back. My dreams about dying had stopped. I hadn't punched a table top in more than a year. My periods had stopped. I was close to, if not at, the other side.

Sophia and Ellie announced that they had sleepovers with friends and would both be out the same evening.

'Date night for us then?' I said to Seán.

Despite our best intentions, time and money constraints meant the last time we had had a date night was on the truffling weekend almost four years before.

'Maybe,' said Seán.

Spring had been cold and wet but the day dawned with perfect sunshine and a fresh breeze. We packed our daughters off to the respective friends.

'So should we go out?' I asked.

'No, let's stay in,' said Seán. 'I picked up our organic beef box and I have two steaks in the fridge. If you do the starter I'll do the main.'

'Deal,' I said.

I set a small table for two with tablecloth, cloth napkins and candles, angled to take advantage of the magnificent view in our *salon*. The setting and table looked idyllic and romantic. Satisfied with my decorative efforts, I returned to the kitchen where Seán had music playing and cooking preparations under way.

While I made herbed goat's cheese toasts for our starter, Seán's knife flashed through spinach and onions fresh from the garden. We found the music of Sophie B. Hawkins online, a CD we had fallen in love to. Her erotic lyrics were backed by smoky rock, perfect music for a date night. 'California, Here I Come' started playing as I poured glasses of Sauvignon Blanc, a Californian biodynamic wine made under the advice of Philippe Coderey, a friend we met in Santa Cruz who had passed by to visit a couple of months before bearing it as a gift. It was delicious, balanced with good acidity and a roundness we didn't usually find on Sauvignon Blanc in France.

With wine and goat's cheese in hand, we chatted, looking intermittently on to the breathtaking view and into each other's eyes. It was the first time in years that we had had an evening together and talked about things that were not to do with the business or immediate day-to-day concerns. Our conversation flowed through current affairs, new adventures, dreams.

Seán served the organic steak pan-fried to perfection with a side of homegrown spinach and beans, and I poured us each a glass of our no-sulphites-added *Grâce* red wine. We soaked in the moment, the exceptional food, the view on to the vineyard and Seán's bountiful *potager*, the music.

I felt like scales had been lifted off my eyes, like I was seeing Seán clearly for the first time in ages. He was still the man I had fallen in love with. We chatted into the night, candles burning and lights twinkling in the valley, enjoying each other's company like we had when we first fell in love. After being missing for most of the perimenopause, my libido returned. The valley of despair was officially over – perhaps Seán had slipped a little truffle aphrodisiac into the sauce.

I could see why so many long relationships broke up around this point. Menopause was a tough transition. We had to keep reinventing ourselves to keep us and our relationship strong. Seán was the love of my life, the only shoe that fit. I could not imagine growing out of him but it was frightening how close we had come to tearing apart. We had so much shared history, so much shared happiness together, a family, a life.

Each morning I rose at 5.45 a.m., went downstairs and did two salutations to the sun and the Five Tibetans. Seán was usually up with the dawn with me, out doing handwork in the vineyard and the *potager* before the heat of the day. We kissed each other hello instead of passing like two strangers. After our greeting I took my tea and crossed the courtyard, the crunch of the gravel under my feet, my eyes turned heavenwards to marvel at the sky. Earlier in the spring the brilliance of the stars was exceptional; I saw formations and clusters I had never noticed.

As the days grew longer, I watched the ever-changing sunrise and saw Seán's evolving garden and vines in a different light every day. We debated options long and hard. We weren't earning what we could have in the city but we were stewards of the land; we were taking care of a small part of the earth, and each year we saw progress that filled us with hope and joy.

Like any work there were days where we felt down, like it was an uphill battle, but we were making a difference to this earth where we had rooted and to the people that came in contact with our passion for organic wine and organic farming. Our plans were evolving: we were looking at ways to increase our self-sufficiency and at equipment that would ease Seán's work in the winery. Sophia started giving Seán lessons to improve his French grammar. The inspirational vineyards we had seen in South Africa had sparked new ideas for our vineyard and wine tourism. I wanted to share our passion for organic beyond our farm gate and to do more writing. With intense debate we were working out what we wanted to do. We hadn't found the perfect balance yet but we felt renewed energy for what we were doing and we had reignited our passion for each other. I had a feeling our vineyard adventures were far from over.

MESSAGE FROM THE AUTHOR

Reading this book you will have realised that I am passionate about organic and how critical it is to choose organic and to grow local food. Each of us can make change happen. We don't have time to wait for governments to legislate it. We can do it ourselves by making informed choices every day. If no one buys chemically grown food farmers will stop producing it and will turn to organic methods.

Over the coming years, I wish to share my passion beyond our farm, to do more outreach, more book festivals and book tours. If you would like me to chat with your book club online or if you wish to host a local event, please get in touch at **caro@carofeely.com**.

I also invite you to join our mailing list at **www.chateaufeely. com**, to like **Chateau Feely** on **www.facebook.com/chateaufeely** and follow me on Twitter **@CaroFeely**, where I regularly share information about farming, ecology and how we can make a difference.

You can find out more about our certified organic and biodynamic vineyard at **www.chateaufeely.com**, our walking tours and wine school at **www.frenchwineadventures.com** and our accommodation at **www.luxurydordognegites.com**.

I look forward to seeing you online, in the Dordogne or beyond. Thank you for joining me on this journey.

À bientôt et merci,
Caro

ACKNOWLEDGEMENTS

A memoir is a personal journey, a way of making sense of the past, so my biggest thank you goes to my family, Seán, Sophia and Ellie, for their participation in this adventure and for supporting me in sharing these intimate portraits of our lives – from my perspective *bien sûr*. Seán says I write great fiction.

Thank you to our family: my mum and dad, Cliff and Lyn Wardle; Dad Feely; the Bristow family; my sister Jacquie and brother Garth. Thank you also to the friends that are part of this story: Thierry and Isabelle Daulhiac, Pierre and Laurence de St Viance, Antoine Mariau, Dave and Amanda Moore, Ian, Brigit and Chiara Wilson, Chris and Dave Drake, Fearn and Andrea King, and Cécile Rousseau.

An important thank you to the team at Summersdale and particularly to Claire Plimmer, Robert Drew, Madeleine Stevens, Nicky Douglas and Lizzie Curtin.

Last but not least, thank you to my readers for reading my books. A special thank you to readers who have written to me over the years – your emails and letters have provided great motivation to keep writing.

WINE

THE ESSENTIAL GUIDE TO TASTING, HISTORY, CULTURE AND MORE

CARO FEELY

WINE
The Essential Guide to Tasting, History, Culture and More

Caro Feely

£9.99

Hardback

ISBN: 978-1-84953-749-0

No other beverage has created the excitement and emotion that wine has over its vast history. It fills our mouths with flavour and our hearts with joy. It's also a subject whose complexities can be baffling and mysterious to the uninitiated – but wine expert Caro Feely is here to unveil all the secrets of this most marvellous drink.

Packed with engaging anecdotes, fascinating history and a wealth of information on the world of wine, this miscellany is perfect for any wine fan, from the expert to the casual drinker. So let's raise a glass to the red, the white and the rosé!

'Wine is sunlight, held together by water.'
GALILEO GALILEI

GRAPE EXPECTATIONS

'a beautifully written tale of passion and guts'
Alice Feiring, author of *Naked Wine*

A Family's
Vineyard Adventure
in France

Château
Haut
Garrigue

Caro Feely

GRAPE EXPECTATIONS
A Family's Vineyard Adventure in France

Caro Feely

£9.99

Paperback

ISBN: 978-1-84953-257-0

Filled with vivid descriptions of delicious wines, great food and stunning views, this is a unique insight into the world of the winemaker, and a story of passion, dedication, and love

When Caro and Sean find the perfect 10-hectare vineyard in Saussignac, it seems like their dreams of becoming winemakers in the south of France are about to come true. But they arrive in France with their young family (a toddler and a newborn) to be faced with a dilapidated 18th-century farmhouse and an enterprise that may never, ever make them a living. Undeterred by mouse infestations, a leaking roof, treacherous hordes of insects, visits from the local farm 'police,' and a nasty accident with an agricultural trimmer, Caro and Sean set about transforming their 'beyond eccentric' winery into a successful business as they embark on the biggest adventure of their lives – learning to make wine from the roots up.

'beautifully written... in turn, it seduced and terrified me'
Samantha Brick

Saving Our Skins

Building a Vineyard Dream in France

CARO FEELY

SAVING OUR SKINS
Building a Vineyard Dream in France

Caro Feely

£9.99

Paperback

ISBN: 978-1-84953-609-7

Frost can be fatal to a fledgling wine business... gorgeous glitter with a high price tag. On a winter's day it is beautiful, but on a spring day after bud burst it spells devastation. For Sean and Caro Feely, a couple whose love affair with wine and France has taken them through financial and physical struggle to create their organic vineyard, it could spell the end. Until they receive an unexpected call that could save their skins...

This book is about life, love and taking risks, while transforming a piece of land into a flourishing vineyard and making a new life in France.

Have you enjoyed this book?
If so, why not write a review on your favourite website?

If you're interested in finding out more about our books,
find us on Facebook at **Summersdale Publishers** and
follow us on Twitter at **@Summersdale**.

Thanks very much for buying this Summersdale book.

www.summersdale.com

Praise for MISS EMILY by Nuala O'Connor

'Secrets will always out. In the same way as Emily Dickinson's poems were once the best kept secret in Massachusetts, Nuala O'Connor's luminous prose has long been one of Ireland's most treasured literary secrets. Now through her superb evocation of 19th century Amherst, an international audience is likely to be held rapt by the sparse lyricism and exactitude of O'Connor's writing. Through a fusion of historical ventriloquism and imaginative dexterity, O'Connor vividly conjures up – in the real-life Emily Dickinson and the fictional Ada Concannon – two equally unforgettable characters who pulsate with life in this study of the slowly blossoming friendship between a delicate literary recluse and a young Irish emigrant eager to embrace the new world around her.'

Dermot Bolger, award-winning playwright and author of *The Journey Home*, *The Venice Suite*.

'Like a Dickinson poem, *Miss Emily* seems at first a simple story of friendship, but gradually reveals itself as a profound meditation on the human condition. O'Connor accomplishes this unfolding, just as Dickinson did, with her exquisite use of language. I lost myself in the beautiful detail of 1860s Amherst, a cast of characters that leapt off the page with life, and the constant reminder that words, properly wielded, can transcend time, transmit love, and, above all, inspire hope.'

Cha   *Tale*